International Studies in Educational Achievement

VOLUME 11

The IEA Study of Reading Literacy:

Achievement and Instruction in Thirty-Two School Systems

International Studies in Educational Achievement

Other titles in the Series include

TRAVERS & WESTBURY
The IEA Study of Mathematics I: Analysis of Mathematics Curricula

ROBITAILLE & GARDEN
The IEA Study of Mathematics II: Contexts and Outcomes of School Mathematics

BURSTEIN
The IEA Study of Mathematics III: Student Growth and Classroom Processes

GORMAN, PURVES & DEGENHART
The IEA Study of Written Composition I: The International Writing Tasks and Scoring Scales

PURVES
The IEA Study of Written Composition II: Education and Performance in Fourteen Countries

ANDERSON, RYAN & SHAPIRO
The IEA Classroom Environment Study

ROSIER & KEEVES
The IEA Study of Science I: Science Education and Curricula in Twenty-Three Countries

POSTLETHWAITE & WILEY
The IEA Study of Science II: Science Achievement in Twenty-Three Countries

KEEVES
The IEA Study of Science III: Changes in Science Education and Achievement: 1970 to 1984

The IEA Study of Reading Literacy:

Achievement and Instruction in Thirty-Two School Systems

Edited by

WARWICK B. ELLEY
University of Canterbury, Christchurch, New Zealand

Published for the International Association
for the Evaluation of Educational Achievement

PERGAMON

U.K.   Elsevier Science Ltd, Headington Hill Hall,
          Oxford OX3 0BW, England
U.S.A.   Elsevier Science Inc, 660 White Plains Road,
          Tarrytown, New York 10591-5153, U.S.A.
JAPAN   Elsevier Science Japan, Tsunashima Building Annex,
          3-20-12 Yushima, Bunkyo-ku, Tokyo 113, Japan

First edition 1994

Library of Congress Cataloging-in-Publication Data

The IEA study of reading literacy/edited by Warwick B. Elley. -- 1st ed.
p. cm. -- (International studies in educational achievement; v. 11)
Includes index.
1. Reading--Statistics. 2. Comparative education--Statistics.
I. Elley, Warwick B. II. International Association for the Evaluation of
Educational Achievement. III. Series.
LB1050.I3 1994
428.4--dc20

British Library Cataloguing in Publication Data

A catalogue for this book is available from the British Library

ISBN 0-08-041933X

Printed in Great Britain by BPCC Wheatons, Exeter

Contents

vi   *Contents*

List of Tables

Chapter 4

Chapter 5

List of Figures

Figure 3.3   Voluntary reading: Countries with students favoring books: Population B

Figure 3.4   Population B: Contrasts in relationships between reading achievement and voluntary reading levels

Chapter 4

Figure 4.1   Pattern of decreasing reading achievement with increasing TV viewing: Population A

Figure 4.2   Pattern of increasing reading achievement with moderately heavy TV viewing: Population A

Figure 4.3   Mean gender differences (girls minus boys) for countries which begin instruction at age 5 and all other countries

Figure 4.4   Gender differences on word recognition for countries which begin instruction at age 5 and all other countries

Figure 4.5   Achievement score differences between urban and rural school areas: Population A (positive value favors urban schools)

Figure 4.6   Differences in overall reading achievement between urban and rural schools: Population B (positive score indicates urban advantage)

Figure 4.7   Percentage of countries reporting negative correlations of metacognitive categories with achievement: Population A

Figure 4.8   Percentage of countries reporting positive correlations of metacognitive categories with achievement: Population A

Chapter 6

Figure 6.1   The average reading achievement of boys and girls as related to the teacher's gender in three countries (Ireland, Singapore, Spain) with a significant interaction between student gender and teacher gender (Population A)

Foreword

T.J. PLOMP
(CHAIRMAN, IEA)

One of the assumptions underlying the formation of the IEA is that educators from different systems of education have much to learn from one another in making decisions about how to improve their own systems. This is particularly the case in literacy. Many diverse views exist about the best way to teach children to read, yet little is known about which countries are most successful in achieving this aim, or what the most productive strategies are for doing so. Moreover, the campaigns for turning around the rising tide of illiteracy in the world adds a note of urgency in the efforts of literacy researchers and practitioners.

This report attempts to address some of these issues. Data are presented on the relative achievement levels of comparable samples of students in each of 32 school systems. Attempts are made to elucidate the reasons for the differences that were found, and implications are drawn about the likely effects of different policies. Not all the questions are answered, but a clear measure of progress is evident in the findings in this report.

A study of this magnitude would not have taken place without the dedication and hard work of many people. Above all, IEA studies aim at being cooperative. This is a three-way cooperation among the persons responsible for the study in each education system, the Steering Committee of the study, and the International Coordinating Center. The National Research Coordinators (NRCs) appointed by their own institutions to be in charge of the day-to-day work in their own systems of education were crucial to the study. These 32 people brought research experience and cultural expectations to the many tasks involved. Without their inputs, resourcefulness, and dedication the project would not have succeeded.

As Chairman of the Steering Committee, Warwick Elley (New Zealand) exerted a major influence on the design and conduct of the project, and was very ably assisted in these endeavors by the other members of the Steering Committee: Al Beaton (USA), John Guthrie (USA), Ingvar Lundberg (Sweden), Francis Mangubhai (Australia), Ken Ross (Australia), and Alan Purves (USA), who was an ex-officio member of the Committee. Very helpful technical assistance was also received from . Peter Allerup (Denmark), Nadir Atash (USA), and Ingrid Munck (Sweden).

Neville Postlethwaite provided the driving force and directed the project from the International Coordinating Center for the first three years. Without his enthusiasm, the study would not have begun. Andreas Schleicher was an outstanding data manager and took over the reins of International Coordinator with a wisdom well beyond his years. Without his expertise the mass of data could not have been analyzed so quickly. Dieter Kotte and Elaine Degenhart served as assistant international coordinators from 1988 to mid-1990 and from mid-1990 to the end of 1992 respectively. Both handled well the task of organizing complex filing systems, communicating with NRCs on a very regular basis, and running the accounts. Elaine Degenhart provided invaluable editorial assistance for various documents and booklets emerging from the study.

The support staff deserve heartfelt thanks, too, for their valuable contribution behind the scenes. Special thanks should go to the data-processing staff of Stefan Seyfert, Michael Bruneforth, Dirk Hastedt, Heiko Jungclaus, and Knut Schwippert under the direction of Andreas Schleicher. This book was also prepared for publication by two members of the secretarial staff, namely, Julianne Friedrich, assisted by Jedidiah Harris. The secretarial and accounting staff consisted of part-time people: Petra Lietz, Britta Niemann, Bettina Westphalen, and Ellen Ziesmann.

Professor Mona Beebe at Memorial University, New Foundland, Canada, Dame Marie Clay at the University of Auckland, New Zealand, and Professor Don Spearritt from Sydney, Australia, served as external reviewers for this book. Our gratitude to them.

The funding agencies also merit much gratitude. While the national field work was financed by the research agencies within each country, the funding of the international aspects of the project was provided by the generosity of the MacArthur Foundation, the Mellon Foundation, the U.S. National Academy of Sciences, the European Community, Unesco, and by additional grants from several participating countries (Canada (BC); Denmark; Germany; Hong Kong; Iceland; Italy; Spain; the Netherlands; New Zealand; Sweden; Switzerland; and the Nordic Council). Unicef paid for some NRCs to attend NRC meetings. The overhead expenses incurred by the International Coordinating Center and by members of the Steering Committee would not have been easily met without the goodwill of their own institutions. Clearly, this project, like other previous IEA studies, owes its success to a great range of people and institutions.

Preface

The IEA Reading Literacy study is the second major survey of reading achievement undertaken by IEA. The first, which was conducted in 15 countries, in the years 1970 and 1971, showed that the enterprise was possible, that certain kinds of reading tasks could be translated satisfactorily into different languages. Moreover it did produce valid, interpretable findings of value to member countries in understanding their relative achievement status, and in identifying areas of strength and weakness in their literacy program.

The present study builds on the very useful work undertaken by Robert Thorndike (1973) and his colleagues in that pioneering survey. The findings reported in this volume relate to 32 countries in all continents of the globe, making it the largest IEA study to date. This time, in keeping with more recent conceptions of reading, students were asked to tackle a wider range of reading exercises, including short simple fables, long 1500 word narratives, dense scientific prose, short personal notes, complex graphs, and functional tasks like following directions, interpreting maps, using timetables, and other document-type items. Prodigious efforts were made by the researchers and national representatives to minimize any cultural or linguistic biases, and the statistical machinery of the Rasch model was systematically used, for the first time in a reading survey, both to help identify troublesome items, and to create defensible international scales.

When compared with the previous IEA reading survey, greater efforts were made, in the present study, to assess the volume and character of students' reading, to explore their beliefs about learning to read, and to compare the effects on their achievement of their teachers' various beliefs and instructional emphases. A wider array of statistical and graphical procedures was employed to clarify the patterns in the findings.

Further innovations included new procedures for providing frameworks within which countries could better interpret their findings. In one exercise, national panels of "judges" were asked to specify expected levels of literacy in their country, thus making possible helpful comparisons between the actual and the expected. In another analysis, national achievement levels were compared with expected levels of performance, as determined by economic, health and adult literacy indicators, in their respective societies.

Despite the introduction of these novel technologies, and test materials, it is fair to say that many of the general conclusions of Thorndike's 1970–1971 survey were confirmed, albeit for a larger set of countries. Acceptable levels of literacy are achieved by most pupils, in most systems, despite a diversity of reading methods and traditions. In general, achievement is greatest, however, when the education systems are well endowed financially, when teachers are well educated, when students have ready access to good books, when they enjoy reading and do it often, and when their first language is the same as that of the language of the school. Again, students in all countries achieve more highly when they have the benefit of more literate family backgrounds, including parents who are supportive of the school's efforts, and who restrain their children's TV viewing hours to reasonable levels. Indeed, the influence of the home was pervasive, just as it had been in the earlier IEA survey, and in many other studies conducted within member countries. By contrast, there was no confirmation in this study that an early start in reading instruction (age 5) is an advantage, or that longer school years are beneficial.

Within each country, specific findings have emerged which will surely give their policy-makers pause for thought, and prompts for action. Moreover, the data are available for others to explore further, as pressures of time and finance inevitably limited our efforts. The authors of the chapters in this volume were only too aware of these and other limitations, and they did their best to clarify the assumptions made about such matters as the equivalence of reading tasks and of student samples across countries.

Assessing reading data from 210,000 students and 10,000 teachers in 21 different languages is no mean task. Fortunately, the statistical genius of Andreas Schleicher and the organizational skills of Neville Postlethwaite and their University of Hamburg team, made it all logistically practicable. Any advances in our knowledge which result from this massive study must owe much to their combined efforts.

Warwick B. Elley
September 1, 1993

1

Introduction

WARWICK B. ELLEY, ANDREAS SCHLEICHER, AND HANS
WAGEMAKER

> The value of literacy for achieving fulfilling, productive, expanding and
> participating lives of freedom in modern societies is undoubted, and
> unquestioned. At the same time, however, literacy does not seem to be well
> understood (H. Graff 1981, p.1).

The Importance of Literacy

Most governments are interested in raising the levels of literacy of their
citizens, and school systems around the globe accord high priority to the
development of reading competence. Nevertheless, it is clear that the ability to
read, taken for granted by the highly literate, is denied to one in four of the
earth's adult population. Valiant efforts by generations of international and
local agencies to reduce the relative proportion of illiterates have been only
partially successful, while 100 million school-age children can still find no
place to learn (World Declaration on Education for All, 1990). Even in the
developed world, large numbers of students pass through the school system
unable or unwilling to read and write, while teachers and researchers continue
to debate the reasons.

Meanwhile, predictions indicate that over 911 million people will be
classified as illiterate in the year 2000 (Carceles, 1990). The implications of
such figures must be disturbing when they are translated into restricted
opportunities of employment, social participation, and enjoyment of life.
Furthermore, in an increasingly complex, information-ridden world, demands
on literacy continue to rise in all nations. Illiterates are at a serious
disadvantage in most countries today.

Expanding enrollments in primary schools in developing countries
during the 1980s brought some hope that the literacy situation would improve,
but the continuing lack of educational resources, trained teachers and quality
instruction in many countries resulted in widespread disappointments.
Schooling alone does not necessarily produce literate students, ready to
become independent learners who can take their place in a complex society.

It is widely accepted in most countries that literacy is a valuable human
right, a source of individual dignity, a prerequisite for further learning in many
areas of knowledge, and a key skill needed for many occupations. World Bank

reports have also argued that a strong relationship has been found to exist between educational investment and economic growth in developing countries (Haddad et al., 1990). But there is more to learn about this relationship. On present evidence, Wagner (1987) claims that literacy may just as well be an outcome of economic development as it is a cause (p. 12).

Meanwhile, there is an obvious need for more accurate figures on the relative achievement levels of students in countries over time. Unesco publishes regular reports of adult literacy and school enrollment ratios by nation (e.g., Unesco, 1991), but the quality of the former data sets is uncertain, based as it is on a variety of criteria (Wagner, 1990), while the school enrollment figures per se carry no information about the quality of the students' learning. Years at school do not guarantee achievement levels adequate for coping with the literacy tasks of a modern society. In the words of the World Bank report, "poor quality schooling has serious implications for a country's future ability to compete economically" (Haddad et al., 1990, p. 69).

In a genuine attempt to provide valid and reliable information about reading literacy levels of students' learning in a diversity of school systems, the IEA resolved to undertake a study of the achievement levels of students at two age levels. The driving purposes were to produce "hard" data on the achievement levels of students in those countries, and to study the relationships between those indicators which vary among and within countries and the achievement levels of students in those countries. An International Steering Committee was established to plan and oversee the project. Thirty-two systems of education in 31 countries agreed to participate, and all countries' National Research Coordinators (NRCs) met regularly with the Steering Committee and members of the International Coordinating and Data Processing Center for the study so that a collaboratively planned survey, fair to all participants, could be undertaken. This report outlines the procedures and major findings of this project.

In 1990–1991 data were collected from some 210,000 students and 10,000 teachers in the 32 systems located on five continents and representing more than 20 different languages. Information on the students' achievement and voluntary reading activities was linked to information about the students' home, school and community circumstances in an effort to increase our knowledge about the world's school literacy scene.

The Aims of the Study

After prolonged discussion among all involved in the study, the following aims were proposed and established:

To describe the achievement levels in reading literacy of comparable samples of students in all education systems. Data on reading literacy levels across countries had not been produced since the first IEA survey of reading achievement in 15 countries, conducted 20 years earlier (Thorndike, 1973). Two grade levels were selected (those in which the majority of 9- and 14-year-olds were found), and these groups of students were referred to as Population A and Population B respectively. While the production of comparative "league tables" was not a major priority of the researchers, it became clear that many governments were interested in the relative performance of their students, first as indicators of the success of their educational efforts, and second as a basis for identifying strengths and weaknesses in their policies and practices. This aim is addressed chiefly in Chapter 2.

To describe the voluntary reading activities of 9- and 14-year-olds. One aim of a reading curriculum in most countries is to instill in students a desire to read voluntarily in their own time. An international survey provides the opportunity to assess the extent and variety of student reading cross-nationally. This aim is addressed in Chapter 3.

To identify differences in policies and instructional practices in reading, and to study the ways in which they relate to students' achievement and voluntary reading. It is clear that educators in the participating countries have different conceptions of the optimal ways to teach reading. Some stress phonics from the outset; others see that as counter-productive. Some begin reading instruction at age five; others delay it until age seven. Some teach all students as a single unit; others prefer to group children by ability. Some teachers stay with a class for six or more years; others change classes every year. Many of these policies are uniform within countries, so that their ramifications can be investigated only by comparing achievement levels of students of comparable age across countries where these policies are found to differ. When testing is conducted under standardized conditions, and the data are subjected to multivariate analyses, there is potential for identifying relationships not revealed by other methods. This aim is addressed in Chapters 4 to 7.

To produce valid international tests and questionnaires which could be used to investigate reading literacy development in other countries. The IEA has accumulated considerable experience in cross-national assessment. The techniques used to develop, edit, translate, pilot test, and analyze data have led the IEA to believe that its measuring instruments would be of value in many nations, whether or not they had the resources and opportunity to participate in the planned international survey of 1990–1991.

To provide national baseline data suitable for monitoring changes in literacy levels and patterns over time. Most governments would benefit from information about whether, and to what extent, literacy standards are changing over time in their school system. Debate on this matter in many countries is often heated, but seldom is it informed by evidence of the kind collected by IEA surveys with standard assessment tasks given under uniform conditions to carefully selected samples. A data archive has been established and is available from the IEA Headquarters.

Additional aims, espoused by some participants, included: the prospect of increased research capability of key personnel as a result of participating in the survey; the possibility of improved theory generation in the area of literacy and national development; and the opportunity to study the links between literacy demand in a country and the levels attained by its school leavers.

The Organization of the Study

The IEA Reading Literacy study was launched in August 1988 by the IEA General Assembly. In November of the same year, the National Research Coordinators (NRCs) from the IEA member centers wishing to participate in the study met in Washington, DC, together with the International Steering Committee members and members of the International Coordinating Center (ICC). For personnel involved in the study, see Appendix A.

Initially 30 countries accepted the invitation to participate. This number rose to 35 in 1990, but some countries dropped out, chiefly due to a lack of funding. In the end there were 31 countries that participated. Germany participated as two systems, East and West, as the country was not unified when the study began. Hence, there were 32 education systems. Thirty-one systems of education were involved in the final survey for Population B, and 27 for Population A. Botswana, Nigeria, the Philippines, Thailand, and Zimbabwe participated only in the Population B survey, while Indonesia took part only in Population A.

In each country, the designated research institute was responsible for funding and conducting the data collection exercises in its own schools, and for preparing a national report. The development of all tests and questionnaires, and decisions about research design, definitions, age levels, methodology, timetabling, and reporting were collective decisions, made by the Steering Committee in consultation with the NRCs. Each country also set up a National Advisory Committee to assist its NRC, especially in relation to test development, questionnaire items, editing of instruments, test administration, translations, and report writing.

Thus, every effort was made to ensure that national circumstances were taken into account in the preparation of instruments and design of the survey. The NRCs played a key role in providing items for the instruments, rating and editing them, pilot testing them on judgment samples, and reviewing them before their final administration. It was the NRCs who collectively developed the questionnaires. The vigilance and competence of the NRCs was crucial to the efficient organization of the whole project, and it is testimony to their efforts that it was completed on time.

The International Coordinating Center (ICC) in Hamburg had responsibility for: communicating with the NRCs; organizing funding; calling meetings; ensuring that high quality instruments were prepared; ensuring that good probability samples of students from the defined target population were drawn in each country; preparing all manuals required; preparing data management procedures; cleaning, weighting, and merging all data and data files; conducting the complex analyses required for processing 600 megabytes of data; and organizing the writing and publishing of the international reports.

The writing of international reports such as this one was undertaken by the Steering Committee with the collaboration of the ICC and NRCs in each country. However, each country undertook to produce a national report, focusing on the results of its own school system, and on issues which were of particular interest in its system.

Definition of Reading Literacy

Quality measurement requires, first and foremost, clear definitions of concepts. The concept of literacy has a long and colorful history (see Graff, 1981; Levine, 1986; Kirsch & Guthrie, 1984; Clifford, 1984; Wagner, 1989) and there is much debate over the meaning and importance of such concepts as basic literacy, functional literacy, cultural literacy, workplace literacy, and the like. The International Steering Committee, mindful of the constraints imposed by the need to include thousands of students in many countries, speaking a multiplicity of languages, and operating in various cultural traditions, searched for a working concept that would be widely acceptable and would provide guidelines for a set of tests which would measure central aspects of literacy.

At the outset, writing ability was excluded from the definition. A recent project of the IEA had focused on writing (Gorman, Purves & Degenhart, 1988) and the problems entailed in making international comparisons in this curriculum area had been extensively explored (Purves, 1992).

The notion of functional literacy, with its connotations of being able to use one's literacy skill to function effectively within one's own society, was popular with most NRCs, but some wanted to extend the notion beyond the basic levels needed for survival, to include higher-level thinking and the reading of literature, for example.

In an attempt to embrace such viewpoints, and to provide some link with the earlier IEA study of reading (Thorndike, 1973), the Steering Committee proposed the following definition, which was subsequently accepted by the NRCs:

> Reading Literacy is the ability to understand and use those written language forms that are required by society and/or valued by the individual.

The category of language forms "required by society" refers to those kinds of literacy tasks which are needed to cope with the business of living in an organized society: reading notices, directions, maps, graphs, and government circulars, to name a few; the latter part of the definition allowed for the inclusion of leisure reading (narrative prose, or popular magazine articles) which may be valued by individual readers, but are less often required for survival in a society. The Committee proposed that the criterion of "value for individuals" in a country could be rated by the NRCs during the test development phase.

Participating NRCs agreed that both "understanding" and "use" of these written forms were important in the definition, and various attempts were made to incorporate both aspects, although the constraints of mass testing and the assessment traditions existing in most countries inevitably meant that the major operational focus was placed on "understanding." In the event, it was found possible to measure the students' ability to follow instructions correctly in a few tasks.

Definitions of Domains to be Tested

The particular "domains" of reading literacy to be assessed were debated at length with the NRCs, until agreement was reached on the following components. The main reason for selecting these domains was that reading specialists traditionally think in these terms (see Barr, Kamil, Mosenthal & Pearson, 1991) and they are considered to be different types of reading which all individuals require.

1.   Narrative Prose: Continuous texts in which the author's aim is to tell a story, whether fact or fiction. Such texts normally follow a linear time sequence and are usually intended to entertain or to involve the reader emotionally. The selected passages to be read ranged from short fables to lengthy stories in excess of 1000 words.

2.   Expository Prose: Continuous texts which are intended to describe, explain, or otherwise convey factual information or opinion to the reader. The IEA tests contained, for instance, short family letters, descriptions of animals, as well as elaborate descriptions of lasers and the dangers of smoking.

3.   Documents: Structured presentations of information, set out in the form of graphs, charts, maps, lists, or sets of instructions. Such materials were organized in such a way that students could search, locate, and process information without reading the whole text.

The three domains defined above were used in the tests for both age levels. Scores were calculated and reported for each domain.

Target Populations

The grade levels in which most 9- and 14-year-olds were to be found were agreed to by the NRCs as representing points in the school systems of importance for reading. The first population was at a point where most children had passed the encoding/decoding phase. It was agreed to be the earliest stage that children in most countries could cope adequately with written tests and questionnaires given under conditions of group administration. It was agreed that teacher effects were more likely to be found at this level of the education system. The second population was at a point in the school systems near the end of compulsory schooling. It was expected that this population would probably reflect the reading ability of the next generation of the majority of people in the workforce.

Some NRCs were concerned that the majority of their 14-year-olds remained at school for several years and probably increased their literacy skills before entering the workforce. This limitation of the proposed study was acknowledged. However, the prospect of including a third population for a minority of countries was agreed to be impractical within the financial and temporal constraints of this study. This alternative was therefore left to the initiative of a few NRCs who resolved to design a study for students of 17 years, outside the framework of the present study, but capitalizing on some of its measures and administrative networks. The original design of the study allowed for pretesting students early in the school year in order to reveal more clearly the impact of current instruction on student outcomes, but this feature proved to be impractical in most countries and was therefore abandoned at the outset.

Population A: All students attending mainstream schools on a full-time basis at the grade level in which most students were aged 9.00–9.11 years during the first week of the eighth month of the school year.

Population B: All students attending mainstream schools on a full-time basis at the grade level in which most students were aged 14.00–14.11 years during the first week of the eighth month of the school year.

Appendix B presents a summary of some key features of the sample designs. The tables in Appendix B show the number of students tested in each country and the percentages of students and schools excluded. Also included is a comment on the target population to indicate any deviation from the desired national coverage of schools. Information about the grade levels tested and the average age levels of national samples is given in Chapter 2, Tables 2.2 and 2.3. Further details can be found in the Technical Report (Beaton, 1993).

It is important to note that these target population definitions were grade-based rather than age-based. That is, students in a grade were selected. It was recognized at that time that several educational systems had students who were 9 or 14 years of age in other grades than the grades selected. Hence, there could be no question of comparing the achievement of 9- or 14-year-olds, as age groups, across systems. At the final stage of sampling, intact classes within the target grade were selected in the selected schools. The use of intact classes was an essential part of the study design because stable estimates of class performance were required so as to be able to link teacher data with the reading literacy levels of their own classes.

Developing the Reading Literacy Tests

To ensure maximum content validity in every country, the NRCs participated in decisions about test development at every stage. Discussions were held at the first NRC meeting about content, format, blueprints, and guidelines for suitable passages and items. Subsequently, NRCs from 20 countries submitted materials for inclusion. After the Steering Committee had selected and adapted the most appropriate passages and items, the NRCs commented on them, in consultation with their National Advisory Committees, and rated them for suitability at the NRC meeting in June 1989. Further screening and editing took place at that meeting, item by item, and all countries were invited to participate in the pilot testing phase.

For these trials, four parallel forms with common anchor items were prepared, allowing for the pilot testing of approximately 300 items at each population level, considerably more than were planned for the final tests.

Translation was undertaken, where necessary, by NRCs according to commonly agreed upon guidelines. The goal of the translators was to capture the essence of meaning rather than to produce verbatim translations. Good translation is more art than science.

The guidelines to translators indicated that two independent persons should undertake a forward translation, that each should be bilingual and familiar with children's language, that no simplification should be made, that translators should be sensitive to differences between verbatim and paraphrase items, that any deviations from the original content should be noted, that changes in the length of the text should be noted, that the independent translations should be compared and differences resolved, that backward translations of selected passages should be undertaken, and that translators should provide reports on their experiences. Statistical checks on the success of the translations were undertaken, and are reported in Table 1.8.

Minor cultural adaptations in English and non-English versions of the tests were encouraged in order to ensure face validity in each country. Thus, place names, units of measurement, seasonal differences, and common terms could be changed to fit local circumstances, provided that they did not affect the difficulty levels of the items.

Item Format

Most NRCs opted for multiple-choice items at both age levels. However, some NRCs preferred that there be some open-ended items. After lengthy debate, an empirical study was undertaken by the Steering Committee to study the differences between multiple-choice and open-ended items on the same passages administered to 9-year-old students. This study showed comparable findings to those conducted with older students, namely, that multiple-choice items produce very similar results to those produced by open-ended questions, in less time, and that multiple-choice items are more popular with students (Elley & Mangubhai, 1992). It was found that the rank order of students was very similar in both cases. Additionally, no significant difference in the relationships of test scores with the same response format and the relationship between test scores gained from two different response formats could be found.

Another empirical study was undertaken involving 9-year-olds, to investigate the importance of print size and line length in test layout. Four parallel versions of a reading test were prepared, with widely different print size and line length, and students' results on these versions were compared with their performance on an equivalent test given under normal conditions. No differences were found in mean scores, or in interactions with ability (Archer & Elley, 1993). Apparently, 9-year-olds can tolerate wide variations in these layout factors without disadvantage, at least in New Zealand, under typical testing conditions.

Pilot Testing

Twenty-nine countries participated in the pilot test exercises which were administered by the NRCs to students in the target grades in carefully selected judgment samples of schools.

Typically, over 800 students participated at each level in each country. As the four parallel forms were rotated within classes, approximately 150 to 250 students responded to each item.

Data cleaning and processing were undertaken at the ICC, and the Steering Committee and five NRCs met in May 1990 to review the results of the item analysis and to select the items for the final tests. Classical item analysis and item response theory, in particular the Rasch model, provided the basis for this exercise after evidence was obtained that the Rasch model would fit the data adequately. This model was useful in such a context because it produced a single measurement scale across all national samples and allowed estimates to be made both of the students' ability and the difficulty of the items. Then any departures from expected patterns either on the part of students or of items were signaled. Items which did not fit the pattern could then be studied and revised or omitted.

The pilot study was designed so that for every item to be selected for the final test, and for every cell of the test blueprint, there would be at least three items in the pilot study. Those passages and items with good psychometric properties within and between countries were identified and selected in such a way as to allow for an appropriate balance of topic, reading skill, and passage length. A further important criterion in the selection process was that the test items would cover the whole range of student abilities in reading, both within and between countries. A problem was that very difficult items rarely survived the pilot tests, as they often showed a highly differential functioning between countries and, in particular, did not function effectively in countries where reading levels were low. A further criterion for the item selection was that items would fit the international and national Rasch domain scales and were sufficiently discriminating between good and poor readers.

Items with poor psychometric characteristics in particular countries were also identified so as to check for culture bias, gender bias or translation faults.

The pilot test also enabled the researchers to check on time limits, to consider item sequencing, and to revise, where necessary, instructions to students. NRCs agreed that this provided them with valuable experience for the final testing. After further review by the NRCs and their Advisory Committees, the final tests, time limits, and instructions were agreed to by all at a meeting of the NRCs and Steering Committee in Frascati, Italy, in July 1990.

The Final Tests

The tests for Population A consisted of 106 test items which were administered in two testing sessions of 35 and 40 min respectively. The beginning of the test contained a short Word Recognition test which consisted of 40 items and asked the students under time-restricted conditions to match simple, individual words with their corresponding pictures. The test provided weaker students with a task on which they might be expected to succeed, and was designed to show whether weaknesses found in the reading comprehension domains could be attributed to the students' inability to decode rapidly words of high familiarity. The Word Recognition part was followed by a number of reading passages and documents, for each of which a set of test items were asked. Four reading passages with 22 items were selected from the narrative domain, five passages with 21 items were selected from the expository domain, and six documents with 23 items were selected from the documents domain. Four test items required a word or phrase to be written by the students, two items asked the students to write an extended response in their own words, and the remaining items had multiple-choice response format, with four choices for each item.

The tests for Population B consisted of 89 test items, which were administered in two testing sessions of 40 and 45 min respectively. Five passages with 29 items were selected from the narrative domain, five passages with 26 items were selected from the expository domain, and 9 documents with 34 items were selected from the documents domain. Twenty of the test items required the students to write a word or phrase, two items asked the students to write an extended response in their own words, and the remaining items were multiple-choice items, with four options for each item. The extended response-items were scored locally as an international option on the basis of an international scoring scheme. They were located toward the end of the testing sessions.

Except for the Word Recognition test, which had a strict time limit of 1 min and 30 sec, the tests were designed so that in most countries the students would have sufficient time to respond to each item. The students were instructed to respond to all items even if they were not sure of the correct answer, and there was no penalty for a wrong answer.

Tables 1.1 and 1.2 show the final blueprints (or two-way grids) for each test. The three domains are listed on the left; the various skills (or mental processes) which it was hypothesized that the students used in responding to each item are listed across the top of each table. The classification of these skills was undertaken initially by the Steering Committee, and confirmed in an exercise conducted by 27 volunteer raters (or judges) in 12 countries. All raters were given copies of the tests and a set of definitions of each skill, with examples, and asked to rate each item. This exercise resulted in a relatively high degree of agreement (over 80%) on most items, but some divergence on a few. In cases of doubt, the modal (most popular) choice was accepted.

Table 1.1 shows that eight items required a verbatim response, i.e., the answer resided in the text, in much the same wording as in the question. Twenty items required students to paraphrase or recognize the answer in the text in different wording from that of the question; 15 items required students to go beyond the information given and make an inference in arriving at the correct answer. In the Documents domain, 11 items required students merely to locate a fact or figure, while a further 12 asked them to locate and process (count, compare, or infer).

Table 1.2 shows the frequencies of skills for Population B. At this level, the few verbatim items were incorporated with the paraphrase items, and a separate category, inferring the main idea or theme of the passage, was introduced. For Population B, it is clear that 35% of items required inferential thinking on prose passages, and another 22% required multilevel processing of information in the Documentary domain.

As expected, these categories of items varied somewhat in difficulty. Verbatim, paraphrase, and locating items proved easier, while inferential items were generally more difficult. However, a detailed analysis of achievement levels by skills across nations did not reveal any patterns which were not identified in comparisons by domains. Items which proved easier in one country tended to be easier in all countries.

Tables C.1 and C.2 in Appendix C list the passages in the final tests, with a brief descriptive comment on each passage.

One potential weakness of a test designed to be acceptable in a wide range of cultures is that it might be one which is very narrow in terms of the range of topics presented to the students. However, a close examination of Tables C.1 and C.2 reveals that the tests cover a broad range of topics which, in fact, is wider than the range found in many standardized reading tests in the participating countries.

The tests contained three bridging passages, common to both populations (labelled Shark, Marmots and Temperature). These passages provided 14 items which formed a link between the performance of the two grade levels (Populations A and B) and thus offered some basis for estimating the amount of growth between the two populations. Two passages (Marmots and Paracutin) were included from the 1970–1971 international survey of Reading Literacy (Thorndike, 1973) to provide some indication of change over time.

Table 1.1

Final Blueprint for Population A. Test Skills

Domain	Verbatim	Paraphrase	Inference	Locate Information	Locate and Process	Total
Narrative	1	11	10	---	---	22
Expository	7	9	5	---	---	21
Documents	---	---	---	11	12	23
Total	8	20	15	11	12	66

Table 1.2

Final Blueprint for Population B. Test Skills

Domain	Paraphrase	Main Idea	Inference	Locate Information	Locate and Process	Total
Narrative	9	3	17	---	---	29
Expository	15	4	7	---	---	26
Documents	---	---	---	14	20	34
Total	24	7	24	14	20	89

Measures of student abilities in reading literacy were estimated and reported for each population for each domain separately (referred to as domain scores in this volume) as well as for the total item scale (referred to as total scores in this volume). The Word Recognition items were not included in any of the scales, since this part of the test was used as a screening test only. Additionally the domain scores were sometimes combined for reporting purposes to produce average domain scores (referred to as overall domain scores in this volume) in which each domain was given equal weight.

From all items in the final tests, six items in Population A and seven items in Population B had to be excluded from the calculation of student ability measures because of poor psychometric properties on the international scale. The omitted items were evenly distributed across the domains. Additionally, in a few cases particular items had to be excluded for particular countries because of mistranslations, problems in administration, or because of poor national psychometric properties. The Rasch scale was able to accommodate such omissions and ensured that, on the basis of some reasonable assumptions, accurate and internationally comparable student ability estimates could nevertheless be calculated.

Figure 1.1 presents the difficulty levels of the test items in the final tests in relation to the international distribution of student abilities. In this figure both populations are presented on a single common scale, anchored on the basis of 12 of the common items on the assumption that the items in both populations would address a common latent trait (for details on this issue readers are referred to Beaton (1993)). Two common items were deleted because of ceiling effects.

The vertical plots on the left-hand side of Figure 1.1 show the international distribution of student ability measures for both populations as derived from the anchored total item scale. The distributions were calculated on an international pooled dataset in which all participating countries were included with equal weight. The scales were chosen so that the mean total score for students in Population A (focusing on 9-year-old students) would be 9 and the mean score in Population B (focusing on 14-year-old students) would be 14, in order to enable the reader to make some inferences concerning the growth in reading ability in relation to the students' age. It is recommended that such inferences should be made with due caution. The horizontal bars in the center of the plots indicate the international mean score, the dark shaded area ranges from the 40th to the 60th percentile, the light shaded area ranges from the 25th to the 75th percentile, the bars outside the shaded areas indicate the 10th and 90th percentile, and the borders indicate the 1st and 99th percentile.

The right-hand side of Figure 1.1 presents the names of the test items that compose the reading tests. The test items for each domain are presented in a separate column, with an indication of the population, the passage, and the sequential number of the item within the passage. Tables C.1 and C.2 provide further information and references for the test items. The vertical position of the items in the figure indicates the item difficulty. The scale value which corresponds to the vertical position of the item in this figure indicates the ability score which a student would need in order to answer this item correctly with a probability of .80. For example, the item GRANDPA 5 has a scale value of 10.9. For students with scores greater than 10.9 on this scale, the probability of answering this item correctly would be greater than .80. As can be seen from the international distribution of the scores, for this item less than 43% of the students in Population A achieved this level. It can be seen from this figure that, under the assumptions by which the populations were anchored, if this item had been administered in Population B, more than 63% of the students in Population B would have answered it correctly. The figure thus provides some indication of the growth in reading ability between both target populations.

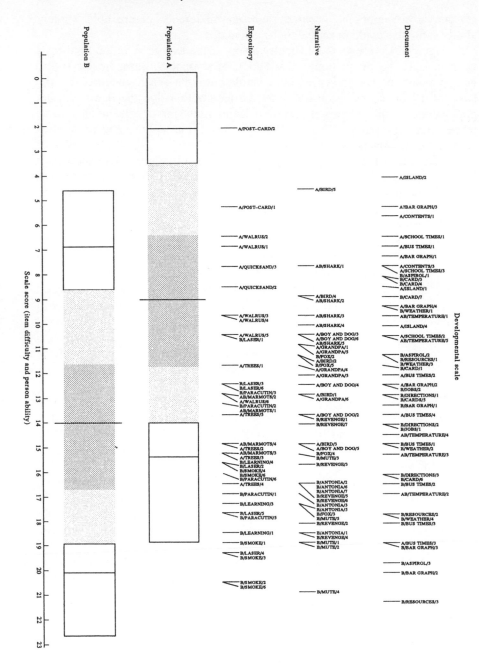

Figure 1.1: Developmental Scale (Items Grouped by Domain)

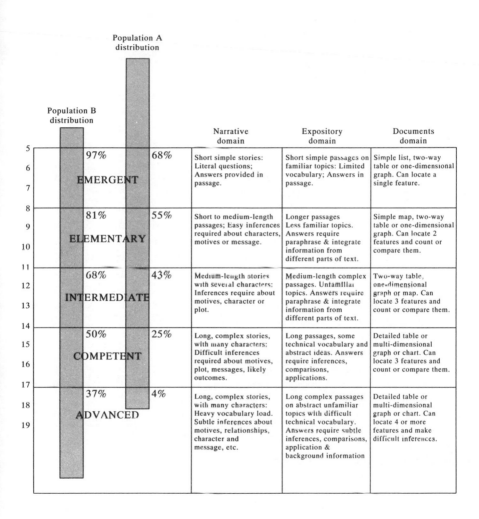

			Narrative domain	Expository domain	Documents domain
5					
6	97% EMERGENT	68%	Short simple stories: Literal questions; Answers provided in passage.	Short simple passages on familiar topics: Limited vocabulary; Answers in passage.	Simple list, two-way table or one-dimensional graph. Can locate a single feature.
7					
8					
9	81% ELEMENTARY	55%	Short to medium-length passages; Easy inferences required about characters, motives or message.	Longer passages Less familiar topics. Answers require paraphrase & integrate information from different parts of text.	Simple map, two-way table or one-dimensional graph. Can locate 2 features and count or compare them.
10					
11					
12	68% INTERMEDIATE	43%	Medium-length stories with several characters; Inferences require about motives, character or plot.	Medium-length complex passages. Unfamiliar topics. Answers require paraphrase & integrate information from different parts of text.	Two-way table, one-dimensional graph or map. Can locate 3 features and count or compare them.
13					
14					
15	50% COMPETENT	25%	Long, complex stories with many characters; Difficult inferences required about motives, plot, messages, likely outcomes.	Long passages, some technical vocabulary and abstract ideas. Answers require inferences, comparisons, applications.	Detailed table or multi-dimensional graph or chart. Can locate 3 features and count or compare them.
16					
17					
18	37% ADVANCED	4%	Long, complex stories with many characters: Heavy vocabulary load. Subtle inferences about motives, relationships, character and message, etc.	Long complex passages on abstract unfamiliar topics with difficult technical vocabulary. Answers require subtle inferences, comparisons, application & background information	Detailed table or multi-dimensional graph or chart. Can locate 4 or more features and make difficult inferences.
19					

Figure 1.2: Developmental scale showing levels of reading ability required to score at selected scale points in each domain

Figure 1.2 is designed to provide the reader with some understanding of the levels of reading ability required to score at selected scale points on this development scale. Thus, students who score below a scale point of 8 are described as reading at the Emergent Level. In the Narrative domain, this means that they typically are able to read (with a .80 probability of success) only short simple stories and respond to literal questions for which the answers are provided in the passage. In the Documents domain, a score at this level means that they can study a simple list, two-way table or one-dimensional graph and locate a single feature correctly.

At the other end of the scale, Advanced Level tasks (over 17 on the scale) involve long complex or abstract texts, with heavy vocabulary load and require difficult or subtle inferences to be performed by the reader. Only 37% of students in Population B were estimated to be reading at the level of 17 or above. Many more may do so with less than .80 probability of success, of course.

The percentage figures presented on the right of each distribution column show the percentage of all students who scored at each level with .80 probability of success. Thus, 50% of all Population B students scored at the Competent Level or above; 25% of Population A did. Meanwhile, 32% of all Population A were not able to read the easiest tasks consistently.

To illustrate more clearly the differences between the levels, sample test passages and selected items are presented below, along with the scaled scores required to read and correctly answer each one.

At the Emergent Level, the examples given are from the Expository and Documents domains. Thus, all Population A students were required to read a relatively short expository passage, in simple language, about the Walrus, and answer five items. (The illustrations have been omitted from this presentation.) The two items given (1 and 2) required the students to respond verbatim, using information given in the passage, in much the same words. These two items are scaled at 6.8 and 6.4 respectively, indicating that they would be answered correctly with .80 probability by 6-year-old students on the assumptions of the scale, as described above.

Example: Expository Domain, Emergent Level

The Walrus
The walrus is easy to recognize because it has two large teeth sticking out of its mouth. These teeth are called eye teeth. The walrus lives in cold seas. If the water freezes over, the walrus keeps a hole free of ice either by swimming round and round in the water, or by hacking off the edge of the ice with its eye teeth. The walrus can also use its skull to knock a hole in the ice.

The walrus depends on its eye teeth for many things. For example, when looking for food a walrus dives to the bottom of the sea and uses its eye teeth to scrape off clams. The walrus also uses its eye teeth to pull itself onto the ice. It needs its eye teeth to attack or kill a seal and eat it, or to defend itself if attacked by a polar bear.
The walrus may grow very big and very old. A full-grown male is almost 4 metres long and weighs more than 1000 kg. It may reach an age of 30 years. The walrus sleeps on the ice or on a piece of rock sticking out of the water, but it is also able to sleep in the water.

1. Where does the walrus live?
   A. ☐ In very cold water   (6.8)
   B. ☐ In tropical countries
   C. ☐ On the bottom of lakes
   D. ☐ In cold forest country

2. How long can a walrus live?
   A. ☐ 2 years
   B. ☐ 4 years
   C. ☐ 30 years   (6.4)
   D. ☐ 100 years

The example from the Documents domain is taken from a short Table of Contents. Students had to locate one feature, the name of the author of "The Rice Bowl." The difficulty scale level for this item was 7.6 and 56% of students in Population A can answer this question with .80 probability of success.

Example: Documents Domain, Emergent Level

Table of Contents

This is a part of the table of contents in a book. Use it to answer the questions below.

CONTENTS

Title	Author	Pages
Let's Look at Tracks	Ann Zim	3–9
What's Inside of Me?	Herb Martin	10–15
The Rice Bowl	Les Jones	16–19
The Ant and the Elephant	Bill Guthrie	20–24
Ring of Roses	Pat Brooke	25–32
Making Model Aeroplanes	Andy Purves	33–35

> 2. Who wrote the passage: "The Rice Bowl"?
>   A. ☐ Les Jones   (7.6)
>   B. ☐ Ann Zim
>   C. ☐ Herb Martin
>   D. ☐ Bill Guthrie

At the Elementary Level, a sample passage and item are given for the Narrative domain. All Population A students had to read a short simple fable about a bird and an elephant and answer five questions to test their comprehension. Item 4 required them to paraphrase the climax of the story and the item proved to have a scale value of 8.8. Fifty-two percent of Population A students and 74% of Population B students would be expected to answer such a question with .80 probability of success.

Example: Narrative Domain, Elementary Level

The Bird and the Elephant

A large tree grew in the middle of the jungle. At the top, a small bird had made a nest for her family of three baby birds. One day, an elephant came by. He leaned against the trunk, and scratched his back. The tree started to crack and sway. The baby birds, full of fear, huddled against their mother. She stuck the tip of her beak out of the nest and said: "*Hey, big animal, there are many trees around here! Why shake this one? My children are afraid, and could fall out of their nest.*"

The elephant said nothing, but he looked at the bird with his small eye, flapped his large ears in the wind, and left.

The next day the elephant returned and scratched against the trunk once more. The tree began to sway. The frightened baby birds once again huddled against their mother's wings. Now Mother Bird was angry. "I order you to stop shaking our tree," she cried, "or I will teach you a lesson!"

"*What could you do* to a giant like me?" laughed the elephant. "If I wanted to, I could give such a push to this tree that your nest and your children would be flung far and wide."

The mother bird said nothing.

The next day, the elephant returned and scratched again. Quick as a flash, the mother bird flew into one of the elephant's enormous ears, and there, tickled the elephant by scratching him with her feet. The elephant shook his head   nothing happened. So he begged the bird to leave and promised to stop scratching against the trunk.

The bird then left the elephant's ear and returned to her nest beside her children.

Never again did the elephant return to scratch his back.

4. What did the mother bird do to stop the elephant from returning to that tree?
   A. ☐ Ordered him to stop
   B. ☐ Scratched his back
   C. ☐ Tickled his ear   (8.8)
   D. ☐ Stuck her beak into him

At the Intermediate Level, examples are presented from the Expository and Narrative domains. All students in Population B had to read Paracutin, a 250 word factual description of a volcano which erupted unexpectedly in Mexico. Item 2 required them to paraphrase and integrate facts from different parts of the passage. The scale value of this item is 12.8 and it was answered correctly, at the .80 level, by 55% of Population B students.

Example: Expository Domain, Intermediate Level

Paracutin

Paracutin was born in Mexico in February, 1943. At the end of one week, Paracutin was 500 feet high and it is now over 9,000 feet high. Today Paracutin is asleep.

What is Paracutin? It was the first volcano in the world which was seen from its birth right up to the present day. On February 20, 1943, a peasant and his wife set out to work in their maize fields from the Mexican village of Paracutin. They were surprised to find the earth warm under their feet. Suddenly, they heard noises deep in the earth and a small hollow appeared in their field. In the afternoon there was a sudden loud noise and stones were flung high in the air. The peasants ran from the field and turned to watch. They saw the birth of a volcano.

There were great bursts of stone and lava and a little hill began to form. By evening this hill was 100 feet high and hot ashes were falling on the village. At night the glare of the hot lava lit up the countryside. The trees near the village were killed and the villagers had to leave their houses. When the village was abandoned its name was given to the volcano. The news quickly spread to Mexico City, far to the east. Many sightseers and scientists flocked to the scene. The volcano grew and grew for ten years and hundreds of square miles of forest were destroyed. Then Paracutin went to sleep. In spite of all the explosions, not one person was killed.

2. What was destroyed in the eruption?
   A. ☐ Only a village
   B. ☐ The villagers living close by
   C. ☐ The forests and fields round Paracutin (12.8)
   D. ☐ Two peasants

The Narrative passage, Grandpa, was given to Population A students. It is a longer passage (340 words), still with relatively simple language, but it includes several characters, and has a somewhat abstract moral message. Item

6 required students to understand the reason for the parents' change of attitude, and was found to have a scale value of 12.6. It was answered with .80 probability of success by 35% of Population A students.

Example: Narrative Domain, Intermediate Level

Grandpa
Once upon a time, there was a very old man. His eyes had become weak. His ears were deaf, and his knees would shake. When he sat at the table, he was hardly able to hold the spoon. He spilled soup on the tablecloth, and he often slobbered. He lived with his son and daughter-in-law. They also had a small boy who was four years old, so the old man was a grandfather. His son and his son's wife found it disgusting to see him spilling food at the table. And so they finally ordered him to sit in a corner behind the stove. Here, they served him his food on a small earthenware plate. Now, Grandpa didn't even get enough to satisfy his hunger. He sat there feeling sad. He looked at the table, where the others were eating, and his eyes filled with tears. Then, one day his shaking hands could not even hold the plate. It fell to the floor, and was broken into many pieces. The young wife scolded him. But the old grandfather said nothing. He just sighed. Then the young wife bought him a very cheap wooden bowl. Now he had to eat from that. One day, while they were having dinner, the grandchild sat on the floor, and was very busy with some small pieces of wood. "What are you doing?" asked his father. "I am making a bowl," the boy answered. "What is it for?" "It is for my father and mother to eat from when I grow up." The man and his wife looked at each other for a long time. Then, they started crying. At once, they asked the old grandpa back to the table, and from then on he always ate with them. After that, even if he sometimes spilt his food, they never said a word about it.

6. The son and his wife cried because
    A. ☐ the boy could not make a wooden bowl.
    B. ☐ their old father could not eat properly.
    C. ☐ they understood that they too would grow old. (12.5)
    D. ☐ the wooden bowl was also broken.

To illustrate the Competent Level, a Document domain set is used, presenting a Bus Timetable. To answer the questions 1 and 2, students had to locate and compare at least three items of information in arriving at the correct response. These questions are scaled at 14.8 and 16.4. Item 1 would be answered correctly, with .80 probability of success, by 18% of Population A and 47% of Population B students; item 2 would be answered at this level by 7% of Population A students and 41% of Population B students.

Example: Documents Domain, Competent Level

Bus
This is a part of a bus timetable; use it to answer the questions below.

INWARD – TO CITY   OUTWARD – FROM CITY

Leaves Weston	Leaves Trump St.	Leaves Monument	Leaves Hilltop	Arrives City	Leaves City	Leaves Hilltop	Leaves Monument	Leaves Trump St.	Arrives Weston
					5.20	5.24	5.30	5.45	5.55
					5.50	5.54	6.00	6.15	6.25
					6.20	6.24	6.30	6.45	6.55
6.00	6.10	6.25	6.31	6.35	6.40	6.44	6.50	7.05	7.15
6.30	6.40	6.55	7.01	7.05	7.10	7.14	7.20	7.35	7.45
7.00	7.10	7.25	7.31	7.35	7.40	7.44	7.50	8.05	8.15
7.20	7.30	7.45	7.51	7.55	8.00	8.04	8.10	8.25	8.35
7.50	8.00	8.15	8.21	8.25	8.30	8.34	8.40	8.55	9.05
8.20	8.30	8.45	8.51	8.55	9.00	9.04	9.10	9.25	9.35
8.50	9.00	9.15	9.21	9.25	9.30	9.34	9.40	9.55	10.05
9.20	9.30	9.45	9.51	9.55	10.00	10.04	10.10	10.25	10.35
10.00	10.10	10.35	10.41	10.45	10.50	10.54	11.00	11.15	11.25
10.30	10.40	10.55	11.01	11.05	11.10	11.14	11.20	11.35	11.45
11.30	11.40	11.55	12.01	12.05	12.10	12.14	12.20	12.35	12.45

1. When does the <u>first</u> bus from Weston to the city leave the Monument each day?   6.25   (14.8)
2. If you miss the 8.21 am bus from Hilltop to the City, what time would you arrive in the city if you took the next one?   8.55   (16.4)

The Advanced Level is illustrated by items drawn from the Documents and Expository domains. The Documents set shows a complex bar graph, depicting the number of hares and lynxes in a given population over an 11-year period. For item 2, Population B students had to use the key to interpret the graph, study each bar to work out the overall pattern, and then identify the year in which the pattern was disrupted. This was a very difficult item (Scale 19.9). For item 3, the students had to again establish the overall pattern of the graph and make a further inference (Scale 18.7).

For the Expository passage, Population B students had to read a 330 word, difficult technical passage on the effects of smoking on human bodily functions. The two items shown (2 and 6) required students to understand the text well enough to integrate information from different parts of the passage and, in the last item, to make an inference about the author's attitude. The scale values are both over 20, and only 8% of Population B were successful on such items.

Example: Documents Domain, Advanced Level

The Snowshoe Hare And The Canadian Lynx
(A Prey And Predator Cycle)
Use the bar graph below to answer the questions.

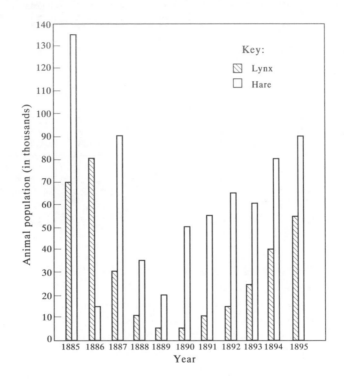

---

2. Which year is not consistent with the general pattern shown by the graph?

    A. ❒   1885
    B. ❒   1886   (19.9)
    C. ❒   1889
    D. ❒   1891

3. If there was a sudden decline in the hare population, due to disease or overcrowding, which of the following would also probably occur?

    A. ☐   The lynx would suddenly increase in numbers.
    B. ☐   The hare population would take a decade to recover.
    C. ☐   The lynx population would also decline soon after.
    D. ☐   The hares would double their number the following year.

Example: Expository Domain, Advanced Level

Smoke

The relationship between smoking and cancer, smoking and heart attacks and many other serious diseases is undeniable. Convincing evidence comes from many statistical studies that show the close relationship between the number of cigarettes smoked daily and the probability of dying of cancer or a heart attack.

The explanation for this terrible phenomenon comes from research laboratories. It has been shown that a single puff of smoke can break down the DNA in human cells, this being the long molecule which contains the cell's genetic and metabolic information. What destroys the genetic code are some tar-like substances produced by the process of combustion. In chemical terms, these are oxidizing molecules, but one can also accurately describe them as little ravenous monsters that tear apart the bonds that keep the DNA together. After each poisonous whiff the DNA patiently reconstructs itself again but clearly at each restoration the probability of errors increases and in the end some malignant genes (which are always present in unstressed DNA) manage to get the upper hand and thus stimulate cancer. This is the destructive process that the cells of the organs which carry the smoke to the lungs have to undergo every time. It is not surprising that mouth, tongue, larynx, windpipe and bronchi in smokers are more often affected by malignant tumours.

The smoke's final destination is in the lungs where, besides tar, it deposits natural radioactive substances concentrated by combustion. Each day a heavy smoker (one who smokes more than 20 cigarettes a day) absorbs the same amount of radiation which he would receive when having a chest X-ray. Nicotine, on the other hand, goes straight into the blood stream and has a strong constrictive action on the arteries. This way the circulation of blood to all the tissues diminishes. That is why skin temperature decreases, sexual organs produce fewer hormones and nervous metabolism slows down. The brain become less efficient, dizziness and giddiness appear but such sensations are barely perceived by the heavy smoker. On the contrary, these are very strong sensations in those who smoke for the first time and they constitute the "drug effect" that has led many towards becoming habitual smokers.

---

2. The destruction of DNA caused by smoke is dangerous because

    A. ☐ it leads to the deposit of tar-like substances in the lungs.
    B. ☐ it causes cancer of the blood.
    C. ☐ it may bring about error in the reconstitution of DNA.
    D. ☐ it prevents DNA from reconstructing.

6. Which of these phrases best indicates the writer's attitude to smoking?
    A. ☐ "patiently reconstructs"
    B. ☐ "ravenous monsters"
    C. ☐ "constrictive action"
    D. ☐ "habitual smokers"

Other Characteristics of the Final Tests

Difficulty Levels

The test plans provided for a wide range of difficulty levels in the reading tasks prepared. In order to accommodate the needs of weaker readers, a number of relatively easy tasks were included at each age level. Indeed, the item selection criteria adopted meant that very difficult items rarely survived the pilot tests, as they did not function effectively in countries where reading levels were low.

Table 1.3

Distribution of International Logit Values for Items in
Population A Test

Logit value	Narrative	Expository	Documents	Total
Over 2.00	0	2	3	5
1.50 to 1.99	1	1	2	4
1.00 to 1.49	2	4	0	6
0.50 to 0.99	5	4	3	12
0.00 to 0.49	3	1	2	6
-0.00 to -0.49	5	3	2	10
-0.50 to -0.99	3	1	4	8
-1.00 to -1.49	0	2	3	5
-0.50 to -1.99	1	1	2	4
Under -2.00	0	0	0	0
Total	20	19	21	60

Tables 1.3 and 1.4 present distributions of international logit values (difficulty indices) for each test, broken down by domain.

Table 1.4

Distribution of International Logit Values for Items in
Population B Test

Logit value	Narrative	Expository	Documents	Total
2.00 to 2.49	0	0	1	1
1.50 to 1.99	1	0	3	4
1.00 to 1.49	3	3	3	9
0.50 to 0.99	5	5	4	14
0.00 to 0.49	6	3	5	13
-0.00 to -0.49	4	6	5	15
-0.50 to -0.99	1	3	5	9
-1.00 to -1.49	2	3	3	8
-1.50 to -1.99	3	1	3	7
Under -2.00	1	0	0	1
Total	26	24	32	82

Item Discrimination Levels

All test items showed positive discrimination within domains. Internationally, most produced a mean point-biserial index between .30 and .50; only two items fell below this level in the Population A test, and none in the Population B test. In the few cases where an item in one country was found to have a deviant discrimination index (usually because of a misprint or a fault in translation), it was identified as not fitting the Rasch scale, and was deleted from that country's data set. The Rasch scale was able to accommodate such omissions and still provide accurate score estimates. Tables 1.5 and 1.6 present the mean point-biserial indices for all countries for Populations A and B.

Table 1.5

Distribution of Point-Biserial Indices for Items in
Population A Test

Point Biserial Index	Narrative	Expository	Documents	Total
Over 0.60	2	0	0	2
0.55 to 0.59	4	5	1	10
0.50 to 0.54	5	5	6	16
0.45 to 0.49	7	2	5	14
0.40 to 0.44	2	4	4	10
0.35 to 0.39	0	1	4	5
0.30 to 0.34	0	1	0	1
0.25 to 0.29	0	1	1	2
Below 0.25	0	0	0	0
Total	20	19	21	60

Table 1.6

Distribution of Point-Biserial Indices for Items in Population B Test

Point Biserial Index	Narrative	Expository	Documents	Total
Over 0.55	5	0	0	5
0.50 to 0.54	3	2	1	6
0.45 to 0.49	5	6	2	13
0.40 to 0.44	3	7	9	19
0.35 to 0.39	6	5	14	25
0.30 to 0.34	4	4	6	14
Below 0.30	0	0	0	0
Total	26	24	32	82

Reliability

Most conclusions drawn in this survey were based on grouped data, often of many hundreds of students, so the question of individual reliability of scores is of lesser significance. However, the individual reliability figures are relevant for some of the multivariate analyses, and are summarized below in Table 1.7. Country-by-country figures are provided in Appendix I.

Table 1.7

Mean Reliability Coefficients for Individual Domain Scores and
Total Scores

	Population A	Population B
Domain Scores		
Narrative	0.84	0.85
Expository	0.81	0.79
Documents	0.79	0.80
Total Scores		
Cronbach alpha	0.93	0.92
Equivalent forms	0.87	0.89

Most domain score reliability coefficients (KR20) for both populations clustered around .80–.85, while those for Total Scores were typically between .90 and .95 when calculated by an equivalent forms method in which students' scores on the two test sessions were correlated and corrected for length by the Spearman–Brown correction formula.

International Equivalence of Items

One important feature of an acceptable international test is its item equivalence across nations. To what extent do the test items behave in a similar fashion in all countries? Are the most difficult items in one country the most difficult in all countries?

To investigate this matter, the difficulty indices for all items were correlated with the mean difficulty index for all countries in an attempt to identify any items which deviated from the expected pattern. For this purpose, international and national p values were used, but the Rasch logit score would have shown similar patterns as the two indices were correlated over .99.

Table 1.8

Correlations Between *p*-Values for Each Country and International
p-Values

Country	Population A	Population B
Bel/Fr	0.96	0.92
Bot	—	0.77
Can/BC	0.96	0.92
Cyp	0.94	0.91
Den	0.93	0.93
Fin	0.91	0.85
Fra	0.96	0.91
Ger/E	0.93	0.90
Ger/W	0.94	0.92
Gre	0.94	0.89
HK	0.90	0.82
Hun	0.91	0.88
Ice	0.94	0.89
Ire	0.95	0.94
Ita	0.93	0.91
Net	0.95	0.91
NZ	0.95	0.94
Nig	—	0.85
Nor	0.95	0.89
Phi	—	0.84
Por	0.94	0.87
Sin	0.91	0.87
Slo	0.95	0.90
Spa	0.96	0.86
Swe	0.96	0.91
Swi	0.96	0.93
Tha	—	0.74
T/T	0.95	—
USA	0.91	0.91
Ven	0.87	0.89
Median	0.94	0.90
Median English Countries	0.95	0.91

The Rasch analysis itself provided confirmation that the test was functioning in similar fashion in each country. However, this additional analysis was undertaken to investigate the extent to which translation may have distorted the scores. If all English-speaking countries showed more similar patterns than those revealed in countries with other languages, for example, one would have to conclude that the translation process had an influence on the scores.

Table 1.8 shows for each population the correlation between the difficulty values of each country on each item and the mean (international) difficulty value, based on a pooled random sample of 200 students from each country. The median rs for all countries were correlated and compared with the median rs for the six English-speaking countries.

The median correlations in Table 1.8 are sufficiently high, with minor exceptions, to generate confidence that the translation process did not have a marked effect on the results, and the tests functioned in a similar fashion in each education system. As the median rs for English-speaking countries were only slightly higher than those for all countries, it is reasonable to conclude that the order of item difficulty in English was virtually identical to the order of item difficulty in the non-English tests. As Thorndike (1973) pointed out, given sensible translation guidelines, the weight of difficulty in most reading comprehension exercises is largely a function of the concepts, rather than the specific language in which they are couched.

Questionnaires

In addition to the reading literacy test data, information was collected from all countries by means of questionnaires about the students' voluntary reading activities, about their homes, and about their school circumstances, as described by teachers, principals, and the students themselves. The researchers recognized the limitations of questionnaires for obtaining reliable data, but in view of the enormous scope of the planned study, questionnaires were judged to be the only practicable approach. While some issues cannot be addressed by questionnaire, and others can be addressed only in an oblique fashion, there are still many questions, of interest to educators, which can be asked and genuinely answered in this way. When large numbers of students and teachers are involved, corroboration of their responses in determining group trends is relatively straightforward, and deviant responses can be readily identified.

Appendix D outlines the procedures adopted in developing the questionnaires used to collect data from four groups of respondents: students, teachers, school principals, and NRCs. As in the case of the test development exercise, all countries' NRCs and their National Advisory Committees were invited to contribute to the conceptual framework and the questions, and to comment on the questions prepared. Past experience of IEA studies had some influence on the choice of indicators to be measured and on the style of questions selected for inclusion. All questions were edited repeatedly by Steering Committee and the NRCs, and the pilot tests of 1990 enabled the researchers to refine them further.

Conceptual Framework

There is no limit to the kinds of background questions which can be put to students and their teachers about the context of their reading development. To delimit the area of investigation, the researchers developed a theoretical framework which guided both the development of the questionnaires and the subsequent analysis. Although this framework was modified slightly as the study progressed, the framework which most influenced the choice of background questions for Population A is given below in Table 1.9. The questionnaires for Population B followed similar lines, but an early decision to confine multivariate analyses to Population A data only ,resulted in a restriction in the number of questions asked in some areas for Population B (This decision was strongly influenced by lack of funds). Table 1.9 presents four sets of variables. The Background Variables column on the left includes those home variables for which information can be collected from students, and which were believed to exert considerable influence on students' achievement levels in reading literacy. There is evidence from most countries, for instance, that students who are brought up in well-resourced homes will achieve more highly in school reading tests than those from homes which lack certain advantages, such as an ample supply of reading materials at home and parents who take a strong interest in their children's progress in reading. There is also sufficient evidence that children whose home language is different from that of the school are typically at a disadvantage in school reading tasks. In addition, pupil gender shows differences in achievement, favoring girls in most countries, while children from large towns frequently achieve at higher levels than those from rural areas. Furthermore, children who watch TV a great deal have less time available for reading, and therefore achieve less highly. On the basis of this kind of rationale, questions were prepared for the student questionnaires. It was hypothesized that the responses treated as singletons or grouped together to form latent variables would yield correlations with student achievement.

Further questions were developed to provide data on School Inputs, the second column of Table 1.9. It is widely assumed by policy-makers that well-resourced schools will enable students to raise their achievement levels. This is an assumption fraught with implications for government spending. In addition to the availability of books it was predicted that student achievement would be assisted by such school inputs as class size, and several presumed beneficial qualities of the school principal, such as principal engagement in the reading program, principal's length of service in the school, principal's initiative in

Table 1.9

Overall Theoretical Framework of the Reading Literacy Indicators:
Population A

I BACKGROUND VARIABLES		II SCHOOL INPUTS		III SCHOOL/ TEACHER POLICIES		IV OUTCOMES	
1	Economic status	7	Teacher gender	25	Comprehension instruction	38	Narrative achievement
2	Home literacy resources	8	Teacher education	26	Skills instruction	39	Expository achievement
3	Home literacy interactions	9	Teacher training	27	Literature emphasis	40	Documents achievement
4	Home language	10	Teacher in-service	28	Assessment emphasis	41	Voluntary reading activity
5	Pupil gender	11	Teacher experience	29	Homework (Teacher)		
6	Urban–rural	12	Instructional time (Total)	30	Homework (Student)		
6a	TV viewing time	13	Instructional time (Lang.)	31	Reading in class		
		14	Instructional time (Reading)	32	Access to reading mat.		
		15	Teacher readership	33	Frquency lib. visits (Class)		
		16	Reading mat. in class	34	Freq. borrowing books		
		17	Reading mat. in school	35	Encouragement to parents		
		18	School pupil–teacher ratio	36	School reading initiatives		
		19	Class size	37	Principal engagement		
		20	Pupil special teacher ratio				
		21	Public/ private				
		22	Principal experience				
		23	Principal time in school				
		24	Unmet remedial demand				

reading practices, principal's encouragement of parents and the extent of unmet demand for remedial help for slow readers. All such variables need to be adjusted for differences in students' home background, however, in order to show to what extent their beneficial effects are a function of advantages already brought by students to school, as a result of residing in well-resourced homes.

Teachers are educated and trained on the assumption that certain processes will improve their ability to raise students' achievement levels. A set of questions surrounding teachers' education level, pre-service training, and in-service training were used to test this assumption in all countries, once again with home background and certain school resource factors partialled out. There is evidence from some countries that female teachers regularly produce higher achievement in students, and this hypothesis was also proposed, while adjusting for school resource differences. Teachers with longer experience were also presumed to be more effective, and this relationship was to be tested after controlling for home and school resources. A self-report of the extent to which teachers read outside of school was designed to show whether this factor is important for teaching 9-year-old students.

The third column of Table 1.9 lists a number of Teacher and School Policies which were presumed to have an influence on student achievement, over and above the variables identified in the previous two columns. While there are many ways of being an effective teacher, and many of these cannot be assessed without close observation, the researchers assumed that some of the key factors can be tapped by means of self-report questionnaires. In debates on reading instruction, one prominent issue revolves around the extent to which students' reading skills should be systematically developed in structured activities as opposed to a more "whole-language" literature-based approach. These and other general orientations were explored with a series of questions to teachers about their methods, aims, and time allocations. It was planned to assess these approaches by comparing the achievement levels of students whose teachers hold these diverse views, again controlling for the effects of advantages in the students' home backgrounds and school resources. Another major orientation is the general belief that teachers can deliberately teach comprehension. Recent research (Pearson & Dole, 1987; Palincsar & Brown, 1984) demonstrates that it is often effective, and this hypothesis was proposed for investigation in all countries, after controlling for the enhancing influence of home and school variables.

Other variables which previous research indicated as likely to be influential were the extent of homework given and done, the amount of reading undertaken in class, and the availability of books in the classroom. If children do improve their reading best by regular silent reading, as some reading theorists suggest, then these relations should be revealed. It is widely claimed that the opportunity to take frequent tests and the style of testing used may assist some pupils in the kinds of tasks used in the IEA study. To test this hypothesis, the kinds and frequency of testing were also investigated, again with appropriate controls.

The right-hand column of Table 1.9 shows the major Dependent Variables in the study. The three test domains, Narrative, Expository, and Documents achievement scores, were described earlier in this chapter. Voluntary Reading Activity is a generic term used to describe the frequency and type of reading material that students claim to read, either in school or at home. The proposal was to collect this information by student questionnaire, and to study the impact of the home and school factors on the outcomes.

2

International Differences in Achievement Levels

WARWICK B. ELLEY AND ANDREAS SCHLEICHER

National Differences in Context and Resources

One of the first aims of this survey was to produce information on the relative achievement levels of students in each school system. It was anticipated that some countries would produce higher achievement outcomes than others, as their students enjoyed a disproportionate array of advantages. Some governments have been able, for instance, to allocate more resources to literacy instruction than those of less affluent countries. Furthermore, social pressures to foster high levels of literacy are greater in some countries than others. Long-term traditions of literacy may have produced generations of good quality literature; daily newspapers are widely circulated and read, and the reading habit is well modeled by many adults in the society. There are also major differences in the quality of health care, which affect the energy levels of students, and there are differences in the size of the school-age population relative to that of the working population that pay for educating them.

Before reporting the comparative achievement levels obtained by students in each country, it is important to spell out some of the differences in resources between them, differences which are beyond the school and which infringe on the students' opportunity to read and perform well on the kinds of tests used in this study. Such a framework needs to include, at least, indicators of affluence, health, and the value placed on literacy by each participating country.

National Differences in Economic Variables

The 32 systems represented in the survey showed a wide range of differences in wealth. When governments can afford to allocate extensive funds to schools, high quality teacher training, school libraries, and professional advisory services, it would be strange if they did not also produce high levels of achievement in their students. Conversely, poor governments which are unable to afford these facilities will rarely be able to point to high performance levels.

Figure 2.1 presents two kinds of economic indicators which are relevant for providing a framework for assessing the achievement levels attained in each country: GNP per capita, and public expenditure on education per student, both expressed in US dollars.

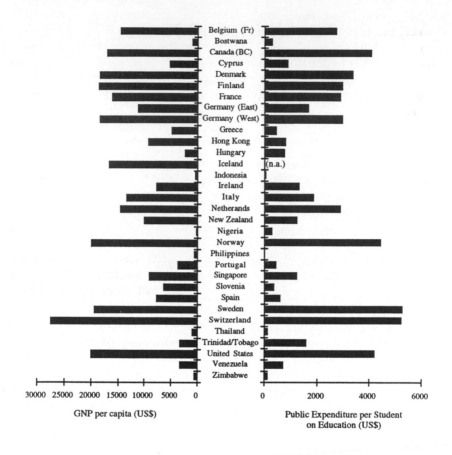

Figure 2.1: Economic Indicators for 32 Participating Countries

The data presented in Figure 2.1 show that seven countries report a GNP per capita of over US$18,000, while four others report figures below US$1000 (it should be noted, however, that these figures are not adjusted for the purchasing power of the US$ with respect to educational resources in each country). Highly correlated with these data is the public expenditure on education per student in each country. The seven most affluent countries report an annual expenditure of over US$3000 per student; the nine least affluent countries report less than US$500 per student.

It is clear that Switzerland, Sweden, Finland, Denmark, Norway, West Germany, Canada/BC, and the United States can allocate extensive resources to their school systems; by contrast, countries like Botswana, Indonesia, Nigeria, the Philippines, Thailand, and Zimbabwe can manage very little by comparison. Not surprisingly, the majority of the wealthy countries also have a relatively small "age dependency ratio." In Scandinavian countries, for instance, there are only 29 children in the 0- to 14-year-old age group for every 100 adults (15 to 64 years). By contrast, the average dependency ratio for the six developing countries is 77 children per 100 adults. Some have more than one child for each adult. These countries not only have less money to spend on the school system, but they must also spread this money more thinly over more students.

Other Indicators of National Welfare and Development

Among the other indicators of development which would influence differences in educational outcomes are those related to the general health and welfare of the population and measures of adult literacy.

Ten countries report population life-expectancy figures at birth of 77 years; six others estimate a figure of less than 70 years. Highly correlated with these data are the national estimates of infant mortality and low birth weight. On the assumption that healthy students will attend school more often and learn better than unhealthy ones, and that healthy teachers will be more effective instructors, one would expect countries with more positive health indicators to show an advantage in this study.

Likewise, 16 countries report 99% adult literacy rate, very high circulation figures for daily newspapers and library books, and very high sales of paper and books. The mean adult literacy rate for the six developing countries was only 75%, while their daily newspaper sales were only 31.7 per 1000 inhabitants. By contrast, several western European countries report over 400 newspapers per 1000 people. On a wide range of relevant indicators, then, it is clear that young people in some countries enjoy considerable advantages in their literacy development. They have teachers with more education, a wider range of reading material, and more obvious reasons for reading than those in developing countries who lack these amenities.

In an effort to set the achievement results in a context which reflects these variations in social pressures to become literate, the scores are reported below in relation to an index known as the Composite Development Index, or CDI. This is a numerical index which is based on six indicators combined with equal weight, and is designed to show the extent of advantage enjoyed by students brought up in wealthier, more literate countries. The six dimensions selected for inclusion in the CDI are two measures of wealth, two measures of health, and two measures of adult literacy.

1.   GNP per capita, in US dollars.
2.   Expenditure on education per student, in US dollars.
3.   Life expectancy at birth.
4.   Percent low birth weight (below 2500 grams).
5.   Newspaper circulation per 1000 inhabitants.
6.   Adult literacy rate.

These six indicators represent the same basic dimensions as the three indicators chosen for the Human Development Index (HDI) produced by the United Nations.

Table 2.1 lists for all 32 systems of education the standard scores calculated for these six indicators, and the total CDI, formed by combining them with equal weights and adding a constant of three to remove negative signs. The countries are listed alphabetically.

Table 2.1

Selected National Indicators of Development for 32 Participating
Systems of Education and the Composite Development Index

Country	(1) GNP per capita ($US)	(2) Public expenditure on education ($US)	(3) Life expectancy	(4) % Low birth weight	(5) Newspapers per 1000	(6) % adult literacy	Composite Development Index	CDI Rank
Belgium/French	14,490	2772	75	5	219	99	3.41	13
Botswana	1010	292	67	8	16	71	1.97	28
Canada/BC	16,960	4096	77	6	254	99	3.66	7
Cyprus	5200	902	75	--	125	94	2.75	22
Denmark	18,450	3390	75	6	359	99	3.64	8
Finland	18,590	2989	75	4	551	99	3.89	5
France	16,090	2912	76	5	193	99	3.48	11
Germany/East	11,300	1697	73	6	585	99	3.44	12
Germany/West	18,480	3021	75	5	347	99	3.65	9
Greece	4800	462	77	6	102	93	2.81	20.5
Hong Kong	9220	843	77	--	239	88	2.94	17.5
Hungary	2460	768	70	10	273	98	2.68	24
Iceland	16,596	--	77	3	562	99	3.98	4
Indonesia	440	54	61	14	21	74	1.59	31
Ireland	7,750	1349	74	4	175	99	3.09	16
Italy	13,330	1894	77	7	105	97	3.17	15
Netherlands	14,520	2910	77	4	314	99	3.65	10
New Zealand	10,000	1261	75	5	327	99	3.28	14
Nigeria	290	294	51	20	22	43	0.68	32
Norway	19,990	4462	77	4	551	99	4.15	3
Philippines	630	29	64	18	56	86	1.73	30
Portugal	3650	459	74	8	41	85	2.46	25
Singapore	9070	1252	74	7	289	86	2.94	17.5
Slovenia	6500	374	73	5	151	99	2.90	19
Spain	7740	630	77	--	75	95	2.81	20.5
Sweden	19,300	5317	77	4	526	99	4.20	2
Switzerland	27,500	5274	77	5	504	99	4.29	1
Thailand	1000	139	65	12	48	91	2.06	27
Trinidad/Tobago	3350	1600	71	--	139	96	2.70	23
United States	19,840	4220	76	7	259	99	3.67	6
Venezuela	3250	756	70	9	164	87	2.47	26
Zimbabwe	650	141	63	15	24	83	1.75	29

From Table 2.1 it can be seen that Switzerland, Sweden, and Norway, with CDI scores above 4.00, stand out on all variables. In the socioeconomically advantaged group of thirteen countries, only 4 of the 78 values listed fell below the international average. Likewise, countries low on one variable tend to be low on all variables.

Appendix E presents the actual mean values and the intercorrelation table for these six variables, plus the total achievement means for all countries. It can be seen that the correlations among these variables are typically 0.7 or higher.

National Differences in Achievement

The Achievement Score Distributions

In Chapter 1, the development of the achievement tests was described in detail. Once the tests were administered in each country and the results coded, all data were then cleaned and processed at the International Coordinating Center (ICC) in Hamburg. On the basis of the Rasch domain item scales referred to in Chapter 1, student Rasch ability measures were computed. The scale for these domain scores was chosen in such a way that the international mean score (giving each participating country equal weight) would be 500 and the standard deviation would be 100.

The final Rasch scores were based on the number of items which students had answered correctly, with no adjustment for omitted items or not reached items. As a considerable number of students in a few countries failed to finish in the time allotted, there was some debate as to whether they should have their scores estimated by the Rasch procedure as if they had finished. However, such an adjustment was not made for reasons presented in Appendix F.

Age and Grade Differences in the Samples Tested

The students in some national samples were older than in others, and some had accumulated more years of schooling at the point of testing. Differences in policies for school entrance and for repeating grades meant that comparisons made between grade groups where most 9-year-olds were found were unlikely to be completely fair. Indeed, Canada (BC) drew a Population A sample which had a mean age of only 8.9 years, while the mean over all countries was 9.8 years. On the other hand France, Indonesia, Portugal, and Venezuela tested samples whose mean ages were slightly over 10.0 years. Similarly, in the Population B sample, Canada (BC) had a mean age of 13.9, while France, Portugal, Hong Kong, and four developing countries had samples with mean ages over 15.0 years.

These discrepancies were not large, and their impact on the comparisons made was not considered very serious for most analyses. Nevertheless, a number of small studies were undertaken to estimate the extent to which the national means would be affected, and these are reported in Appendix G. As the adjustments that resulted from these studies are only approximations, they are not reported in the tables of this chapter. Suffice it to say that the countries most affected were Canada (BC) and the Netherlands in Population A, with possible score underestimates of about 14 and 9 points respectively. For Population B, those most affected were Canada (BC), Italy, Hungary, Spain, and Belgium (French), with possible underestimates of approximately 18, 16, 14, 12, and 11 points respectively. Portugal and France may be overestimated by 20 and 16 points in Population B, along with three developing countries. The remaining differences due to age variations were considered of little consequence. Nevertheless, the mean age of each sample is presented alongside the score distributions in the relevant tables. To put this problem in perspective, it should be noted that a correlation of .99 was found between the reported national mean scores and those means adjusted for differences in mean age.

Eight countries in the survey began formal schooling at age seven, while three others started children at age five and one at five and a half years. The rest began formal schooling at age six. Thus, at age nine, one would anticipate considerable differences in exposure to reading materials, differences which would be reflected in higher test scores for the earlier starters. It is interesting to note that the pattern was different from expectation, and the highest scoring countries proved to be late starters. Furthermore some countries began forms of reading instruction in their preschool institutions, and it should also be borne in mind that the term "formal schooling" has a different meaning in different countries. For example, the preschool in one country might be more "formal" than the first or even second grade of the formal school in another country. Since no internationally comparable definition of the grade could be found, it was decided not to attempt adjustments for grade differences. Nevertheless, the grade levels tested are represented in the relevant tables so that they can be used when interpreting the results.

The reader should also be aware that in different countries different proportions of students in the respective target grades were excluded from testing (see Appendix B) and that in a few developing countries, less than 95% of 14-year-olds were enrolled in school.

National Achievement Scores

Interpreting the Figures

Figures 2.2, 2.3, and 2.4 present the distributions of reading literacy achievement scores by domain for the countries participating in Population A. Figures 2.7, 2.8, and 2.9 present the same data for Population B.

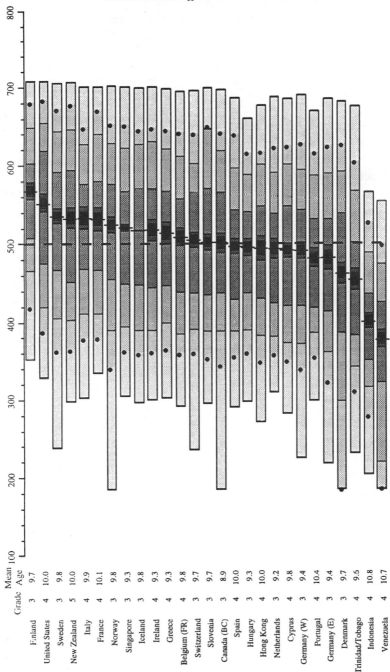

Figure 2.2: The Distribution of Rasch Scaled Scores for the Narrative Domain,
Population A

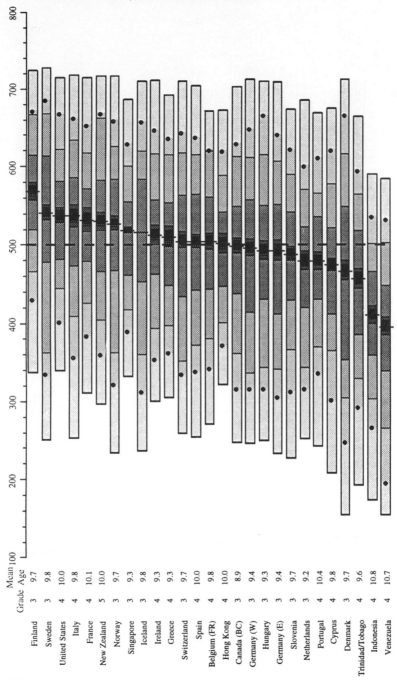

Figure 2.3: The Distribution of Rasch Scaled Scores for the Expository Domain,
Population A

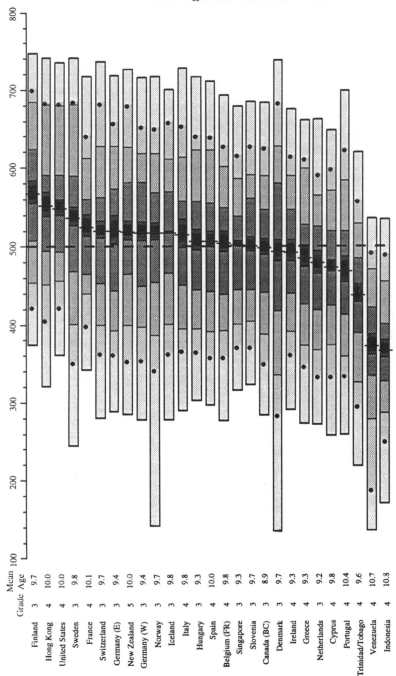

Figure 2.4: The Distribution of Rasch Scaled Scores for the Documents
Domain, Population A

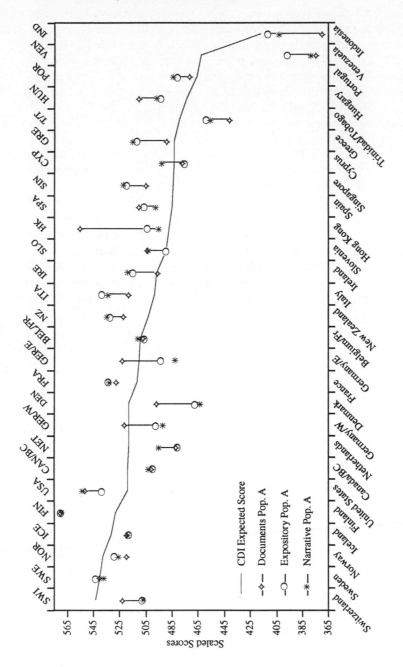

Figure 2.5: Scaled Scores by Domain Compared with Composite Development
Index (CDI), Population A

Each figure presents the country name, grade level tested, and mean age of the sample on the left-hand side. The graphs on the right show the mean score for each domain in the middle, and eight percentile points (p 1, p 5, p 10, p 25, p 75, p 90, p 95, and p 99) on each side. These percentile points are represented in sequence by the vertical lines and dots. Thus, for Finland, the percentile points in Figure 2.2 for Narrative are: p 1, 351; p 5, 419; p 10, 465; p 25, 508; p 75, 602; p 90, 650; p 95, 679; p 99, 709. In addition, the international mean of 500 is represented by a dotted vertical line running through the figure from top to bottom.

The inner band of dark shading on either side of each national mean shows the size of the standard error of sampling, and enables the reader to determine when a mean difference is statistically significant. Thus, for Belgium (French), the mean score on the Narrative test for Population A is 510, and the standard error extends from 504 to 516. This is the area within which the actual mean score probably lies (95% confidence interval). The outer band of shading shows the more conservative Bonferroni interval (500 to 521). The Bonferroni significance testing procedure is recommended when multiple comparisons are being made. Briefly, it is a method of adjusting significance levels so that the probability of falsely rejecting one or more null hypotheses when many comparisons are made is kept to a fixed level. As the standard error for Belgium (French) is three points, domain mean scores clearly overlap; it cannot be claimed that Belgian students differ significantly in their performance levels from those of countries immediately above and below them. However, they do differ from those of Finland on the one hand, and from Denmark on the other.

Figures 2.3 and 2.4 are structured in the same way. Such a presentation allows the reader to compare, at a glance, the relative performance levels between countries for each domain.

Figure 2.5 shows the same means again, presented in the order of each nation's Composite Developmental Index (CDI). The sloping line in this figure shows the scaled score for each country expected on the basis of the CDI (these predicted scores were derived from a regression equation based on the correlation between CDI and mean achievement across countries). Thus, Switzerland, with a high CDI value of 4.29 (see Table 2.1) produces a high expected overall average score of 541. The actual mean domain scores for Switzerland are 506, 507, and 522 for Narrative, Expository, and Documents scales respectively. The figure shows which countries scored above and below the CDI prediction in each domain, and by how much.

Table 2.2 presents the actual mean scores for all countries by separate domains and by an overall average of the three domain scores. The table also shows the standard errors of sampling (in brackets) and the standard deviations for each country. It can be seen that the differences between the mean scores of the developed countries are not very great even though the distributions often look quite different. Thus, 15 countries showed overall mean scaled scores between 500 and 540. There is a clustering of many education systems at this point on the scale. Nevertheless, there were a few countries which showed consistently high patterns of achievement across all domains at both age levels. Likewise a few countries showed consistently low levels of literacy on each domain at both age levels. There is a stability in these patterns which is reflected in a high correlation between the mean national scores at the two age levels (0.83). There are real, stable differences in reading literacy levels between nations. Such differences give rise to interesting questions for research.

Table 2.2

Mean Student Ability Scores (with Standard Errors of Sampling) for all Domains Arranged in Order of Overall Achievement: Population A

Country	Grade tested	Mean Age (in years)	Overall Mean (s.e.)	SD	Narrative Mean (s.e.)	SD	Expository Mean (s.e.)	SD	Documents Mean (s.e.)	SD
Finland	3	9.7	569 (3.4)	70	568 (3.0)	83	569 (3.1)	81	569 (4.0)	88
United States	4	10.0	547 (2.8)	74	553 (3.1)	96	538 (2.6)	80	550 (2.7)	81
Sweden	3	9.8	539 (2.8)	94	536 (2.6)	100	542 (2.7)	112	539 (3.2)	106
France	4	10.1	531 (4.0)	74	532 (4.1)	93	533 (4.1)	84	527 (3.9)	81
Italy	4	9.9	529 (4.3)	80	533 (4.0)	88	538 (4.0)	95	517 (4.9)	92
New Zealand	5	10.0	528 (3.3)	86	534 (3.5)	102	531 (3.1)	93	521 (3.3)	92
Norway	3	9.8	524 (2.6)	91	525 (2.8)	102	528 (2.3)	103	519 (2.8)	101
Iceland*	3	9.8	518 (0.0)	85	518 (0.0)	95	517 (0.0)	101	519 (0.0)	91
Hong Kong	4	10.0	517 (3.9)	71	494 (4.1)	87	503 (3.4)	72	554 (4.2)	89
Singapore	3	9.3	515 (1.0)	72	521 (1.1)	91	519 (1.0)	75	504 (1.0)	78
Switzerland	3	9.7	511 (2.7)	83	506 (2.6)	92	507 (2.7)	100	522 (2.8)	96
Ireland	4	9.3	509 (3.6)	79	518 (3.7)	94	514 (3.2)	89	495 (3.8)	84
Belgium/Fr	4	9.8	507 (3.2)	77	510 (3.3)	92	505 (2.8)	85	506 (3.5)	88
Greece	4	9.3	504 (3.7)	75	514 (3.8)	88	511 (3.6)	85	488 (3.8)	85
Spain	4	10.0	504 (2.5)	78	497 (2.4)	86	505 (2.3)	92	509 (2.7)	89
Germany/W	3	9.4	503 (3.0)	84	491 (2.8)	93	497 (2.9)	104	520 (3.2)	94
Canada/BC	3	8.9	500 (3.0)	80	502 (3.5)	96	499 (2.7)	94	500 (2.8)	86
Germany/E	3	9.5	499 (4.3)	84	482 (4.2)	93	493 (3.6)	103	522 (5.0)	96
Hungary	3	9.3	499 (3.1)	78	496 (2.9)	80	493 (3.1)	101	509 (3.5)	89
Slovenia	3	9.7	498 (2.6)	78	502 (2.7)	94	489 (2.5)	93	503 (2.5)	82
Netherlands	3	9.2	485 (3.6)	73	494 (3.3)	85	480 (3.4)	87	481 (3.9)	82
Cyprus	4	9.8	481 (2.3)	77	492 (2.4)	92	475 (2.3)	91	476 (2.1)	81
Portugal	4	10.4	478 (3.6)	74	483 (3.3)	81	480 (3.0)	84	471 (4.5)	92
Denmark	3	9.8	475 (3.5)	111	463 (3.4)	119	467 (3.5)	127	496 (3.6)	125
Trinidad/Tobago	4	9.6	451 (3.4)	79	455 (3.6)	91	458 (3.4)	93	440 (3.3)	82
Indonesia	4	10.8	394 (3.0)	59	402 (2.8)	66	411 (3.2)	77	369 (3.0)	66
Venezuela	4	10.1	383 (3.4)	74	378 (3.2)	86	396 (3.3)	91	374 (3.7)	84

*Iceland tested all students, therefore no standard error was calculated.
s.e. = 1 standard error of sampling

Commentary on the Findings: Population A

High Achieving Countries

A study of Table 2.2 and Figures 2.2 to 2.4 shows that the students in Finland produced consistently high scores in all three domains at age nine, despite the fact that Finnish students do not begin formal instruction in reading until age seven. In each domain, they scored at least 68 points above the international mean, and at least 15 points ahead of the next country. Furthermore, their mean score is above expectation based on the CDI in each domain by at least 38 points (see Figure 2.5). On 46 of the 66 items, Finnish students had the highest or second highest performance level. A close study of Figures 2.2 to 2.4 shows that in all domains over 75% of Finnish students score above 500, a score obtained by less than 10% of students in the two lowest-scoring countries.

Among the factors which may help account for this outstanding result are the following:

1.   Finland is a relatively affluent country, in the top five countries for GNP per capita at the time of the IEA survey.

2.   Finland's schools are linguistically very homogeneous, as the only significant sub-group speaking another language (Swedish) attends separate schools.

3.   Literacy is highly valued in Finland. The country has the highest figures for library book holdings and adult literacy, and among the highest for newspaper circulation (551) and post-secondary school participation rates in education (41%).

4.   The Finnish language has an extremely regular orthography. In Finnish there is only one symbol for each sound, and one sound for each symbol. Many educators believe that this feature makes learning to read a much easier task than in languages with less regular orthographies (e.g., Kyöstiö, 1980; Downing, 1973).

There may be other reasons for the Finnish high levels of literacy, such as the quality of teaching and the methods of instruction. In that connection, Finnish educators describe their teaching methodology as eclectic: both whole language and phonic methods are used for initial instruction.

Students in the United States had the second highest mean scores in Population A in Narrative Reading (553) and third highest in the Expository and Documents domains (538 and 550). The Narrative scores of American students were outstanding, and significantly higher than those of all other countries except Finland. Their students' performance was consistently high across all passages and very few students in this cohort could be described as non-readers. Less than 2% of students scored below 25% (the mean chance score), which could be regarded as a crude cut-off point in tests with predominantly four-choice items. In the earlier IEA survey of reading comprehension (Thorndike, 1973), American students scored in the top group of countries in the older age groups, so this strong result is not unexpected. It should be noted, however, that the American sample was surprisingly homogeneous linguistically, with only 3.5% of students in the non-English speaking category.

Other countries with very high scores were Sweden and France, while students in Italy and New Zealand showed very similar levels of attainment, though from a lower economic base. Sweden's results are impressive, as they also start reading instruction only at age seven, and have a more diverse language context in schools than Finland does. In the Expository domain, their best readers were outstanding, as their 95th percentile score was the only one over 680 points It is relevant to point out that both Swedish and Finnish children achieved at very high levels in the first IEA reading survey at age 10 (Thorndike, 1973).

Students in France were placed fifth or sixth in each domain, with all mean scores close to 530. Like Finland, they also showed a narrow range of scores. The French sample was slightly older than average (10.1 years), and excluded the private schools (16% of students). These factors probably had small compensating effects, as recent evidence from the French Ministry of Education suggests that private school students achieve at higher levels than public schools in literacy. France did not participate in the earlier IEA Reading Comprehension survey.

Italy and New Zealand were two of the highest scoring countries in the Thorndike IEA survey (1973) and they again produced high scores at age nine in the current survey. As both countries had more modest economic resources than the other top countries, their results were well above expectation on the basis of CDI (See Figure 2.6). Italian students enjoy the advantage of an orthography almost as regular as that of Finnish students. While New Zealand students have no such advantage, it should be noted that they have had reading instruction since age five, a longer period than in most countries. While the New Zealand expenditure on education is relatively low (17th out of 27), they appear to spend more of it on library books than others, and their early teaching programs emphasize the extensive use of storybooks. This fact may help explain their higher scores in the Narrative domain.

The other highest scoring countries from Europe were Norway and Iceland, both of which are in the highest bracket for GNP per capita, and both of which begin formal instruction at age seven. Countries with similar performance levels to these were Hong Kong and Singapore. These two countries have much in common: a heavy urban concentration of population in a small area; a large Chinese population; an average but fast-growing GNP; typically a large school size and class size; and a school starting age of six years. However, Hong Kong students are educated in the native Chinese language, with its complicated ideographic script, while Singapore students acquire their literacy in English, which is commonly spoken in only 25% of homes. This contrast may be related to the fact that Hong Kong students performed especially well in Documents (554), and poorly in Narrative (494), while Singapore's profile showed stronger performance on Narrative and Expository scores (521 and 519) and only modest scores in Documents (504). It is relevant to point out that the Singapore reading program is heavily storybook oriented, like that of New Zealand. Another striking feature of Singapore's impressive result is that at least three-quarters of their students acquire their initial literacy in a non-native language, English. While most educators have traditionally accepted the Unesco position that students should be taught to read first in their native tongue, Singapore authorities ignored this advice, and have produced a generation of bilingual students who speak one language at home, and read competently in another at school. This is a potentially important finding.

Other Countries in Population A

Other European countries with relatively high scores from Table 2.2 were Switzerland, Ireland, Belgium (French), Greece, and Spain, while the two Germanys had similar scores, close to the international mean of 500. Interestingly, the three German-speaking countries showed scores on the Documents scale 15 to 20 points higher than their performance on the other two domains. Narrative scores were lowest in each case.

As mentioned earlier, the scores for Canada (BC) and the Netherlands would probably be 10 to 15 points higher if they had not tested such a young sample. Finally, the students of Denmark showed unexpectedly low means and unusually large standard deviations. Like their counterparts in the Netherlands and the two Germanys, many Danish students failed to finish the tests, and scored well below their CDI expectation at this age level. It should be noted that Danish students only begin formal schooling at age seven and that most of them were unaccustomed to formal testing, as was indicated by their teachers. While the graphs of their performance show that there are many very good readers in Denmark with scores over 700, an inspection of their item statistics suggests that many students chose to omit items they were unsure of, which depressed their scores considerably. Hence the large standard deviations.

Among the less affluent nations, it has already been stated that Singapore and Hong Kong were high scoring countries, well above the levels anticipated on the basis of the CDI estimates. In addition, Hungary, Greece, and Spain had overall means at least 20 points above expectation (see Figure 2.5). Greek students showed relatively high scores in the Narrative domain, as did the students of Cyprus who also speak Greek. It should be noted that Greek and Hungarian students were on average only 9.3 years old, considerably below the international average.

Students of Ireland, Slovenia, Portugal, and Cyprus all show performance levels up to or slightly above expectation, while the three poorest countries Trinidad and Tobago, Indonesia, and Venezuela all fall at least 20 points below expectation. Each of these countries show depressed scores in the Documents domain, but there are readers who score above the international average in all three school systems. Indeed, the top Narrative and Expository scores in Trinidad and Tobago are among the best scoring students in the study.

Differences in Score Distributions

Examination of Figures 2.2 to 2.4 reveals some differences of interest in the distributions of scores. While Finland clearly has the shortest "tail" in each domain, there are other countries with unexpectedly large numbers of low scoring students. For instance, the lowest 5% of students in Sweden, New Zealand, Norway, Canada (BC), and Denmark are clearly below expectation, relative to their overall performance levels, suggesting the presence of a group of nonreaders who need official policy attention. By contrast, some countries show relatively few very weak readers. The lowest 10% of students in Finland, the United States, and France were above the norm in all domains, while those in Singapore, Slovenia, Ireland, and Greece were relatively high in two domains. Such enviable homogeneities may provide lessons for others.

It is revealing, too, that nearly 90% of students in Finland perform at a higher level than the highest 10% in Venezuela. Such comparisons can show the lowest scoring countries what is potentially achievable, and provide policy makers with some idea of what standards might represent feasible long-term goals.

Word Recognition

Although the Word Recognition Test was not incorporated into the other results for Population A, it is appropriate to report the results here. The ability to recognize words is fundamental to the reading process. Students who cannot decode words reasonably quickly cannot read (Calfee & Drum, 1986). Students may be able to recognize words without comprehending what they read, but there is no evidence of the contrary position (Stanovich, 1991). Certainly, there are many other influences on reading ability, but the link between word recognition and comprehension is highlighted in all current models of the reading process.

This relationship is most obvious, of course, in the early stages of reading acquisition. As students mature, the importance of word recognition gradually declines in favor of general language ability or listening comprehension. Nevertheless, it is still a source of variance in adult readers, over and above such other qualities as intelligence, vocabulary, listening skills, and memory factors (Cunningham et al., 1991).

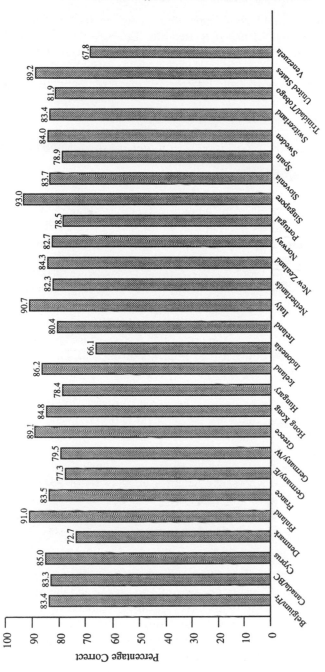

Figure 2.6: Word Recognition Mean Percentage Scores: Population A

It is plausible to assume that many of the students who failed to comprehend well in the IEA Reading Literacy tests had inadequate word recognition skills. Such a belief led the Steering Committee to explore the following issues by means of a short, speeded test:

1.   Are there systematic differences in word recognition speed between countries?

2.   Could these differences help explain international differences in reading achievement?

3.   Is rapid word recognition skill a prerequisite for good comprehension in all languages?

To investigate these issues, a simple Word Recognition Test was administered to the 9-year-old students in each country. It was an adaptation of one prepared for Danish schools (Dansk Psykolgisk Forlag, 1990), and consisted of a series of 40 familiar words, each of which was to be matched, in turn, with one of four pictures, under speeded conditions (one and a half minutes).

This measure, however, is only an indirect test of the real task of word recognition, which was not easy to assess in an international setting because the language has a potentially strong effect on difficulty. The words were presented in isolation and the child responded by selecting a picture rather than saying a word. However, the use of this test was justified in the study because it contained many of the crucial elements of the task. The words were familiar, each was required to be processed without the benefit of context and the speed element helped indicate the level of automation the child had achieved. Those who did not possess adequate decoding skills could not score highly. It is possible, of course, that some might be good decoders and not perform well on this task, but the reverse would not be the case. Pilot studies in most countries confirmed that the test was very easy for good readers, and the results were in line with predictions. After revision, the inclusion of the test was further justified by those who saw a need for an easy set of tasks for readers which might not be as discouraging at the outset as a daunting passage of text. The Word Recognition Test was administered at the beginning of the first test session for Population A only.

National Means for Word Recognition

Figure 2.6 presents the mean scores for each country expressed as percentages. All means fell between 93 and 66%, and the item p values ranged from 98 to 45%. Approximately 37% of all students scored full marks. The highest mean scores were shown by Singapore (93.0%), Finland (91.0%), Italy (90.7%), the United States (89.2%), and Greece (89.1%). Relative to expectations, all of these countries performed well on the Narrative and Expository domains, both of which require efficient decoding of text.

By contrast, low scores in Word Recognition were found in Indonesia (66.1%), Venezuela (67.8%), Denmark (72.7%), and Germany (East) (77.3%).

All of these countries had total reading achievement scores below expectations. The correlation between Word Recognition and Reading Achievement Total, across 27 countries, was 0.81.

A further analysis, comparing the National Mean Reading Score with the proportion of each country's sample who scored less than 50% on the Word Recognition Test, showed an even higher correlation (0.86). Clearly, there are sizable differences between countries in word recognition, differences which predicted and could well help explain their comprehension levels. No country achieved highly with low word recognition scores.

Commentary on the Findings: Population B

High Achieving Countries

Figures 2.7 to 2.9 show the achievement score distributions and the total score distribution for the 31 countries that participated at Population B level; Figure 2.10 shows the same scores in relation to CDI (refer to Table 2.1), and Table 2.3 presents the actual means for each domain and the overall average. Readers should be reminded that Canada (BC), Italy, Hungary, Spain, and Belgium (French) tested students who were several months younger, and that their mean scores are probably lower by 10 to 15 points accordingly. By contrast, the scores of Portugal and France are overestimated by 15 to 20 points because their samples were over age.

As at the younger age, there is a clustering of high achieving (mostly) European countries in the 520 to 540 range, but the differences between them, though small, are remarkably stable across surveys. For instance, the correlations with mean scores in the Population A survey was 0.83, and would have been higher but for some anomalous differences in the relative mean ages of the two samples. The national differences in performance were also very similar to those obtained in the earlier IEA survey (Thorndike, 1973).

For Population B, the highest scoring country was again Finland, with consistently high scores across all parts of the tests. At this age level, the Finnish students also had among the highest means in earlier IEA surveys of reading (Thorndike, 1973) and literature (Purves, 1973), and the result is consistent with many other indicators of literacy. Finland should have some lessons for other educators on the ingredients of a strong literacy program.

Very impressive results were also shown by the students in France, especially in the Narrative (556) and Expository (546) domains. By way of qualification, it should be recalled that their sample was 15.4 years, whereas the mean international age was 14.7. However, the French sample also excluded the 24% of students who attend private schools, and whose literacy levels are known to be higher. French students, at this age as at age nine, are high achievers in literacy. They also have a notably "high floor" in their results, as very few students scored below 450 points in any domain.

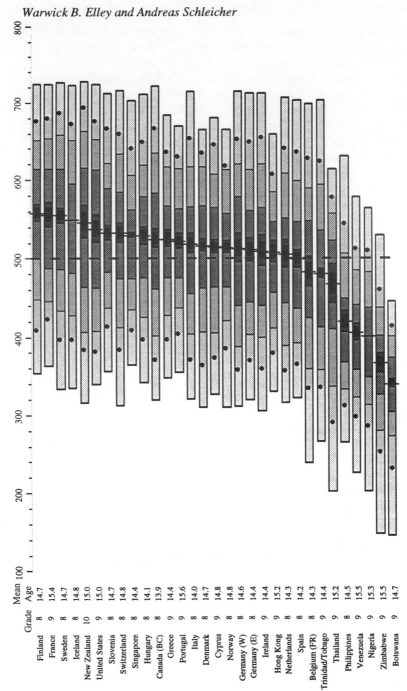

Figure 2.7: The Distribution of Rasch Scaled Scores for the Narrative Domain,
Population B

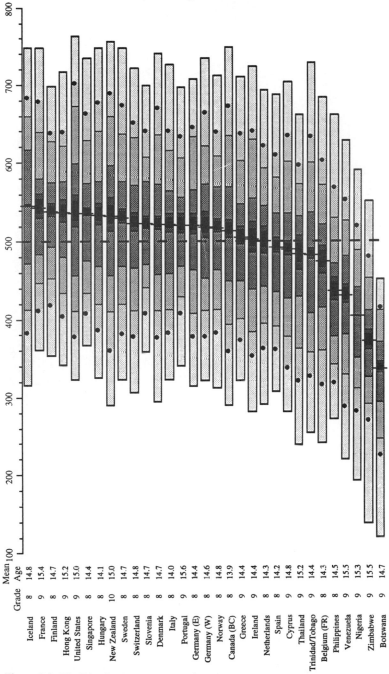

Figure 2.8: The Distribution of Rasch Scaled Scores for the Expository Domain,
Population B

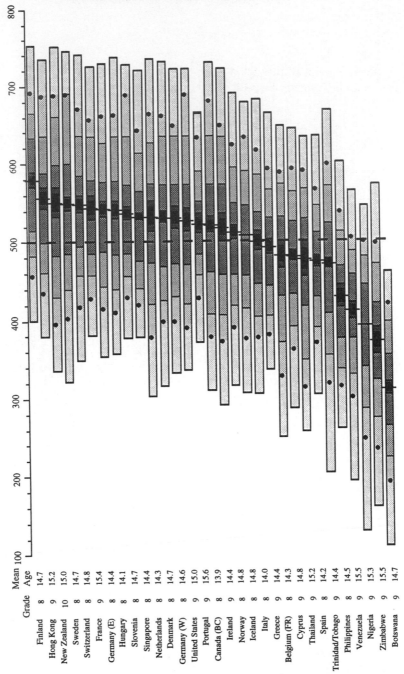

Figure 2.9: The Distribution of Rasch Scaled Scores for the Documents
Domain, Population B

Table 2.3

Mean Student Ability Scores (with Standard Errors of Sampling)
for all Domains Arranged in Order of Overall Achievement:
Population B

Country	Grade tested	Mean age (in years)	Overall Mean (s.e.)	SD	Narrative Mean (s.e.)	SD	Expository Mean (s.e.)	SD	Documents Mean (s.e.)	SD
Finland	8	14.7	560 (2.5)	65	559 (2.8)	84	541 (2.2)	71	580 (2.5)	82
France	9	15.4	549 (4.3)	68	556 (4.2)	86	546 (4.3)	84	544 (4.2)	77
Sweden	8	14.8	546 (2.5)	80	556 (2.6)	93	533 (2.4)	91	550 (2.4)	90
New Zealand	10	15.0	545 (5.6)	92	547 (5.7)	104	535 (5.7)	105	552 (5.3)	98
Hungary	8	14.1	536 (3.3)	73	530 (3.1)	81	536 (3.6)	91	542 (3.2)	82
Iceland	8	14.8	536 (0.0)	78	550 (0.0)	91	548 (0.0)	100	509 (0.0)	77
Switzerland	8	14.9	536 (3.2)	74	534 (3.4)	90	525 (3.2)	87	549 (3.0)	82
Hong Kong	9	15.2	535 (3.7)	64	509 (3.7)	72	540 (3.8)	79	557 (3.8)	76
United States	9	15.0	535 (4.8)	85	539 (4.9)	98	539 (5.6)	107	528 (4.0)	84
Singapore	8	14.4	534 (1.1)	66	530 (1.1)	73	539 (1.2)	82	533 (1.1)	74
Slovenia	8	14.7	532 (2.3)	63	534 (2.6)	76	525 (2.2)	73	537 (2.2)	74
Germany/E	8	14.4	526 (3.5)	73	512 (3.9)	90	523 (3.5)	87	543 (2.9)	81
Denmark	8	14.8	525 (2.1)	77	517 (2.0)	83	524 (2.2)	94	532 (2.1)	88
Portugal	9	15.6	523 (3.1)	60	523 (2.5)	71	523 (3.4)	79	523 (3.4)	67
Canada/BC	8	13.9	522 (3.0)	81	526 (3.1)	94	516 (3.1)	97	522 (2.7)	88
Germany/W	8	14.6	522 (4.4)	78	514 (4.9)	95	521 (4.5)	92	532 (3.9)	82
Norway	8	14.8	516 (2.3)	71	515 (2.1)	76	520 (2.4)	86	512 (2.4)	82
Italy	8	14.1	515 (3.4)	73	520 (3.6)	88	524 (3.2)	85	501 (3.3)	78
Netherlands	8	14.3	514 (4.9)	76	506 (4.8)	88	503 (4.7)	83	533 (5.3)	90
Ireland	9	14.5	511 (5.2)	81	510 (5.3)	93	505 (5.3)	94	518 (4.9)	90
Greece	9	14.4	509 (2.9)	65	526 (2.9)	75	508 (3.1)	84	493 (2.6)	69
Cyprus	9	14.8	497 (2.2)	73	516 (2.2)	82	492 (2.4)	91	482 (2.0)	74
Spain	8	14.2	490 (2.5)	65	500 (3.0)	84	495 (2.6)	79	475 (2.0)	64
Belgium/Fr	8	14.3	481 (4.9)	78	484 (5.1)	95	477 (4.8)	89	483 (4.7)	82
Trinidad/ Tobago	9	14.4	479 (1.7)	87	482 (1.7)	96	485 (1.8)	100	472 (1.7)	92
Thailand*	9	15.2	477 (6.2)	79	468 (6.6)	88	486 (5.9)	87	478 (6.2)	88
Philippines	8	14.5	430 (3.9)	65	421 (3.6)	71	439 (4.1)	78	430 (3.9)	72
Venezuela	9	15.5	417 (3.1)	61	407 (2.9)	67	433 (3.3)	80	412 (3.0)	70
Nigeria†*	9	15.3	401 (---)	65	402 (---)	69	406 (---)	73	394 (---)	81
Zimbabwe*	9	15.5	372 (3.8)	60	367 (3.3)	64	374 (3.6)	70	373 (4.6)	83
Botswana	9	14.7	330 (2.0)	43	340 (1.6)	53	339 (1.9)	58	312 (2.4)	69

† Insufficient data to calculate the Design Effect.
* Sampling response rates of schools was below 80 percent.
s.e. = 1 standard error of sampling

Sweden and New Zealand showed the next highest profiles, with overall mean scores of 546 and 545 respectively. Swedish students have improved their relative status since the 1970 survey (Thorndike, 1973), while New Zealand students have dropped a little from the highest position. Swedish students had very high scores in the Narrative domain (556) at this age, while New Zealanders achieved their highest mean on the Documents scale, quite unlike their 9-year-olds. It should be recalled that Swedish students start formal instruction at age seven, two years later than New Zealand, but any differences in reading development seem to have disappeared by age nine (see Population A results).

Other high scores from Table 2.3 were shown by Hungary, whose students were only 14.1 years, but whose mean scores clustered closely around 536, a full 57 points above expectation. They have clearly improved their literacy levels since the 1970 survey at this age level. Iceland's students stood out in the Expository scale (the highest at 548) but dropped in the Documents scale (509).

Switzerland showed a relatively high mean in Documents (549) as they had at age nine, while Hong Kong had a very unusual profile, with the second highest country mean in Documents (557) but only 21st in Narrative (509). The same pattern was seen in Population A, perhaps reflecting a pervading business-oriented approach to literacy. Once again, Hong Kong students achieved well above expectation (41 points) as did those of Singapore (43 points). Both had high overall means (535 and 534 respectively) and small standard deviations. Relatively few students scored below 450 in either country.

The other high achieving nations at this age level were the United States and Slovenia. The American result ranked lower than that of their 9-year-olds, but was closely in line with CDI prediction, and well up with their high status in the Thorndike survey. The distribution of scores within domains for American students was noticeably wider, particularly in the Expository scale, with more very high and very low scores than usual. Slovenian students achieved well above expectation (by 32 points) and, like the United States, had similar scores in each domain. It is worth commenting that the Slovenian students took their tests against the backdrop of severe civil strife in their country at the time.

Other countries in Population B

Among the middle scoring countries for Population B is Canada (BC) (overall mean of 522), whose student scores were probably underestimated by about 18 points due to the students' younger age. Also at this level are Denmark, Germany (East), Germany (West), Norway, and the Netherlands. All of these countries except Norway showed stronger performance in Documents, as they had in Population A. Denmark's scores are no doubt underestimated because their students were mistakenly given 5 minutes less testing time in one session.

A study of Table 2.3 shows several more countries at this level. Portugal has a perfectly flat profile across domains (523), but its students were well above the average age across countries. Italy's sample, which was much younger (14.1 years), produced similar scores in Narrative (520) and Expository (524) but dropped to 501 in Documents. Ireland has a comparatively flat profile (around 511 points), while the Greek students show a relatively high Narrative score, just as they had at age nine.

Just below the international average of 500 are Cyprus, with a relatively high score in Narrative (like Greece), and Spain, with an unexpected drop in the Document scale. Belgium (French) has a surprisingly low profile for a high socioeconomic country, just ahead of Trinidad and Tobago and Thailand. However, the sampling rate for Thailand was less than 80% and, as the retention rate of their 14-year-old population is low (32%), these mean scores for Thailand are probably inflated.

The remaining countries have low socioeconomic status and therefore low expected means. All countries except Botswana and the Philippines tested over-age samples (by arrangement), and several had difficulty obtaining adequate samples. Most of these countries have relatively low Documents scores, but all except Botswana have some students scoring well above 500 points (see Figures 2.7 to 2.9). All have very long tails to their distributions, however, indicating the presence of many nonreaders.

Distribution of Scores

A study of Figures 2.7, 2.8, and 2.9 reveals a number of interesting patterns. Firstly, it is plain to see that approximately 75% of Finland's students obtained scores above 500 in each domain, while less than 10% of students in the four lowest scoring countries were able to achieve this level. At what is essentially the end of compulsory schooling in such countries, most students are performing, by a huge margin, below the levels which are achieved in the high scoring countries.

Several countries stand out because of the wide dispersion of their scores. In all three domains, New Zealand, the United States, and Canada (BC) showed the widest range of achievement between the lowest 5% and the highest 5%. At the other extreme, Portugal, Singapore, Finland, France, and Greece show a relatively narrow range of achievement, yet several of these countries have substantial minorities with different home languages. In addition, three countries (Belgium (Fr), Thailand, and Trinidad and Tobago) showed relatively long tails to their distributions in each domain.

A study of Figure 2.10 shows the extent to which the national means for each domain deviated from the expected level, based on CDI, as well as how they differed across domains. Here we can see huge deviations between the domains for Hong Kong, Iceland and Finland. On the other hand, Portugal, Belgium (Fr), Norway, and Zimbabwe had almost identical mean scores in each domain.

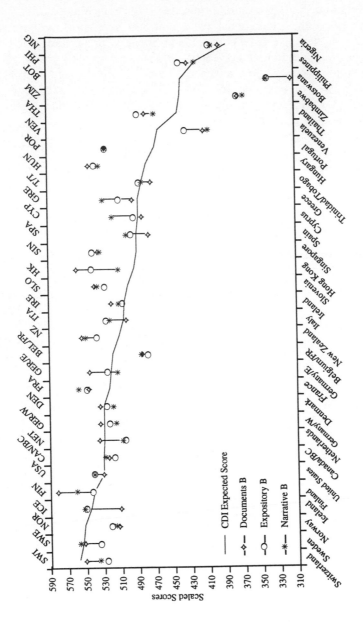

Figure 2.10: Scaled Scores by Domain Compared with Composite Development
Index (CDI), Population B

National Panel Ratings of Expected Achievement Levels

In order to provide an additional framework against which to view their test scores, eleven countries participated in a small study designed to determine the expected levels of proficiency of 14-year-olds on the kinds of tasks included in the Population B tests. As described in more detail in Appendix H and in the Technical Report (Beaton, 1993), a panel of about 20 informed adult judges was selected in each country and asked to read and rate each item in the Population B test. Each judge recorded the percentage of 14-year-olds whom they thought should be able to respond to each item correctly, if they were to be considered "barely literate" in their country. This meant that they could be expected to cope with the literacy demands of running a household, performing a manual job, and using basic community services. The percentages were summed across the items in each domain, and averaged to obtain an expected mean achievement level, following the method of Angoff (1971). The judges made a second estimate to generate the percentage considered "high-level literate."

The experiment was a novel one for the NRCs, and the procedures were not entirely identical in each country. Nevertheless, the exercise provided a number of useful findings. Table 2.4 lists for the eleven countries the number of judges, the expected mean scores for the "barely literate" cut-off point for each domain, and the percentage of students who achieved that level. Table 2.5 does the same for the "high-level literate" cut-off point. The standard errors of the means clustered around 30 points in each domain. This exercise was guided and the analysis undertaken by Dr Nadir Atash of Westat, USA.

A study of Table 2.4 reveals that there was considerable variation between countries in the expected mean scores. Judges in Finland, Hong Kong, and Switzerland expected considerably more than those in Venezuela and New Zealand. Literacy demands in the former group are apparently higher. However, there was also considerable variation in the students' achievement levels. How well do they match up?

For most countries the percentage of 14-year-olds attaining the expected mean for low-level literacy lies between 92 and 97%. Nearly all students in these countries are therefore judged to be "literate" at a lower level, one at which they could at least survive sufficiently in their societies. Only in Hong Kong were expectations consistently well ahead of performance, while Switzerland's students fell short of expectations in Narrative and Expository reading. At the other end of the spectrum, New Zealand students were exceptional with over 99% attainment, largely because the judges' expectations appeared unrealistically low. What is more revealing, however, is that while students in Venezuela and Cyprus achieved at low levels on their tests, their performance was judged to be just as good as those of Sweden or Finland in terms of their panel's literacy expectations.

Table 2.4

Mean Expected Levels of Low-Level Literacy for Population B
Students and Percentages of Students Attaining Those Levels

Country	No. of Judges	Narrative		Expository		Documents	
		Expected Mean	Percent attained	Expected Mean	Percent attained	Expected Mean	Percent attained
Cyprus	28	383	94.8	359	94.3	355	96.1
Finland	30	429	93.2	435	94.3	430	97.8
Germany/W	9	411	86.1	395	93.7	403	95.3
Greece	28	427	92.4	359	98.1	365	97.3
Hong Kong	22	495	58.7	513	64.5	525	65.5
Netherlands	35	374	94.7	355	96.8	363	96.3
New Zealand	19	267	99.9	276	99.5	300	99.7
Slovenia	14	431	92.8	410	96.2	414	96.7
Sweden	23	380	96.8	377	96.7	395	96.7
Switzerland	19	434	86.9	420	89.4	417	96.0
Venezuela	24	293	96.3	284	96.0	264	97.7
Mean		393.1	90.2	380.3	92.7	384.6	94.1
S.D.		63.4	10.7	63.9	9.3	65.8	9.1

Another interesting feature of Table 2.4 is the variation in expectations across domains. In most countries, the expected means are highest in narrative reading. For Greece and Cyprus this is especially the case, and it is in these two countries that students' narrative achievement is much higher than for the other domains. By contrast, Hong Kong and New Zealand expect more in the Documents domain, and it is in this area that students' achievement in these countries is highest. This result provides some supportive evidence for the validity of the procedure. In these cases student performance clearly reflects the relative emphases of their society. Indeed, if the two outliers, Hong Kong and New Zealand, were dropped, the correlation between expected low-level mean and actual mean score would be 0.85 across countries and domains ($N = 27$). The correlations were highest for Documents at 0.91 and 0.82 for the other two domains.

Table 2.5 presents the comparable figures for the high-level literate cut-off points, and the percentage of students in each country attaining them.

At the higher level, judges showed less unanimity in their estimates. Nevertheless the overall pattern shows that the expected achievement levels mirrored the actual levels well except in Hong Kong and New Zealand. Finland and Sweden have the longest history of near universal literacy, and the highest expectations; Venezuela, with the lowest CDI indices, has the lowest expectations. Approximately 20–30% of students reached expected standards in the Narrative, and 15–25% in the Expository and Documents domains. For many countries these figures correspond approximately with the percentage of the population which would attend university and pursue professional careers.

Table 2.5

Mean Expected Levels of High-Level Literacy for Population B
Students and Percentages of Students Attaining Those Levels

Country	No. of Judges	Narrative Expected Mean	Narrative Percent attained	Expository Expected Mean	Expository Percent attained	Documents Expected Mean	Documents Percent attained
Cyprus	28	581	21.6	504	12.4	608	4.2
Finland	30	598	28.0	636	10.1	652	15.4
Greece	28	552	33.5	552	29.4	554	13.9
Hong Kong	22	586	15.5	622	13.6	648	8.6
Netherlands	35	565	26.1	571	20.5	588	25.2
New Zealand	19	541	53.1	542	44.3	566	44.0
Slovenia	14	566	34.9	562	25.3	573	32.3
Sweden	23	599	29.7	610	14.4	638	11.5
Switzerland	19	572	30.9	585	20.6	568	40.3
Venezuela	24	524	4.4	535	10.4	491	7.9
Mean		569.9	27.8	561.9	20.1	588.6	20.3
S.D.		24.2	12.2	34.3	10.1	47.2	13.5

Once again, the Hong Kong panel expected considerably more from their students in the Documents domain, and this is where they excelled. In fact, eight of the national panels expected higher means from their students in Documents, and in six cases the scores reflected this expectation. The correlation between the actual student means and the expected high-level means across all countries and domains ($N = 30$) was 0.67. Once again, the results of low-scoring countries look considerably better in relation to expectation than they do when viewed in absolute terms.

3

Voluntary Reading Activities

WARWICK B. ELLEY

An international survey provides a potentially useful occasion for comparing, across countries the extent to which students read voluntarily in their leisure time. Most education systems emphasize voluntary reading as an important objective, and the majority of teach.. rated highly the instructional aim of fostering students' interest in reading (see Chapter 6). Previous international surveys have attempted to make comparisons across countries, using simple questionnaires. Thorndike (1973) surveyed the reading attitudes of 10- and 14-year-olds in 15 countries, most of which were also represented in the current investigation. He found consistently positive, but low correlations with achievement in most countries. In the IEA study of literature, Purves (1973) found high correlations between professed interest in reading literature and achievement scores. The relationship of achievement to involvement in what was read, however, was less strong. That study also produced data on the specific interests of 14-year-olds, which can be used as a reference point for this study. Guthrie and Siefert (1984) summarized a number of surveys of reading activity in several countries, and Greaney and Neuman (1990) analyzed student perceptions of the functions of reading in 15 countries. They found many uniformities in the reported purposes of students' reading, across age groups and nations. In most of the studies of reading interests and activities, girls are found to read more than boys, and they read about a wider range of topics. It should be a matter of concern to educators that students' reading activity out of school is declining, in line with the rise of television, videos and computers. Recent studies conducted in the United States, Ireland, England, Scotland, and New Zealand, among others, have drawn attention to the small numbers of books read by students in their leisure time (Guthrie & Greaney, 1991). Guthrie points out that such figures mean that many students will not be able to meet the reading demands of adult life. This chapter describes the main trends found in voluntary reading for both populations, for both genders, and for each type of reading material.

Procedures for Assessing Voluntary Reading

In the pilot tests, a separate questionnaire was tried out at each population level, seeking information on the extent to which students claimed to read a wide variety of materials for different purposes. These trials were only partially successful. They revealed the value of having test administrators read the questions aloud, and allowing of ample time for completion. However, they presented many problems for the younger and less able readers, and by general consensus the questions were radically shortened and incorporated into the background questionnaires.

In the main survey, some of the problems were found to persist. Many students apparently found it difficult to estimate how frequently they read different kinds of materials, and in some countries there was evidence of strong compliance effects. Students apparently wished to show themselves in as good a light as possible. Thus, the absolute numbers given for some countries must be treated with caution. Interpretations will be more revealing on the relative weights given to the various categories of reading materials within countries. The limitations of questionnaire surveys became very obvious in this part of the investigation.

For Population A, students were asked in a series of questions to state whether they had read any books, comics, magazines, or newspapers "for fun" in the previous week (yes/no) and how often they did so (on a four-point scale). Population B students had similar questions, but they were also asked to classify the materials they read, by type or purpose. Students were not asked to state the length of time they read these materials on any one occasion.

Voluntary Reading Patterns in Population A

Table 3.1 presents for Population A the voluntary reading mean values for four different kinds of reading materials: books, comics, magazines, and newspapers. In each column, the left-hand figure shows the percentage of students in each country who reported reading books (or comics, etc.) for fun in the previous week; the right-hand figure shows the students' estimates of how often they read them, on a recoded scale of 0–6 (to approximate the number of times per week). Thus, 70% of Belgian students reported having read a book last week; the mean value for frequency of reading books was 2.91, which indicates a value close to three times per week. While the two columns are highly correlated across countries (.78), it is clear that they do not correspond exactly.

Taking both sets of figures into account, it can be seen that the heaviest readers of books at age nine are reportedly found in Hungary, the Netherlands, Portugal, Slovenia, Switzerland, and Sweden. Students in all of these countries report reading books more than three times a week on average and over 65% of them read a book for fun in the previous week. By contrast, students in Hong Kong, Indonesia, and Trinidad and Tobago report that they read books only rarely.

The picture for comics is quite different. Here the highest percentages of students reporting that they read a comic last week were in Finland (88%),

Norway (78%), and Sweden (75%). Students in these countries read comics more frequently than books. The light comic readers were in the United States (23%), New Zealand (27%), and Indonesia (28%). It is reassuring to note that the mean frequency figures match those percentages almost exactly ($r = .95$). Comics are generally popular with 9-year-olds, although they claim to read them somewhat less than books.

Table 3.1

Frequency of Reading Books, Comics, Magazines and Newspapers:
Population A

Country	Books Last week %	Books Fre-quency	Comics Last week %	Comics Fre-quency	Magazines Last week %	Magazines Fre-quency	Newspapers Last week %	Newspapers Fre-quency
Belgium/French	70	2.91	59	2.46	50	1.26	35	0.75
Canada/BC	58	2.84	37	1.22	29	0.73	26	0.58
Cyprus	58	2.48	40	1.58	43	1.51	43	1.21
Denmark	71	2.69	62	2.50	38	1.21	41	1.25
Finland	70	2.66	88	3.93	41	1.05	62	2.27
France	70	2.91	50	1.84	37	1.07	34	0.79
Germany/East	67	2.65	52	1.92	32	0.96	27	0.68
Germany/West	66	2.68	44	1.50	22	0.53	27	0.63
Greece	70	2.67	51	1.60	40	1.37	44	1.08
Hong Kong	47	1.72	34	1.13	21	0.64	64	1.97
Hungary	80	3.10	47	1.42	29	1.00	45	1.34
Iceland	62	3.06	44	1.79	29	0.68	50	1.89
Indonesia	54	2.08	28	0.97	42	1.29	32	1.04
Ireland	62	2.60	39	1.29	28	0.62	48	1.24
Italy	56	2.24	60	2.06	24	0.64	26	0.67
Netherlands	78	3.34	63	2.31	40	0.83	34	0.80
New Zealand	67	2.82	27	0.79	31	0.65	49	1.24
Norway	65	3.01	78	3.73	31	0.66	48	1.48
Portugal	79	3.57	53	2.34	52	1.40	29	0.53
Singapore	55	2.45	30	1.03	28	0.85	54	2.46
Slovenia	78	3.28	51	1.73	44	1.21	46	1.13
Spain	79	2.76	56	1.93	41	1.05	37	0.51
Sweden	65	3.20	75	3.40	22	0.66	46	1.92
Switzerland	72	3.12	52	1.95	37	1.11	27	0.70
Trinidad/Tobago	49	2.15	31	1.26	17	0.67	55	2.02
United States	63	2.64	23	0.72	34	0.82	40	0.94
Venezuela	56	2.93	41	2.16	30	1.67	68	2.44
Mean	65.44	2.76	48.70	1.87	33.78	0.97	42.11	1.24
S.D.	9.08	0.40	15.71	0.81	8.73	0.31	11.81	0.60
r with achievmt.	0.26	0.23	0.36	0.24	-0.08	-0.53	-0.05	-0.07

The correlations given at the foot of Table 3.1 show that good readers tend to read more books and more comics. While the positive relationship with book reading was expected, the correlation with comic reading is surprising.

There may well be reading benefits to be gained from a medium in which students are continually matching pictures with words, under highly motivating conditions, and making repeated inferences to create a story. Comics also tend to use metaphors and word play and so contribute to close reading.

Magazine and newspaper reading are less common at this age and the differences between countries are less striking. Frequent magazine reading is reported only in Venezuela, Portugal, and Cyprus, and the overall mean frequency is less than once a week. More intriguing is the fact that a negative relationship was found between achievement and both indicators of magazine reading ($r = -.08, -.53$). Apparently, poor readers are more inclined to enjoy reading magazines, and/or they receive little benefit from doing so at this age level.

The highest reported frequencies for newspaper reading were found among the Nordic countries and in Singapore, Hong Kong, Trinidad and Tobago, and Venezuela, and the lowest were found in Canada (BC), Spain, Portugal, and Italy. The two indicators for frequency of newspaper reading correlate very highly across countries ($r = .91$) and reflect closely the percentage of homes reported as receiving a daily newspaper.

Within-Country Analyses: Population A

Table 3.2 presents for each country the correlations between overall achievement scores and the frequency with which Population A students report reading books, comics, magazines, newspapers, and directions. On the right is the correlation with a total frequency score based on the summation of all these five media. As expected, the correlations are nearly all positive. In all countries, students who read most tend to achieve better in reading. The total frequency correlations cluster around .20 but range from .35 in Denmark to .05 in Indonesia. No doubt, the modest reliability of individual 9-year-olds' responses to such questions has constrained the size of these correlations.

A close perusal of Table 3.2 reveals that achievement shows the highest correlations with regularity of book reading (median $r = .20$), followed by comics ($r = .14$), newspapers ($r = .11$), magazines ($r = .10$), and directions ($r = .02$). Once again, comic reading shows up ahead of all other media except books. In the book column, the countries which stand out are New Zealand (.29), and Canada (BC) (.27), both of which espouse a book-based philosophy. Teachers in both of these countries allow much time for reading. Four of the Nordic countries (Denmark, Iceland, Norway, and Sweden) show consistently high correlations across the first four media, and their total frequencies all show coefficients above .30. Their range of available reading materials is greater than in most countries and the mean frequencies are also high. By contrast, students in the countries less well-provided for show consistently low correlations. These contrasting relationships are consistent with the finding, reported below, that the ready availability of reading materials is a key factor in raising reading levels. Without a rich stock of books and other materials of interest to young readers, achievement scores will probably remain low. The fact that Finland, France, and the United States showed lower correlations cannot be overlooked, however. Perhaps the smaller range of achievement scores reduced the correlations in these cases.

Table 3.2

Within-Country Correlations Between Overall Achievement and Frequency of Reading of Books, Comics and Other Media: Population A

Country	Books	Comics	Maga-zines	News-papers	Direc-tions	Total
Belgium/French	.19	.20	.10	-.01	-.05	.15
Canada/BC	.27	.11	.16	.13	.06	.24
Cyprus	.19	.19	.12	.16	.05	.26
Denmark	.24	.26	.20	.27	.04	.35
Finland	.13	.19	.08	.11	-.05	.17
France	.15	.14	.16	.02	-.01	.14
Germany/East	.22	.21	.13	.08	.03	.25
Germany/West	.23	.12	.11	.09	.05	.23
Greece	.18	.10	-.01	.13	.02	.18
Hong Kong	.13	.00	.02	.19	-.08	.13
Hungary	.22	.07	-.03	.09	.01	.16
Iceland	.25	.20	.13	.27	.04	.33
Indonesia	-.02	.02	.08	.10	.02	.05
Ireland	.22	.14	.04	.11	.03	.21
Italy	.09	.13	.08	.18	.03	.19
Netherlands	.22	.19	.10	.05	-.02	.21
New Zealand	.29	.04	.13	.17	.12	.25
Norway	.22	.30	.14	.24	.02	.34
Portugal	.20	.18	.13	.05	.08	.19
Singapore	.14	-.03	.03	.16	.04	.14
Slovenia	.20	.10	.08	.06	.02	.15
Spain	.16	.13	.06	.05	-.06	.12
Sweden	.19	.22	.11	.26	.06	.32
Switzerland	.25	.22	.25	.14	.09	.29
Trinidad/Tobago	.16	.14	.04	.31	.10	.27
United States	.20	-.13	.09	.10	-.02	.07
Venezuela	.05	.02	-.01	.07	-.02	.06
Median	.20	.14	.10	.11	.02	.20

Gender Differences in Voluntary Reading

Most surveys show that girls enjoy reading more than boys do, and that they read more often (Guthrie & Greaney, 1991). To investigate this phenomenon across countries in Population A, the data from all students' questionnaires on the frequency of their reading books, comics, magazines, and newspapers were examined and the results shown in Table 3.3.

Book Reading: Population A

As predicted, girls reported a higher frequency of voluntary book reading than did boys in every country except Hong Kong, where the difference was negligible (-0.08). On a recoded six-point scale, from "hardly ever" (0) to "nearly every day" (6), girls in 18 of the 27 countries produced a mean greater than 3.00 (i.e., three times a week), while boys did so in only one country.

Table 3.3

Mean Frequency of Voluntary Reading of Books by Gender:
Population A

Country	Boys	Girls	Difference
Belgium/French	2.75	3.09	.34
Canada/BC	2.35	3.37	1.02
Cyprus	2.33	2.64	.31
Denmark	2.23	3.15	.92
Finland	2.16	3.22	1.06
France	2.72	3.06	.34
Germany/East	2.17	3.19	1.02
Germany/West	2.22	3.02	.80
Greece	2.50	2.84	.34
Hong Kong	1.73	1.68	-.08
Hungary	2.79	3.43	.64
Iceland	2.64	3.50	.86
Indonesia	1.86	2.31	.45
Ireland	2.46	2.75	.29
Italy	2.03	2.48	.45
Netherlands	2.72	3.97	1.25
New Zealand	2.51	3.16	.55
Norway	2.35	3.65	1.30
Portugal	3.32	3.82	.50
Singapore	2.31	2.60	.29
Slovenia	2.98	3.59	.61
Spain	2.60	2.91	.31
Sweden	2.62	3.82	1.20
Switzerland	2.81	3.46	.65
Trinidad/Tobago	2.05	2.25	.20
United States	2.19	3.09	.90
Venezuela	2.76	3.09	.33

The most frequent book reading was reported by girls in the Netherlands, Sweden, Norway, Iceland, Portugal, and Slovenia. Further inspection of Table 3.3 shows that the largest gender differences, favoring girls, were found in relatively affluent countries such as Norway (1.30), the Netherlands (1.25), Sweden (1.20), and Finland (1.06). It is conceivable that boys in these countries are more attracted by other kinds of leisure pursuits less available to students in other countries. The smallest gender differences were found in Hong Kong (-0.08), Ireland (0.29), Singapore (0.29),.and Trinidad and Tobago (0.20).

Other Voluntary Reading: Population A

Table 3.4 sets out the gender differences in frequency of reading for comics, magazines, newspapers and directions. Whereas boys showed relatively less interest in books at age nine, they compensated by reporting consistently greater reading of comics than girls did. In every country, boys reported more comic reading than girls, and in eight countries, boys read more comics than books. There is apparently a universal tendency for boys to be attracted to comics. At this age, the largest gender differences were found in Finland (1.36), Germany (East) (.88), Sweden (0.99), the Netherlands (0.89), and New Zealand (0.85); the smallest were found in Indonesia (0.12), Portugal (0.17), and Venezuela (0.08).

Gender differences in magazine reading were relatively small across countries at age nine. Indeed, the frequency of reported magazine reading was consistently low at this age level, over all countries, reflecting the relative dearth of magazines produced for this age group. In 15 countries girls showed slightly higher figures; in 15 other countries the boys did. Only in Norway, Portugal, Indonesia, Italy, and the Netherlands did the gender differences exceed 0.20, all favoring girls, but none of these differences was significant.

In 18 of the 27 countries boys reported somewhat more frequent reading of newspapers at this age than girls did, but the differences were relatively small.

Finally, boys in 21 countries reported more reading of directions on how to make or perform something than girls did. The largest frequencies on this variable were reported by the United States, Canada (BC), and Spain, the smallest by Denmark, Germany (East and West), Norway, and Switzerland. Gender differences greater than 0.4, favoring boys, were found only in Belgium (French), Finland, Hong Kong, Norway and the Netherlands. The differences in the other countries were negligible.

Overall Patterns of Gender Differences in Voluntary Reading: Population A

Although girls reported more voluntary reading of books than boys, the pattern was reversed for the reading of comics and directions.

In spite of the problems associated with collecting information by questionnaire from 9-year-olds, certain generalizations can be confidently drawn: consistent gender variations in voluntary reading do exist across different kinds of reading materials, and reading scores are positively associated across countries with greater frequency of reading of books and comics, but not of magazines.

Table 3.4

Gender Differences in Mean Frequency of Voluntary Reading of
Comics, Magazines, Newspapers and Directions: Populatin A

Country	Comics		Magazines		Newspapers		Directions	
	Boys	Girls	Boys	Girls	Boys	Girls	Boys	Girls
Belgium/Fr	2.84	2.07	1.31	1.21	0.76	0.74	1.83	1.39
Canada/BC	1.37	1.05	0.79	0.66	0.63	0.53	1.99	1.99
Cyprus	1.77	1.39	1.43	1.59	1.18	1.24	1.40	1.47
Denmark	2.68	2.32	1.11	1.31	1.33	1.17	0.66	0.63
Finland	4.57	3.21	1.02	1.07	2.34	2.20	1.91	1.22
France	2.16	1.53	1.10	1.04	0.88	0.71	1.46	1.44
Germany/E	1.93	1.05	0.51	0.54	0.68	0.58	0.91	0.71
Germany/W	2.30	1.57	1.03	0.89	0.58	0.75	0.88	0.73
Greece	1.86	1.33	1.37	1.37	1.16	1.00	1.63	1.52
Hong Kong	1.31	0.91	0.61	0.66	1.84	2.11	1.11	0.68
Hungary	1.68	1.15	1.01	0.98	1.31	1.37	1.22	0.98
Iceland	2.09	1.47	0.72	0.63	2.06	1.71	1.21	1.03
Indonesia	1.01	0.89	1.17	1.40	1.03	1.03	1.05	1.29
Ireland	1.63	0.94	0.65	0.59	1.41	1.07	1.25	0.97
Italy	2.19	1.96	0.51	0.78	0.79	0.52	1.65	1.47
Netherlands	2.77	1.88	0.70	0.96	0.96	0.65	1.32	0.55
New Zealand	1.19	0.34	0.57	0.73	1.29	1.19	1.39	1.38
Norway	4.06	3.42	0.50	0.82	1.57	1.40	0.95	0.47
Portugal	2.42	2.25	1.22	1.60	0.64	0.42	1.86	1.76
Singapore	1.22	0.83	0.86	0.85	2.38	2.53	1.60	1.40
Slovenia	2.00	1.44	1.12	1.30	1.17	1.07	1.60	1.68
Spain	2.28	1.56	1.01	1.09	0.59	0.42	2.04	1.78
Sweden	3.88	2.89	0.63	0.70	1.89	1.94	1.19	0.97
Switzerland	2.34	1.53	1.15	1.03	0.84	0.55	0.89	0.52
Trinidad/ Tobago	1.37	1.16	0.63	0.69	1.89	2.12	1.67	1.71
United States	1.01	0.43	0.92	0.72	0.97	0.91	2.02	2.20
Venezuela	2.19	2.11	1.70	1.62	2.41	2.46	1.77	1.68

Voluntary Reading Patterns in Population B

How do voluntary reading patterns differ across countries at the
Population B level? As students are exposed to a greater range of reading
materials, do they report different reading activities from their 9-year-old
counterparts? To investigate these questions the total voluntary reading scores
on each category of reading material (books, magazines, and newspapers)
were compared across countries (see Table 3.5). The means reported in this
table are derived from student ratings (on a six-point scale) of the frequency
with which they read 15 kinds of books, 8 kinds of magazines, and 7 sections

of newspapers. Just as in Population A it was found that in certain countries newspapers are more widely read than books or magazines. In others the pattern is reversed.

Table 3.5

Mean Frequency of Voluntary Reading of Books, Magazines, and Newspapers: Population B

Country	Books	Magazines	News-papers	Total
Belgium/Fr	9.55	10.42	8.86	28.83
Botswana	14.21	8.30	6.87	29.38
Canada/BC	9.62	7.85	9.74	27.21
Cyprus	15.38	15.05	13.48	43.91
Denmark	7.04	9.53	11.72	28.29
Finland	6.31	13.45	18.12	37.88
France	9.97	10.49	8.95	29.41
Germany/E	7.38	10.97	9.47	27.82
Germany/W	7.56	10.51	10.22	28.29
Greece	15.36	14.07	12.32	41.75
Hong Kong	6.54	9.49	11.01	27.04
Hungary	14.87	14.90	14.26	44.03
Iceland	7.52	9.83	15.04	32.39
Ireland	10.18	10.32	11.85	32.35
Italy	14.65	14.80	10.81	40.26
Netherlands	7.05	9.64	8.94	25.63
New Zealand	7.65	8.09	11.24	26.98
Nigeria	21.98	14.36	12.99	49.33
Norway	6.13	10.01	16.92	33.06
Philippines	21.75	12.56	11.76	46.07
Portugal	11.30	12.64	8.69	32.63
Singapore	12.17	10.43	16.87	39.47
Slovenia	17.97	10.81	10.01	38.79
Spain	13.58	11.91	8.69	34.18
Sweden	8.01	12.54	16.34	36.89
Switzerland	8.76	10.74	10.77	30.27
Thailand	10.27	11.47	14.42	36.16
Trinidad/Tobago	18.79	12.58	15.76	47.13
United States	12.20	11.57	11.69	35.46
Venezuela	15.66	13.07	13.15	41.88
Zimbabwe	10.84	12.43	10.25	33.52
Mean	11.62	11.45	11.97	35.04
S.D.	4.42	1.97	2.82	6.65

In interpreting Table 3.5 it should be remembered, once again, that some countries' mean values are suspect because of a noticeable compliance effect which prompted many students to raise their judgments about their reading habits to unrealistic levels. The voluntary reading totals presented on the right of the table show unexpectedly high values for most of the developing countries and should be regarded with caution.

Thus, the relative size of the reported values across topics will be given more weight than the absolute figures in the interpretation which follows. The heavy book readers are best identified, then, by comparing for each country the means given in the left-hand column of Table 3.5 with those of the other columns. Thus, students of Botswana, Greece, Nigeria, the Philippines, Slovenia, Trinidad and Tobago, and Venezuela stand out because they prefer book reading to the reading of magazines or newspapers. Perhaps books are more accessible than other media in these countries. More disconcerting, however, is the discovery that for almost half the countries, book reading is the least popular of the media.

Countries in which students rated magazines highest of all media are Belgium (French), Germany (East), Portugal, and Zimbabwe, while the frequent readers of newspapers are found in the Nordic countries, Singapore and Hong Kong, just as they were in Population A. Just what they read in their newspapers will be examined in the next section. The clear contrasts between the heavy readers of newspapers, magazines, and books are illustrated in Figures 3.1, 3.2, and 3.3.

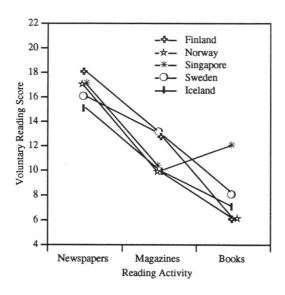

Values
Fin 18/13/6
Nor 17/10/6
Sin 17/10/12
Swe 16/13/8
Ice 15/10/7

Figure 3.1: Voluntary Reading: Countries With Students Favoring Newspapers:
Population B

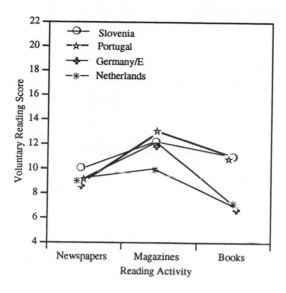

Figure 3.2: Voluntary Reading: Countries With Students Favoring Magazines:
Population B

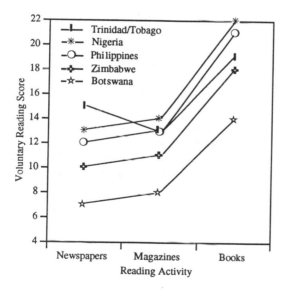

Figure 3.3: Voluntary Reading: Countries With Students Favoring Books:
Population B

Patterns of Book Reading: Population B

In order to throw more light on the differences between countries' reading activity profiles, all students in Population B were asked to rate the frequency with which they read 15 kinds of books, ranging from mystery and romance to history/politics and classical literature. The absolute levels of frequency claimed were suspect in a few countries, but the most and least popular choices in each country were meaningful, and generally in line with prediction. For instance, in most countries books on humor and sports were rated relatively high, while books on poetry and classical literature were rated relatively low.

To clarify the relative popularity of the 15 topics across countries, the six highest rated topics were identified for each country and ranked from one to six. These rankings are presented in Table 3.6. Thus, students in Belgium (French) ranked Sports/Health (SH) as their most preferred category of books, followed by Humor (second), Adventure, Nature, Music and Horror (sixth). The other categories were ranked lower than sixth by these students.

It is clear from the weighted Ns at the foot of Table 3.6 that books of humor are the most popular with 14-year-olds. In 18 of the 31 countries books of humor were ranked first, and only the students in Italy, Botswana, Nigeria, the Philippines, and Zimbabwe ranked them lower than second. Also, books dealing with sports or health are very popular in all countries except Germany (East) and are especially so in Belgium (French), Ireland, and the Netherlands, where they ranked well ahead of the next choice. Asian, African and Nordic countries tended to rate sports lower than the remainder. The third most popular, overall, were books about music, especially in Botswana, Germany (East), Hong Kong, the Philippines, and Zimbabwe. Then followed books about adventure, nature, romance and horror.

Least popular overall were classical literature, biography and poetry, which were ranked in the last three places in most countries. It would be of concern to literature teachers that only in Botswana, Hungary, Italy, Nigeria, Norway, Spain, the United States, and Zimbabwe did poetry reach as high as eighth or ninth choice. Travel and history books also showed consistently low ratings, and science fiction, science/technology and mystery were not very popular in most countries either.

Distinctive patterns were found in only a few countries. Hong Kong students downplayed fiction themes, such as adventure, mystery and romance, and opted more for non-fictional science-technology and nature. Students in Thailand had similar priorities. By contrast, students in several Nordic countries preferred romance and mystery themes and gave lower priority to sports. Italian and Nigerian students were the only ones to give priority to the less popular classical literature.

Table 3.6

Ranking of Six Highest Preferences For Book Reading Topics: Population B

Country	H	SH	M	A	N	R	HO	HP	SF	ST	MS	P	CL	T	B
Belgium/Fr	2	1	5	3	4		6								
Botswana		5	1						2	4		6	3		
Canada/BC	1	2	5	3		4	6								
Cyprus	1	2	3	4	5						6				
Denmark	1	5	2	4	3	6									
Finland	1	5	6	4	2					3					
France	1	2	3	5	4	6									
Germany/E	2		1	5	4	2	6								
Germany/W	1	4	2		3	6	5								
Greece	1	2	3	4			6		5						
Hong Kong	2	6	1		4		3			5					
Hungary	1	2	6	3	5	4									
Iceland	1	3	2		6	5					4				
Ireland	2	1	4	3	5		6								
Italy	5	1	2	4	3								6		
Netherlands	2	1	4	3		6					5				
New Zealand	1	4	3	2		6	5								
Nigeria		3	2						5	1		6	4		
Norway	2	5			3	1	4		6						
Philippines		3	1	4					6	4	2				
Portugal	1	4	2	3	5							6			
Singapore	1	5	4	3					2			6			
Slovenia	1	3	4	2	5							6			
Spain	1	3		2	4		5	6							
Sweden	1	2	5	3	3	6									
Switzerland	1	2	4	3	5	6									
Thailand	1	2	5			6			4		3				
Trinidad/Tobago	2	3	4	1	5					6					
United States	1	2	3	5	6	4									
Venezuela	3	1	2	4	5	6									
Zimbabwe		5	1						4	3	2	6			
Weighted N	150	121	113	84	42	36	30	7	20	26	12	3	4	4	0

Key

H - Humor	SF - Science Fiction
SH - Sports/Health	ST - Science/Technology
M - Music	MS - Mystery/Spy
A - Adventure	P - Poetry
N - Nature/wildlife	CL - Classical Literature
R - Romance	T - Travel
HO - Horror	B - Biography
HP - History/Politics	

Apart from these minor deviations, inter-cultural differences in book reading preferences were of minor significance. There appear to be underlying tendencies which transcend national and linguistic barriers in the way students choose their reading topics. By and large, 14-year-old students enjoy reading about humor, sports, music and adventure. They do not express interest in poetry, biography, classical literature, travel or history/politics.

Patterns of Newspaper Reading: Population B

Students at both age levels reported frequent reading of newspapers, especially in the Nordic countries, Singapore, and Hong Kong. Are they using this time profitably, learning about current political and economic affairs, and extending their reading skills, or are they restricting themselves to the TV programs and comic strips? To clarify this matter, 14-year-olds were asked to rate how often they read various parts of the newspaper. The results for each country were ranked according to their relative popularity within countries and are presented in Table 3.7.

The pattern is conspicuously clear. In almost every country, students report that they use the newspaper primarily to gain information about TV and movies. The reported figures showed more than three times per week on average, and virtually every day in Finland, Sweden, Norway, and Singapore. Only in the countries with limited access to TV were the average frequencies below once per week.

Second in popularity overall were the comic sections of the newspaper. In Canada (BC), the Netherlands, Trinidad and Tobago, and the United States they were read even more than the entertainment sections. Comic strips were also highly rated in Finland, Iceland, Norway, Sweden, and Singapore, where they were reportedly read on average four or five times per week. The third preference of students in most countries was the sports section of the newspaper, and the preference was highlighted especially in Venezuela and Cyprus at three to four times per week. Indeed, only in Germany (East) did the sports mean fall below once per week. Interest in sports is virtually a universal phenomenon at this age.

The similarities across nations in newspaper reading habits are striking. Students read them primarily to gain information about current entertainment, to follow a popular comic strip, and to read about the current sports scene. The remainder of the newspaper appears to hold little interest for 14-year-olds in any country. Students in a few developing countries claim to read the news or politics as often as two or three times a week, but no other section was chosen that often by students in any other country. Classified advertisements might be consulted once per week in many cases, but the business and finance scene has very little appeal.

Patterns in Magazine Reading: Population B

Table 3.8 presents the national preferences for reading various sections of magazines, again in terms of ranks within countries. Eight commonly found sections of magazines were listed in the student questionnaires, and students rated each for frequency of reading on a six-point scale. The absolute values between countries were again felt to be distorted by compliance effects in a few countries, so the focus of analysis in Table 3.8 is again on the relative popularity of each section within each country.

Table 3.7

Ranking of Three Highest Preferences for Newspaper Reading Topics: Population B

Country	M/TV	SH	C	NP	RF	CA	BF
Belgium/Fr	1	3	2				
Botswana		2		1		3	
Canada/BC	2	3	1				
Cyprus	1	2	3				
Denmark	1		2	3			
Finland	1	3	2				
France	1	2	3				
Germany/E	1		2	3			
Germany/W	1	3	2				
Greece	1	2	3				
Hong Kong	1		3	2			
Hungary	1	2			3		
Iceland	1	3	2				
Ireland	1	3	2				
Italy	1	2	3				
Netherlands	2		1			3	
New Zealand	1	3	2				
Nigeria	1	2					3
Norway	1	3	2				
Philippines	1	3	2				
Portugal	1	3	2				
Singapore	1		2	3			
Slovenia	1	2			3		
Spain	1	3	2				
Sweden	1	3	2				
Switzerland	1	2	3				
Thailand	1		3	2			
Trinidad/Tobago	2	3	1				
United States	3	2	1				
Venezuela	2	1	3				
Zimbabwe		3		1		2	
Weighted N	81	37	47	12	2	2	1

Key

M/TV Movies/TV
C - Comic Strips
SH - Sports/Health
NP - News/Politics
RF - Romance/Fashion
CA - Classified Advertisements
BF - Business/Finance

Table 3.8

Ranking of Four Highest Preferences for Magazine Reading Topics: Population B

Country	TV/M	SH	M	NP	RF	CM	N	CT
Belgium/Fr	1	2	3			4		
Botswana		4	1	2		3		
Canada/BC	1	2	3		4			
Cyprus	1	2	4	3				
Denmark	1	4	3	2				
Finland	1	2	4	3				
France	1	2	3		4	4		
Germany/E	1		2	3	4			
Germany/W	1	3	2		4			
Greece	1	2	4	3				
Hong Kong	2		3	1	4			
Hungary	1	2	4		3			
Iceland	1	3	2			4		
Ireland	1	2	3	4	4			
Italy	1	2	3			4		
Netherlands	1	3	2	4				
New Zealand	1	3	2		4			
Nigeria	1	4	3	2				
Norway	1	4	3	2				
Philippines	2	3	1	4				
Portugal	1	3	2			4		
Singapore	1	3	4	2				
Slovenia	1	2	3		4			
Spain	1	2	3			4		
Sweden	1	2	4	3				
Switzerland	1	2	4	3				
Thailand	1		3	2	4			
Trinidad/Tobago	1	3	4	2				
United States	2	1	4	3				
Venezuela	1	3	2		4			
Zimbabwe	4	3	1	2				
Weighted N	114	67	66	45	12	8	0	0

Key

TV/M	TV/Movies
SH -	Sports/Health
M -	Music
NP -	News/Politics
RF -	Romance/Fashion
CM -	Cars/Motorcycles
N -	Nature
CT -	Computer/Technology

It takes only a glance to discern the pattern. In all except five countries, students reported reading the entertainment section of magazines (TV, movies) most often, and this fact is reflected in a weighted total of the ranks of 114, nearly twice that of the second topic. In Finland, Sweden, Italy, Hungary, Denmark, Slovenia, and Spain, 14-year-olds claim to read these sections four or five times a week.

The second most popular part of magazines is, not surprisingly, the sports section, with a weighted total of 67. Only in Germany (East), Hong Kong, and Thailand did sports fail to rank in the top four choices of 14-year-olds. In the United States it is ranked first. Following closely is the music section, which was judged most popular in Botswana, the Philippines, and Zimbabwe, and ranked in the top four choices in every country. For 14-year-olds, music probably includes popular music, jazz, rock, and pop stars.

The news and politics sections receive somewhat more attention in magazines than they do in newspapers, especially in Hong Kong, Singapore, and Thailand, but they are ranked very low in Belgium (French), Canada (BC), France, Italy, and Spain.

The category romance/fashion captures the attention of a few, especially in Hungary and in Slovenia and Venezuela who ranked it close to third, while cars/motorcycles is more frequently read by students in Spain, France, Belgium (French), Iceland, Portugal, Italy, and Botswana than those in the other countries. No doubt these two categories would show clear-cut gender differences.

The remaining two magazine topics, nature and computers/technology, were ranked last in all countries, with no perceptible national differences in absolute values.

Gender Differences in Voluntary Reading: Population B

Gender differences in the voluntary reading patterns of 14-year-olds have changed somewhat from that of their younger brothers and sisters. Table 3.9 presents the gender differences by country for frequency of reading of books, newspapers, magazines, and documents. To clarify a complex picture, the higher frequency is simply denoted by B (for boys) and G (for girls), and the asterisks show when the differences are significant. Thus, for Belgium (French), boys report more reading of books and of magazines than girls do, but only the latter difference was large enough to be significant.

It can be seen that by age 14 boys reported more reading of books in 21 out of the 31 countries, and 12 of these differences were significant. Only in five countries did the girls read significantly more books than boys. These five include Finland, Norway, and Slovenia as well as the Philippines and Trinidad and Tobago. Thus, there is a clear reversal of gender differences from age nine to age fourteen.

For newspaper reading there is no clear pattern: nine countries showed significant differences favoring boys and eight favoring girls. In magazine reading, the boys showed significant differences over girls in 22 cases, whereas the girls showed no significant difference over boys in any country for this variable. This represents a change in pattern from Population A where boys and girls showed similar preferences.

Table 3.9

Gender Differences in Reading of Books, Newspapers, Magazines and Documents: Population B

Country	Books	Newspapers	Magazines	Documents
Belgium/Fr	B	G	B**	G**
Botswana	G	G	B	G**
Canada/BC	B**	B**	B**	G
Cyprus	B**	G	B**	G*
Denmark	B	B**	B**	G
Finland	G**	G*	G	G**
France	B**	B	B**	G
Germany/E	G	B	B**	G**
Germany/W	B*	B**	B**	B**
Greece	B**	B**	B**	B*
Hong Kong	B**	B**	B**	G
Hungary	G	G**	B**	G**
Iceland	B	B	B**	B
Ireland	B	G**	B**	G**
Italy	B	G***	B**	G*
Netherlands	B**	B**	B**	G
New Zealand	B**	B	B	G**
Nigeria	B	G	G	G
Norway	G*	G	B	G
Philippines	G**	B	B	G*
Portugal	B**	B	B**	B
Singapore	B**	B**	B**	G
Slovenia	G**	G**	G	G**
Spain	B**	B**	B**	G**
Sweden	G	B	B*	B**
Switzerland	B	B**	B**	B**
Thailand	B	G**	B*	G**
Trinidad/Tobago	G**	G**	G	G**
United States	B**	B	B**	G*
Venezuela	B	G**	B**	G**
Zimbabwe	G	B	G	G**

*   Significant at .05 level
**   Significant at .01 level

However, for the reading of documents (e.g., charts, forms, directions), girls were well ahead of boys with 17 to 4 significant differences. In the course of a day, girls in many countries are apparently more likely to be reading instructions than boys, although this conclusion does not apply to Germany (West), Greece, Sweden, and Switzerland. Once again, the gender difference points in the opposite way from that of Population A. Nine-year-old boys reported more reading of directions than girls did.

Achievement and Voluntary Reading

To what extent do the most competent readers read more? If it is true that one learns to read by reading, as many specialists claim, then one would expect a positive relationship between reading scores and time spent reading. Certainly, there is data from a number of countries to support the conclusion that regular reading does improve achievement (Fielding & Anderson, 1987; Elley, 1991).

To investigate this relationship within countries, the achievement scores for Population A were first correlated with the total voluntary reading scores. The resultant correlations were generally positive but low, ranging from near zero in the United States and Indonesia to .27 in Switzerland.

Closer investigation showed that the relationship was generally higher with Expository and Narrative prose scores, as one would expect. Practice at reading continuous text is less likely to be beneficial for processing graphs and charts. There is also a hint of curvilinear relationships in some countries, suggesting that a plateau may occur in the benefits of regular reading, as assessed by IEA-type tests. Table 3.10 demonstrates this relationship by reporting the students' Expository mean scores for four levels of voluntary reading. The pattern was similar for Narrative scores. Thus, for 9-year-old students in Belgium (French) the lowest quarter of voluntary readers had a mean Expository score of 486, and the highest quarter had 523. In this case, those who report themselves to be frequent readers are the most competent at reading. In Finland, however, the best readers cluster in the second highest quarter and in the most exceptional cases, Greece and Hong Kong, in the third quarter. On the whole, examination of the table shows that in every country the least frequent readers performed worst, and in 15 out of the 27 countries the most frequent readers performed best. In all cases except Greece and Hong Kong, there is a definite upward trend. Although it is capable of other interpretations, this result is consistent with the old adage that one learns to read by reading. Also, the students who read the least show the lowest literacy levels in all countries.

At the Population B level, the relationship between regular reading and achievement declines somewhat. In a few countries (Botswana, Zimbabwe, Venezuela, the Philippines, Finland, Sweden, and Slovenia) frequent readers still read best, but in 24 countries the trend has changed. The highest achievement was shown not by the most frequent readers, but by those in the second or third quarters. If there are direct benefits to be obtained from more frequent reading at this age, they appear to reach a peak at relatively low levels of voluntary reading in most school systems. In the developing countries, this threshold level is only met by the most frequent readers. The contrast between these countries and some western countries, portrayed in Figure 3.4, is most striking. Of course, no account is taken of the quality of the material read in such analyses.

Table 3.10

Relationship Between Voluntary Reading, by Quarters, and
Expository Scores: Population A

Country	Lowest quarter	Third highest quarter	Second highest quarter	Highest quarter
Belgium/Fr	486	501	514	523
Canada/BC	471	501	513	512
Cyprus	451	472	488	490
Denmark	407	462	482	515
Finland	550	571	584	570
France	511	532	550	539
Germany/E	441	487	517	525
Germany/W	439	495	524	532
Greece	491	521	517	519
Hong Kong	486	510	507	507
Hungary	461	488	510	514
Iceland	472	516	536	545
Indonesia	398	413	415	417
Ireland	494	517	524	521
Italy	516	541	550	547
Netherlands	454	476	500	493
New Zealand	496	533	549	543
Norway	477	528	547	555
Portugal	462	477	491	491
Singapore	503	518	529	527
Slovenia	460	484	504	505
Spain	482	505	516	518
Sweden	498	543	558	568
Switzerland	464	492	532	535
Trinidad/Tobago	425	451	474	484
United States	526	543	548	540
Venezuela	378	404	412	403

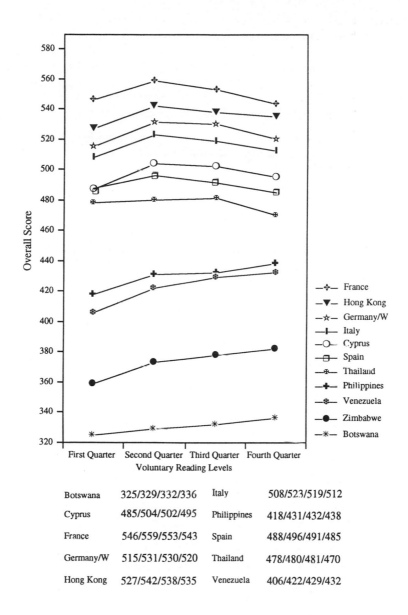

Botswana	325/329/332/336	Italy	508/523/519/512
Cyprus	485/504/502/495	Philippines	418/431/432/438
France	546/559/553/543	Spain	488/496/491/485
Germany/W	515/531/530/520	Thailand	478/480/481/470
Hong Kong	527/542/538/535	Venezuela	406/422/429/432

Figure 3.4: Population B: Contrasts in Relationships Between Reading
Achievement and Voluntary Reading Levels

Table 3.11

Comparison of Voluntary Book Reading Choices, 1971 and 1991,
Population B

Listed in 1971	Listed in 1991	1971 Rank	1991 Rank
Adventure		2	4
History		11	11
Science Fact		13	9
Sci Fi		10	8
Travel/Nature		7	5
Mystery		4	10
Art		14	no
Politics		15	11
Sports		3	2
Romance		5	7
Humor		1	1
Myths/Legends		9	no
Poetry		12	13
Film Stars		6	no
School Stories		8	no
	Music	no	3
	Classics	no	14
	Horror	no	6
	Biography	no	15

Twenty-Year Trends in Reading Interests of Fourteen-Year-Olds

This study allows an exploration of changes in the pattern of reading
interests of young adolescents over a twenty-year period. In the earlier IEA
study of literature (Purves, 1973), a similar survey of interests of 14-year-olds
was conducted. The study included six countries which are included in the
present study (Belgium, Finland, Italy, New Zealand, Sweden, and the United
States). Many of the same categories also appeared. Without searching for
national patterns of interest, but instead accepting the idea of the possibility of
a broad youth culture, we may look for some shifts in patterns of interest
(Table 3.11). Some of the shifts are apparent in the very make-up of the
questionnaires which reflect changes in the judgment of what would be
available for students of this age to read. Whereas current affairs, art,

philosophy, myths and legends, film stars, and school stories were seen as useful categories twenty years ago, they were given no place in the 1991 questionnaire. Classics as a category includes the earlier myths and legends; music (which most students would interpret as referring to popular music and music stars) has replaced both art and film stars. Horror has emerged as a separate category (perhaps thanks to the popularity of such writers as the American Stephen King and the emergence of horror films); school stories have disappeared, and biography has emerged as a separate category.

The patterns of reading interest reported by the students have clearly undergone some shifts, in addition to those indicated by the added categories. Humor remains number one, but adventure has been replaced by sports as number two, and music at number three is a new phenomenon in the book scene. Mysteries have declined in importance as horror has become popular, but science has increased in popularity. Science fiction has maintained a modest popularity as have travel and wildlife, and romance.

We may hazard that some of the changes in the reading interests of young adolescents have resulted from the emergence of the new culture of music, which has tended to replace film as the major source of entertainment. Mystery has become subdivided as the new genre of horror has been discovered. Sports has become increasingly popular as it has become less bound to the interests of males. At the same time, it is perhaps reassuring that the popularity of humor, adventure, romance and science fiction have remained.

4

The Role of the Home and Student Differences in Reading Performance

ALAN C. PURVES AND WARWICK B. ELLEY

One of the major findings of the first IEA Reading study pointed to the strong effect of the home background of the students on both individual and school-level performance. Although this was not a startling finding (following the earlier studies of Peaker (1967, 1971) and Coleman et al. (1966), which pointed to the same phenomenon), it emphasized the point that such variables as parental occupation and education, home literacy resources, and interactions between parent and child concerning literacy and language, could exert an influence on the performance of children in reading. The findings of the earlier study were confirmed in the more recent IEA Written Composition study (Purves, 1992) and have been explored in other research studies (Langer & Allington, 1992).

This relationship is to be expected, since students are the product of their homes and families. Whether they become avid readers or grow up illiterate or aliterate can depend on their parents and the kinds of home environments provided for them. Where students are favored by stable, economically affluent families with a ready supply of interesting reading materials, by residing in a community where literacy is the norm and there is an abundance of environmental print, and brought up by parents who are themselves readers and models of reading, those students stand to gain more from their teachers' endeavors than do students who have grown up without these "advantages." This idea is summed up in Coleman's metaphor of "social capital" (Coleman, 1990).

Particularly in societies where literacy has become a "social habit" (Connerton, 1989; Foster & Purves, 1990), such a child will be well on the way to understanding the social and cultural uses of literate behavior and will be inclined to learn to read. In this milieu, there is a great deal of environmental print which greets the child from birth: the child is continually encouraged to discriminate visual symbols and texts; s/he is encouraged to read and to engage in other literate activities (word games, writing, mailing letters, etc.); and school work tends to be reinforced in both the home and

89

school environments. As a result, the metaphor of emergent literacy has come to replace that of reading readiness (Teale & Sulzby, 1986); the former suggests an environmental force, as opposed to the developmental force suggested by the latter. This hypothesis was supported by Guthrie in a reanalysis of the first reading and literature studies, when he found that national levels of print availability predicted national reading scores (Guthrie, 1981). A similar finding is reported below (see Table 5.7).

In many societies, of course, such home effects are mitigated by the language spoken in the home, so that children even from a literate environment in a language that is not the language of the school may be at some disadvantage in school reading in the language of instruction. In other situations, however, this may be overcome by tremendous individual and family pressure (Akinnaso, 1991), and the child in an otherwise aliterate environment may become a successful reader.

The effects of home and school on achievement in reading will differ because the quality of home environments differs from that of schools in a particular society. Furthermore, the effects of the home occur prior to those of the school, and are cumulative over time, continuing while the child is in school. Parents may clearly influence their children's attitude towards school, and children spend more time at home than in school. All of these reasons suggest that home and community and student characteristics are worthy of analysis in an international study of reading achievement.

This chapter, however, will explore only the nature and variety of home influence. The kinds of questions addressed in this chapter are concerned with the extent to which different home and community factors are associated with student achievement and voluntary reading, including: television in the home, a ready supply of reading materials, gender, and attitudes towards reading and reading instruction.

In Chapter 1, a model of the multiple influences on reading achievement was presented as a guide to the construction of questionnaires. Under the general heading of home conditions and individual characteristics, the following variables were identified:
1.   socioeconomic status
2.   home literacy resources
3.   home literacy interaction
4.   home language
5.   TV viewing
6.   student gender
7.   urban–rural location
8.   self-rating of achievement.

On the following pages, each of these variables is discussed and the relationship it shares with student reading achievement is described. In each case the first description is an international one in which the pattern of country means is discussed; the second concerns within-country patterns. Where these patterns are strongest or weakest, or where the performance of students within a country or group of countries stands out, comments will follow.

Socioeconomic Status

The socioeconomic status of Population A students was assessed by means of questions on the number of a set of material possessions they reported present in their homes. In the pilot study, the use of years of parental education was also tried out as an indicator, but the responses proved inaccurate in many countries, and the question was prohibited in others. To assess socioeconomic status, therefore, each NRC was asked to prepare a list of 10 home possessions (TV, washing machine, telephone, etc.) which they judged would be found in the more affluent households, but by no means in all households in the country. These lists could not be uniform across countries, as appliances which would be suitable for differentiating students in some countries would be almost universal in others. Students merely responded on a yes/no basis to each item on the list.

A second list, similar to the first but containing eight possessions which might be owned by the students themselves, was also prepared by each NRC. This list included such items as one's own bicycle, computer, bedroom, etc. It was anticipated that a student who responded in the affirmative to a large number of these two sets of items would thus identify herself as belonging to the higher socioeconomic levels of her society.

Country Patterns

In spite of differences in the specifics of the lists used in the various countries, both the family and personal lists predicted mean national achievement levels with moderate correlations (.48 and .50), and when combined (by straight addition), the correlation rose to .57. Results for some countries were found to be missing in more than 20% of cases (in some cases because of privacy laws), and when the two countries with the most omissions were deleted, the correlations rose to .62.

Within-Country Patterns

Table 4.1 presents the correlations for each country of the two indices of possessions with student achievement in each domain for Population A. Most correlations were low and positive. Only in five countries (Cyprus, Hungary, Indonesia, Portugal, and Trinidad and Tobago) did the correlation reach .25. Indeed, in Hong Kong and Iceland some correlations were slightly negative.

In view of the argument that social class correlates less highly with achievement in developing countries than in developed countries (Heynemann & Loxley, 1983; Fuller, 1987; Schiefelbein & Simmons, 1981), it may seem surprising that the highest correlations in this study should be in countries with relatively low wealth indicators, compared with the other countries in the

Alan C. Purves and Warwick B. Elley

study. It should be remembered that the number of possessions is not necessarily an indicator of social class. Apparently inequalities in affluence measured in this way have stronger links with the quality of education in such school systems than those in developed countries.

Table 4.1

Means, Standard Deviations and Correlations with Reading
Literacy Domain Scores of Home and Student Possessions Indices:
Population A

| Country | Home possessions | | | | | Student possessions | | | | |
| | Mean | SD | r with achievement | | | Mean | SD | r with achievement | | |
			Narra-tive	Expos-itory	Docu-ments			Narra-tive	Expos-itory	Docu-ments
Belgium/Fr	7.1	1.9	.14	.12	.18	5.8	2.1	.09	.08	.10
Canada/BC	6.8	2.2	.15	.15	.14	4.1	2.3	-.03	.00	.00
Cyprus	5.6	1.7	.21	.16	.25	5.0	2.5	.14	.13	.14
Denmark	4.4	1.8	.19	.01	.05	3.4	1.5	-.05	-.03	-.02
Finland	6.2	1.8	.08	.11	.15	4.8	2.3	.02	.03	.07
France	7.1	1.8	.10	.09	.16	5.6	2.1	.10	.12	.13
Germany/E	1.0	1.1	.04	.01	.09	5.5	2.0	.13	.13	.17
Germany/W	1.5	1.5	.04	-.02	.06	5.8	2.0	.14	.13	.14
Greece	5.1	2.0	.22	.17	.22	4.3	2.4	.11	.10	.11
Hong Kong	5.1	2.3	-.03	-.03	-.04	4.2	2.3	-.07	-.05	-.03
Hungary	6.4	1.8	.19	.17	.26	5.0	2.1	.08	.10	.12
Iceland	5.4	2.0	-.04	-.03	.03	6.0	1.9	.00	.03	.03
Indonesia	1.7	1.7	.25	.25	.28	2.6	2.2	.21	.22	.24
Ireland	5.9	2.2	.16	.15	.18	4.4	2.1	.01	.01	.02
Italy	3.2	2.1	.05	.02	.00	4.9	2.1	-.04	-.04	-.06
Netherlands	4.4	2.2	.09	.07	.13	5.2	1.8	.04	.06	.06
New Zealand	6.7	2.1	.15	.16	.24	5.1	2.1	.07	.06	.09
Norway	5.3	2.0	.06	.06	.11	3.5	1.8	.01	.00	.03
Portugal	4.9	2.5	.28	.28	.32	5.6	2.4	.11	.15	.16
Singapore	6.6	2.0	.22	.21	.19	4.7	2.2	-.01	-.01	-.02
Slovenia	4.5	2.0	.09	.13	.14	5.0	2.3	.05	.08	.09
Spain	6.8	2.0	.14	.16	.17	6.5	1.9	.05	.10	.09
Sweden	4.9	2.0	.12	.12	.13	4.2	2.0	.00	.02	.02
Switzerland	3.1	1.9	.14	.11	.16	4.9	1.8	.14	.14	.14
Trinidad/ Tobago	4.1	2.4	.22	.24	.25	3.3	2.6	.10	.13	.11
United States	7.7	1.7	.16	.18	.20	7.4	1.8	.20	.22	.25
Venezuela	3.7	2.9	.20	.18	.23	4.0	2.8	.10	.12	.13

The Population B figures reveal a similar picture to that of Population A (Table 4.2). The highest correlations with achievement were shown by the Philippines (*r* = .33 to .36), Venezuela (.20 to .26), Trinidad and Tobago (.21 to .24), and Hungary (.21 to .25). The lowest correlations were again shown in most cases by the wealthiest countries: Norway, Iceland, Canada (BC), Finland, and Denmark. Thus, the two indicators of socioeconomic status used in this study cannot be regarded as sensitive measures of advantage for literacy acquisition in relatively wealthy countries. One reason may well be the lack of variance concerning these possessions in the wealthier countries.

Table 4.2

Means, Standard Deviations and Correlations with Reading
Literacy Domain Scores of Home and Student Possessions Indices:
Population B

Country	Home possessions					Student possessions				
	Mean	SD	r with achievement			Mean	SD	r with achievement		
			Narra-tive	Expos-itory	Docu-ments			Narra-tive	Expos-itory	Docu-ments
Belgium/Fr	7.8	2.0	.16	.15	.20	6.0	1.6	.14	.12	.16
Botswana	4.2	2.2	.09	.09	.18	2.8	1.8	.06	.07	.14
Canada/BC	7.5	1.9	.01	.02	.02	4.9	1.8	-.09	-.09	-.09
Cyprus	5.8	1.6	.09	.16	.21	5.9	1.9	.13	.16	.18
Denmark	4.7	1.9	.02	.00	.02	4.6	1.3	-.02	-.01	-.01
Finland	6.4	1.7	.05	.08	.09	5.2	1.7	-.06	.01	.02
France	7.4	1.7	.08	.10	.15	6.1	1.5	.12	.11	.13
Germany/E	1.4	1.1	.03	.02	.04	6.3	1.5	.05	.06	.00
Germany/W	2.4	1.7	.11	.10	.09	6.4	1.5	.14	.13	.13
Greece	5.6	2.0	.15	.18	.21	5.5	1.9	.09	.12	.10
Hong Kong	6.0	1.9	.00	.00	-.01	4.5	2.0	.02	-.02	-.01
Hungary	6.6	1.5	21	.22	.25	5.7	1.6	.15	.13	.14
Iceland	5.8	1.9	-.06	-.05	-.03	6.2	1.2	-.02	.00	-.01
Ireland	6.1	2.1	.09	.09	.10	5.4	1.7	.09	.09	.09
Italy	3.8	1.9	.06	.05	.05	5.2	1.8	.03	.03	.04
Netherlands	4.4	2.3	.07	.09	.09	4.7	1.3	-.01	.01	-.02
New Zealand	7.2	1.9	.13	.17	.22	6.1	1.5	.08	.09	.11
Nigeria	5.8	2.7	.17	.15	.17	4.1	2.1	.07	.09	.07
Norway	5.7	1.9	-.02	.02	.01	4.2	1.4	-.05	.00	-.04
Philippines	4.0	2.4	.34	.36	.33	4.3	1.8	.10	.10	.10
Portugal	5.0	2.0	.13	.13	.15	6.4	1.6	.09	.06	.07
Singapore	0.5	2.0	.12	.18	.18	4.8	1.9	.00	.03	.01
Slovenia	4.4	1.8	.09	.13	.14	5.2	1.7	.10	.09	.07
Spain	6.8	1.8	.14	.15	.15	6.0	1.6	.13	.12	.10
Sweden	5.3	2.1	.09	.12	.12	4.6	1.7	.03	.04	.06
Switzerland	3.9	2.0	.15	.17	.15	5.3	1.5	.11	.08	.06
Thailand	6.6	2.1	.06	.05	.09	6.5	1.6	.06	.04	.04
Trinidad/	4.5	2.1				3.9	2.0			
Tobago			.21	.22	.24			.14	.12	.13
United States	8.1	1.4	.17	.19	.19	7.2	1.1	.19	.21	.21
Venezuela	4.3	2.5	.20	.24	.26	4.1	2.2	.14	.15	.16
Zimbabwe	3.7	2.3	.26	.24	.32	3.7	1.7	.13	.12	.18

94 *Alan C. Purves and Warwick B. Elley*

Home Literacy

As was suggested earlier in this chapter, the extent to which students are good readers is normally affected by the kind of literacy environment the parents provide in the home, whether it be affluent or not. The main components of this home literacy variable were estimates of the number of books in the students' homes, and whether the families receive a daily newspaper; these are admittedly rough and indirect measures of the literacy environment, but they appear to serve as surrogates for the actual use of these materials. Students estimated the number of books on a four-point scale, ranging from 0, through intervals of 1–10, (recoded 5); 11–50 (recoded 30), 51–100 (recoded 75), 101–200 (recoded 150), and more than 200 (recoded 250).

Country Patterns

There is evidence of wide variation among countries in the average number of books in the students' households. At the Population A level, countries with the most books reported per household were Sweden (174), Iceland (162), the Netherlands (160), Canada (BC) (157), and Norway (157). By contrast, students in Indonesia reported having only 25 books at home. Others with fewer books in the home were Hong Kong (41), Portugal (69), Venezuela (72), and Greece (77) (Table 4.3).

Some might question the ability of 9-year-olds to estimate the number of books in their household. In reply, one can point to the fact that the students were asked for only coarse estimates, and that the correlation with the national estimates of 14-year-olds on the same question was high (.83). If they, too, had made unreliable estimates, one would have expected a much lower correlation. The mean estimates were very similar in all cases except for Portugal and Trinidad and Tobago, where the Population B students estimated over 40 more books per household. At the same time, it should be acknowledged that there may not be a universal concept as to what constitutes a book, so that national differences may be differences in definition as well as in number.

The second component of the home literacy construct was the presence of a daily newspaper in the household. Students at both age levels responded "yes" or "no" to this question. Once again, large variations were seen between countries. In Finland, 92% of Population A students claimed to have a daily newspaper at home, followed closely by Sweden (88%), Switzerland (81%), the United States (80%), Iceland (79%), Hong Kong (78%), and Germany (East) (77%). The lowest newspaper rates were reported by Portugal (17%), France (26%), Indonesia (28%), Spain (29%), and Hungary (32%). To check the validity of the figures, these estimates were correlated with those of the Population B students on the same question, and with those reported by UNESCO for newspaper circulation figures, per 1000 people, in each country.

Again, correlations between national means were high ($r = .90$ and $.81$), suggesting that these figures are reasonably accurate.

More important are the relationships between the Home Literacy variable and achievement level. The theoretical model established at the outset predicted that the literacy resources of the home would be one important indicator of the literacy achievement levels of the students who reside there. A plentiful supply of readily available reading matter is a prerequisite for learning to read and for maintaining that skill.

To investigate the relationship of availability of reading material with achievement, the Books in the Home variable (six categories) was combined with Newspaper at Home (two categories) to form an eight-point scale, and the percentage of students in each country falling in point levels 7 and 8 was correlated with the Population A national achievement means (for all domains combined). The resulting correlation of .47 gives tentative confirmation to the hypothesis that in societies where many children live in homes that have an abundance of print (whether available to the child or not), students will score higher on reading tests. This composite variable of the home may be a proxy for a larger societal variable dealing with the availability of print per capita rather than a comment on parents and homes.

Within-Country Patterns

To explore this relationship within countries, the categories of books and newspapers were kept separate, and the correlations between those two variables and achievement in the three domains is presented in Table 4.3. The correlation of achievement with books in the home is positive in all countries. The countries where the relationship is highest are Hungary, New Zealand, and Portugal. The relationship is lowest in Finland (although the standard deviation of books in the home is among the highest). There may be some cultural explanation for these differences; perhaps that children should learn to read is expected among all sorts of people in Finland, not just among those who have books themselves. In the other three countries there may be at play factors such as the relatively high number of non-native speakers in New Zealand. The correlation of achievement with newspapers in the home is much lower in all countries and not significant in Belgium (French), France, Germany (East), Hungary, Iceland, Indonesia, Portugal, Slovenia, and Venezuela.

Looking across the three domains, one notes relatively little variation among the correlations. The correlation of books in the home with narrative scores is higher in 8 countries, and with document scores it is higher in 13 countries, but the differences are negligible. The differences are even less for newspapers in the home. On the basis of this survey, one cannot make the argument that books and newspapers exert differential effects on the domain scores.

Table 4.3

Correlation of Reading Materials in the Home with Achievement
Scores: Population A

Country	Books in the home					Newspapers			
	Mean	SD	Narra-tive	Expos-itory	Docu-ments	Percent yes	Narra-tive	Expos-itory	Docu-ments
Belgium/Fr	142	95	.22	.18	.22	45	.05	.04	.04
Canada/BC	157	93	.16	.15	.13	60	.10	.09	.08
Cyprus	85	80	.13	.12	.14	45	.05	.06	.08
Denmark	156	88	.11	.10	.15	67	.10	.10	.12
Finland	135	86	.09	.08	.10	92	.07	.11	.09
France	116	92	.18	.15	.21	26	-.02	.00	-.01
Germany/E	102	86	.18	.16	.23	77	.06	.02	.06
Germany/W	103	90	.23	.22	.21	65	.10	.11	.07
Greece	77	80	.22	.18	.21	44	.14	.13	.14
Hong Kong	41	66	.11	.11	.13	78	.08	.08	.08
Hungary	128	90	.25	.25	.30	32	-.04	-.07	-.05
Iceland	162	86	.12	.10	.12	79	.05	.06	.06
Indonesia	25	51	.16	.10	.15	28	.01	.00	.00
Ireland	118	42	.21	.20	.23	59	.12	.12	.12
Italy	86	85	.19	.15	.15	43	.06	.05	.05
Netherlands	160	94	.18	.16	.21	73	.04	.02	.08
New Zealand	146	93	.28	.27	.30	70	.08	.09	.09
Norway	157	91	.16	.11	.15	76	.12	.09	.12
Portugal	69	83	.28	.27	.31	17	.03	.05	.02
Singapore	97	89	.25	.22	.23	77	.11	.10	.09
Slovenia	119	89	.21	.19	.18	48	.02	.05	.03
Spain	115	92	.21	.22	.22	29	.05	.09	.07
Sweden	174	85	.14	.13	.15	88	.08	.08	.10
Switzerland	143	92	.21	.18	.19	81	.10	.10	.08
Trinidad/Tobago	120	97	.21	.21	.21	55	.07	.08	.05
United States	137	94	.19	.18	.20	80	.09	.08	.09
Venezuela	72	88	.11	.11	.14	53	.00	.01	.02

Home Literacy Interaction

This construct was designed in order to indicate the level of parental encouragement to improve students' reading. Students in Population A were asked about the extent to which people at home read to the student, are read to by the student, ask the student about his/her reading, or help the student with homework. Some complications are caused by the fact that students who receive most help at home may, in fact, be those who most need or desire this form of attention, while competent readers will report less interaction of this kind, and by the fact that reading aloud to children may well be a cultural phenomenon.

To illustrate, the students who reported highest values on the extent to which parents read to them at home were those of Trinidad and Tobago (3.7 times per week) and Venezuela (2.9), yet these countries had relatively low achievement means. By contrast, the lowest countries on this variable had moderate to high achievement scores, i.e., Iceland (1.1) (a country where little homework is assigned), Spain (1.2), and the Netherlands (1.3). Given these complications, it is not surprising that most of the correlations with achievement between and within countries on these variables for Population A turned out to be low and negative. For frequency of reading aloud to students 9 out of 27 within-country correlations were negative, and no coefficient was significantly different from zero. This factor is probably more important in influencing reading performance with children of a younger age. Again, for the frequency of the child reading aloud at home, seven correlations with achievement were negative, and none was higher than .16 (Italy). The analysis of home interaction factors was therefore taken no further.

Home Language

Many students in the current survey are taught, and were therefore tested, in a language different from that which they regularly spoke at home. To what extent is this kind of discrepancy a handicap for the child? Is it consistent for all language groups? How does it affect national mean scores? This topic is discussed at the within-country level only.

Within-Country Patterns

To investigate such issues, students were requested to state how often they used the test language at home. They responded on a five-point scale: Always, Most of the Time, Sometimes, Hardly Ever, and Never. Tables 4.4 and 4.5 present for Populations A and B respectively the percentage of students who did not speak the language of the school in their homes, all or most of the time. Next to these percentages are the mean scores averaged across all domains for these students, and the mean scores for the remainder (those who typically spoke the language of the school).

In the right-hand column is the difference in mean scores between both groups. Thus, in Population A, a maximum of 72.5% of Singapore students infrequently speak the language of the school (English) at home. These students achieved a mean score of 505 (with a standard error of 1.1), and the remaining 27.5% of students who normally speak English at home scored 543, which is 38 points higher.

A closer inspection of Table 4.4 shows that in two countries, Singapore and Indonesia, over half of the students typically speak another language at home, while a little more than one-fifth reported doing so in Italy and Switzerland. By contrast, schools in Finland, Germany (East), Hungary, and

Ireland are linguistically very homogeneous, with 3% or less in the category of a different home language.

Table 4.4

Achievement Levels of Students by Language of the Home:
Population A

Country	Non-school language			School language		Diff.
	% in sample	Mean score	s.e.	Mean score	s.e.	in means
Singapore	72.5	505	1.1	543	1.9	38
Indonesia	72.5	394	3.0	403	5.1	9
Italy	26.9	513	6.9	537	4.1	24
Switzerland	20.7	476	6.3	521	3.2	45
Venezuela	17.8	383	6.3	388	3.2	5
Trinidad/Tobago	14.7	439	7.9	456	3.2	17
Spain	13.4	499	6.2	505	2.5	6
Hong Kong	12.6	488	7.3	522	2.8	34
Netherlands	12.5	459	11.0	489	4.0	30
Slovenia	11.5	469	6.8	502	2.5	33
Belgium/French	11.4	481	9.5	512	3.3	31
Canada/BC	11.0	488	10.4	502	4.1	14
Germany/West	10.5	461	8.1	509	2.9	48
Sweden	9.2	486	10.8	544	3.2	58
France	9.1	491	12.2	536	4.2	45
New Zealand	8.4	465	9.6	535	3.0	70
Greece	6.4	472	12.6	508	3.1	36
Denmark	4.7	441	15.9	480	3.8	39
Norway	4.1	471	16.7	527	3.1	56
Cyprus	3.7	476	13.6	482	2.3	6
Iceland	3.5	487	0.0	519	0.0	32
United States	3.5	520	12.3	549	2.5	29
Portugal	3.4	469	19.1	479	3.2	10
Ireland	3.0	495	23.2	510	3.7	15
Hungary	2.8	468	14.3	501	2.7	33
Germany/East	1.7	472	28.4	500	4.4	28
Finland	1.5	532	27.6	569	3.2	37

In the next column, mean achievement scores for the groups who speak a different language at home from that of the school are seen to be relatively low, only four rising above 500 (Singapore, Italy, the United States, and Finland). The groups in Finland and the United States should be thought of as a minority of "special" students who are not in second language programs, but are probably the children of relatively affluent foreigners, and the students in Italy may represent the groups that speak a different dialect not too dissimilar to Italian. The results in Singapore suggest that the language instruction program is unusually effective.

Table 4.5

Achievement Levels of Students by Language of the Home:
Population B

Country	Non-school language			School language		Diff.
	% in sample	Mean score	s.e.	Mean score	s.e.	in means
Philippines	89.6	428	2.1	449	8.1	21
Zimbabwe	83.2	371	3.1	385	9.3	14
Singapore	74.1	523	1.2	566	2.3	43
Botswana	61.4	328	2.7	334	3.4	6
Nigeria	41.2	403	–	400	–	-3
Thailand	38.7	476	6.8	479	6.0	3
Italy	26.1	488	5.1	525	3.3	37
Trinidad/Tobago	16.1	456	3.9	485	1.9	29
Switzerland	15.0	497	6.7	544	2.5	47
Spain	11.4	481	6.8	491	2.4	10
Netherlands	9.1	489	12.6	518	3.7	29
Belgium/French	8.7	435	13.3	491	3.9	56
Germany/West	8.4	455	10.7	530	3.2	75
Canada/BC	7.6	506	8.3	524	2.4	18
Slovenia	6.3	506	8.5	534	2.3	28
New Zealand	5.6	470	15.9	551	4.1	81
Venezuela	5.3	394	11.7	421	2.6	27
Sweden	5.1	501	10.8	549	2.3	48
Hong Kong	4.1	495	14.9	537	2.8	42
France	3.9	516	16.1	552	3.3	36
United States	3.8	478	21.0	539	4.4	61
Greece	2.8	487	13.4	510	2.3	23
Denmark	2.5	470	12.9	527	2.0	57
Norway	1.9	473	19.5	519	2.2	46
Portugal	1.6	504	18.6	524	2.4	20
Ireland	1.2	482	44.7	513	3.6	31
Germany/East	0.8	521	32.1	527	2.8	6
Hungary	0.6	493	35.9	536	2.7	43
Finland	0.6	533	38.1	562	2.6	29
Cyprus	0.4	437	32.1	497	2.2	60
Iceland	0.4	508	0.0	536	0.0	28

Of some interest is the size of the discrepancy between the two means. The largest difference is found in New Zealand (70 points). Many of the minority language students in this case are Pacific Islanders, who are recent immigrants from small nations with Austronesian languages quite dissimilar to the majority English tongue, and with no long-standing literacy traditions of their own. Next highest discrepancy is shown by Sweden (58 points) followed by Norway (56). In addition, Singapore, Germany (West), Italy, and Switzerland also showed a substantial reduction in overall mean score (see Table 2.2) as a result of having in their sample large numbers of students with a different home language, and who achieved at relatively low levels. By contrast, Finland and the United States, the two highest scoring countries, had very few such children in their samples (1.5 and 3.5% respectively). The mean for their school language sample was almost identical to their overall mean scores (Table 2.2).

At Population B level, the countries with the most students who speak another language at home were from Africa and Asia: Philippines (89.6%), Zimbabwe (83.2%), Singapore (74.1%), Botswana (61.4%), Nigeria (41.2%), and Thailand (38.7%). Among the European countries, the proportions of such students were consistently lower than for the younger age group, but highly correlated with them. Why there should be a drop is a matter of interest, and may reflect a variety of demographic and migration patterns.

Once again, the mean scores for the "other" language groups were relatively low. Only those of Singapore, France, Germany (East), and Finland rose above 510. The largest discrepancy between the two language groups was seen in New Zealand (81 points), while Germany (West) showed a large deviation (75), just as they had in Population A. Clearly for both age groups, the language that students typically speak at home should be considered as a key factor in explaining their achievement levels.

Extent of TV Viewing

The number of hours students watch television each day has been widely investigated in many countries, as well as in previous IEA studies. As this variable has been found to show slightly negative correlations with reading achievement in some countries and is often used as the explanation for low achievement scores, it was included in this survey in order to explore the relationship between television viewing and reading achievement in a large number of countries.

All students were asked to estimate the number of hours they usually watch TV or videos, on weekdays, outside of school hours, on a seven-interval rating scale: (0 hr, less than 1 hr, 1–2 hr, 2–3 hr, 3–4 hr, 4–5 hr, and over 5 hr). The limitations of such methods of data collection are obvious, yet the figures for frequency were similar for the two populations and were judged to be in line with national predictions.

Country Differences

Table 4.6 presents the mean reported hours of daily TV viewing for all countries for Populations A and B, and the percentage of students who claimed to watch over 5 hr per day. Inspection of this table shows that the United States has, by far, the highest mean estimate of hours at age nine (3.0). American students also show the largest percentage of students watching over 5 hr per day at both age levels (21.3 and 11.4%). Such children are spending more hours viewing television than they spend in the classroom.

Table 4.6

Mean Hours of TV Viewing and Percent of Students Reporting
over Five Hours Per Day

Country	Population A		Population B	
	Mean hours	% over 5 hours	Mean hours	% over 5 hours
United States	3.0	21.3	2.5	11.4
New Zealand	2.6	14.4	2.4	8.6
Spain	2.6	17.5	2.2	5.8
Portugal	2.5	12.1	2.4	5.5
Venezuela	2.5	16.3	1.9	3.9
Canada/BC	2.4	14.9	2.3	9.0
Finland	2.4	6.1	2.3	2.9
Hong Kong	2.4	13.8	2.6	9.1
Iceland	2.4	9.0	2.6	6.8
Ireland	2.4	11.8	2.0	4.8
Trinidad/Tobago	2.3	13.0	1.9	7.3
Denmark	2.2	6.0	2.4	6.3
Netherlands	2.2	12.6	2.4	8.4
Singapore	2.1	9.3	2.1	3.8
Germany/East	2.0	4.7	2.2	2.8
Italy	2.0	9.2	2.3	5.4
Hungary	2.0	8.0	2.5	5.9
Sweden	2.0	4.7	2.3	5.5
Slovenia	2.0	5.5	1.9	2.5
Belgium/French	1.8	5.9	2.0	6.1
Cyprus	1.8	4.6	1.9	2.2
Germany/West	1.6	4.4	1.9	3.1
Greece	1.6	3.6	2.0	4.0
Norway	1.5	3.7	1.8	3.0
Switzerland	1.4	3.0	1.6	2.6
France	1.4	5.5	1.8	4.3
Indonesia	1.4	4.6	–	–
Thailand	–	–	2.0	5.3
Nigeria	–	–	1.3	3.9
Philippines	–	–	1.2	1.8
Botswana	–	–	0.7	3.6
Zimbabwe	–	–	0.6	2.9

Other countries with heavy viewing hours are New Zealand, Spain, Portugal, and Venezuela at age 9, and Hong Kong, Iceland, Hungary, and New Zealand at age 14. Students in these countries typically spend 2.5 hr in front of their TV sets each day. Of course, many watch sporadically and many combine viewing with other activities, but TV is clearly a major occupier of students' leisure time in most countries. Only in the Philippines and the African countries did the mean value drop below 1.4 hr per day.

Within-Country Patterns

More interesting for this survey are the within-country relationships between TV viewing and reading. A study of the correlations for Population A within countries shows that all correlations were small and negative, except for a few countries with relatively low socioeconomic levels, e.g., Indonesia, Portugal, Trinidad and Tobago, and Venezuela, and even here, the correlations were .10 or lower. The most likely interpretation of their deviant correlations is that students with access to TV sets in these countries come from homes with a higher socioeconomic status than the remainder, as the ownership of TV sets in these countries is far from universal.

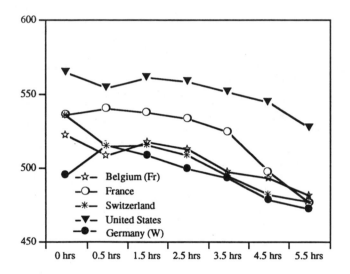

Figure 4.1: Pattern of Decreasing Reading Achievement with Increasing TV
Viewing: Population A

A closer analysis of the relationship between TV viewing hours and achievement in reading comprehension revealed more, however. Figure 4.1 shows the typical pattern observed. Students who watch the most (over 5 hr) had the lowest scores; those who watch only 0–2 hours tended to score best. However, in a small set of European countries this pattern was reversed. Figure 4.2 shows a distinct curvilinear relationship for these six countries, with the highest achievement scores clustering around 3.5 hr daily viewing. Heavy viewers, over 4 hr, still showed very low achievement, which accounts for the negative correlation, but the peak at 3.5 hr was unexpected.

Further inquiry revealed that many students in the countries described in Figure 4.2 watched foreign programming, shown with subtitles in the local language. One could argue that these students were regularly given high-interest reading experiences, under speeded conditions, with visual support from the pictures, as well as the (spoken) foreign language. Such a practice may have contributed much to their elevated reading competence. There is evidence from an experimental study of the learning of students watching captioned television which indicates that this is an effective way of acquiring language (Neuman & Kostinen, 1991). This phenomenon clearly warrants further investigation. Meanwhile, it is clear that heavy TV viewing (over 4 hr daily) is not associated with high reading scores.

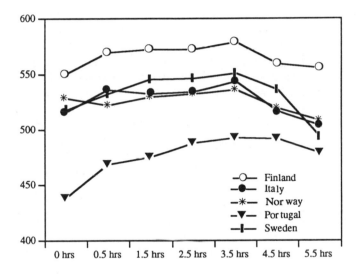

Figure 4.2: Pattern of Increasing Reading Achievement with Moderately Heavy TV Viewing: Population A

Gender

Comparisons of the reading achievement levels of boys and girls in many countries have frequently shown differences in favor of girls (Thorndike, 1973; Downing, 1973). Some researchers have attributed these differences to earlier maturation, others to such environmental influences as the predominance of female teachers (Preston, 1962; Johnson, 1974) or the role modeling presented by mothers.

Country and Within-Country Patterns

In the present study, gender differences in reading literacy were investigated at both age levels. Tables 4.7 and 4.8 present the overall mean scores for Populations A and B respectively for boys and girls, arranged in order of the size of the gender gap.

Inspection of the Population A scores reveals that the girls' overall mean surpassed the boys' in all countries. In 19 countries these differences were statistically significant. The fact that in every country the difference favored girls is itself a highly improbable outcome, if one assumes the equality of boys and girls. While there were six cases where boys performed slightly better in the Documents scale, the girls were consistently ahead in the Narrative and Expository domains. It is clear that 9-year-old girls read better than boys of the same age, and that the largest differences are found in the Narrative domain.

The gender gap, however, is not uniform, and the differences among countries deserve exploration. To test the hypothesis that a predominantly female teaching force would favorably influence the performance of girls, the percentage of female teachers reported in each country's sample (see Tables 4.7 and 4.8) was correlated with the size of the difference between boys' and girls' total achievement means between countries. If the hypothesis is to be supported, the gender gap would be largest when the proportion of female teachers was greatest. For Population A, the correlation was positive and significant at the 5% level ($r = .38$). Although the relationship accounts for only 14% of the variance, it is a plausible interpretation. For Population B, the correlation is also positive and in line with earlier research ($r = .24$) but not significant. Besides the influence of female teachers, there are clearly other cultural or pedagogical factors at work in explaining the variations. The effect of teacher gender on the performance of the students is further explored in Chapter 6.

One new hypothesis emerges from this analysis. Only three countries state that they begin formal reading instruction at age five: New Zealand, Ireland, and Trinidad and Tobago, all anglophone countries whose schooling is based on the British model, and all figure prominently near the top of Tables 4.7 and 4.8. To investigate further, the mean gender difference for these three countries was compared with that of all other countries at both age levels. Figure 4.3 shows these mean differences for both populations.

Clearly the boys who begin reading at age five are further behind the girls by age nine, and the difference appears to have increased even more by age fourteen. Both differences are significant at the 1% level. Interestingly, while boys in Ireland and Trinidad and Tobago have fallen further behind girls by 14 years, those of New Zealand narrowed the gap. The difference among the three countries may result from efforts to help weaker readers or from school retention practices.

As this phenomenon has clear policy implications, it was investigated further by analyzing the item results on the Word Recognition Test. If boys have difficulties in learning to read through lack of maturity, one could reasonably expect their problems to be evident on a measure of word recognition.

Table 4.7

Mean Gender Differences in Overall Reading Literacy Scores by Country: Population A

Country	Mean scores				Difference	% Female teachers
	Boys	s.e.	Girls	s.e.		
Denmark	463	(5.5)	489	(4.9)	26*	79
New Zealand	519	(4.1)	539	(4.0)	20*	76
Iceland	508	(0.0)	528	(0.0)	20*	81
Germany/E	490	(6.3)	509	(6.1)	19*	98
Trinidad/Tobago	443	(4.3)	460	(4.1)	17*	70
Norway	517	(4.6)	533	(4.0)	16*	79
Ireland	502	(5.2)	517	(5.0)	15*	72
Slovenia	491	(3.3)	506	(3.4)	15*	99
Venezuela	379	(4.2)	392	(3.9)	13*	86
Sweden	533	(4.4)	546	(4.3)	13*	97
Hong Kong	512	(3.7)	524	(3.6)	12*	71
Italy	525	(5.2)	537	(5.1)	12*	93
Canada/BC	495	(5.4)	506	(5.4)	11*	90
Finland	564	(4.5)	575	(4.5)	11*	66
Greece	499	(4.4)	510	(4.2)	11*	51
Singapore	510	(1.3)	521	(1.3)	11*	91
Switzerland	507	(4.2)	517	(4.2)	10*	55
United States	543	(3.6)	552	(3.4)	9*	86
Portugal	474	(4.5)	483	(4.5)	9	90
Belgium/Fr	503	(4.5)	512	(4.5)	9	72
Hungary	495	(3.8)	504	(3.6)	9	98
Spain	500	(3.4)	508	(3.3)	8*	76
Germany/W	501	(3.9)	508	(3.8)	7	80
Cyprus	479	(3.2)	484	(3.2)	5	59
Netherlands	483	(5.4)	488	(5.2)	5	42
France	530	(5.7)	533	(5.6)	3	57
Indonesia	394	(3.6)	397	(3.7)	3	46

* Significant difference (p<.05)

Table 4.8

Mean Gender Differences in Overall Reading Literacy Scores by
Country: Population B

Country	Boys		Girls		Differ-ence	% Female teachers
	Mean scores	(s.e.)	Mean scores	(s.e.)		
Trinidad/Tobago	466	(2.6)	492	(2.2)	26*	85
Thailand	464	(7.3)	488	(5.5)	24*	87
Ireland	502	(5.1)	525	(5.0)	23*	61
Canada/BC	513	(3.4)	534	(3.3)	21*	47
Sweden	540	(3.3)	555	(3.2)	15*	69
Finland	554	(3.7)	568	(3.6)	14*	82
Hungary	528	(3.8)	542	(3.7)	14*	92
United States	530	(6.3)	543	(5.9)	13*	71
Iceland	530	(0.0)	543	(0.0)	13*	44
Italy	511	(4.0)	520	(3.9)	9*	82
Netherlands	511	(4.9)	520	(5.2)	9	28
Cyprus	493	(3.0)	501	(3.2)	8*	66
Germany/E	523	(4.0)	530	(4.0)	7	85
Belgium/Fr	480	(5.2)	486	(5.4)	6	61
Botswana	327	(3.2)	333	(2.8)	6	55
Hongkong	533	(4.0)	538	(3.8)	5	57
New Zealand	544	(5.9)	549	(5.5)	5	61
Philippines	427	(3.4)	432	(2.6)	5	89
Slovenia	529	(3.3)	534	(3.3)	5	98
Denmark	523	(2.9)	527	(2.8)	4	65
Germany/W	522	(4.4)	526	(4.4)	4	51
Norway	516	(3.2)	520	(3.1)	4	57
Spain	488	(3.3)	492	(3.1)	4	64
Switzerland	535	(3.5)	538	(3.3)	3	19
Venezuela	419	(4.0)	421	(3.5)	2	78
Greece	509	(3.3)	510	(3.1)	1	77
Nigeria	401	(---)	401	(---)	0	66
Singapore	534	(1.6)	534	(1.5)	0	78
France	553	(5.0)	549	(4.2)	-4	67
Portugal	528	(3.4)	520	(3.2)	-8*	70
Zimbabwe	380	(4.4)	363	(4.1)	-17*	34

* Significant difference

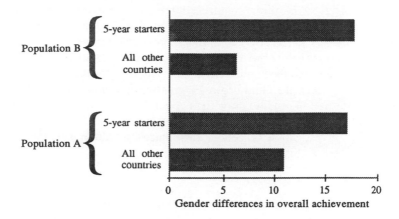

Figure 4.3: Mean Gender Differences (Girls Minus Boys) for Countries which
Begin Instruction at Age Five and all Other Countries

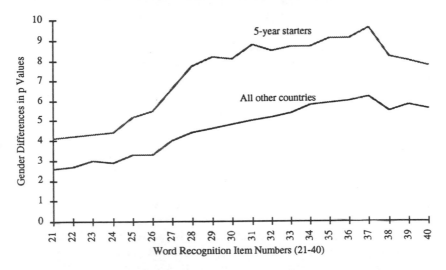

Figure 4.4: Gender Differences on Word Recognition for Countries which
Begin Instruction at Age Five and all Other Countries

Figure 4.4 shows the mean p values for the countries where children start
school at age 5 on items 21–40, compared with the mean p values for all other
countries. The earlier items were too "close to the ceiling" (too easy) to
provide helpful comparative data. Once again the differences are large and
consistent. A plausible interpretation of these trends is that a policy of an
earlier start in formal reading instruction is too early for many boys, and

implies persisting problems for many of them. One possible alternative explanation is that the three countries all have English as the medium of instruction. However, this can be ruled out as a major causative influence as the United States, Canada (BC), and Singapore also teach in English, and their gender gaps are all below the international average. It is possible that there is an interaction between the complexity of the language for the beginning reader and the age at which the child begins instruction that is at work. While more evidence is desired in order to draw firm conclusions, the trends observed here can certainly provide policy-makers with food for thought.

Further investigation of gender differences is undertaken in a booklet which is devoted to this topic (Wagemaker et al., 1993).

Urban–Rural Differences

In many countries, it has been claimed that city students enjoy educational advantages which are denied to their rural counterparts. Urban students tend to have teachers with longer training, access to more school resources, and to more cultural amenities in the community. Therefore, research findings have often shown higher achievement scores in city and suburban schools than in small rural areas. At the same time, improved rural transportation and school consolidation have occurred in many countries, and the inner cities in some metropolitan areas around the world have become increasingly depressed, so that the advantage given to urban schools has come into question. The school principals in this survey were asked to indicate in which of four community sizes (from large urban to small rural area) their school was located. It was hypothesized that the larger communities would produce higher means in achievement than the smaller ones.

Country Differences

Figure 4.5 shows that for 9-year-olds in some countries the expected pattern of urban advantage did appear. One should note that Singapore and Hong Kong are excluded since they have few or no rural schools. In five countries (New Zealand, Germany (West), Switzerland, France, and the Netherlands) the advantage to rural schools is greater than the standard error of sampling, and in Sweden, Norway, Belgium (French), the United States, Finland, and Iceland, the differences are negligible. One suspects that although urbanization might be an advantage in these countries, the large town and the city have both a depressed core and an affluent fringe which would produce an overall evenness of score (See NAEP (1985) p. 42 for evidence of this phenomenon in the United States). Nevertheless, the rural disadvantage which was so often found in previous studies is no longer uniform in all countries, through either changes in transportation patterns, policy initiatives towards education in rural areas, or neglect of the inner cities.

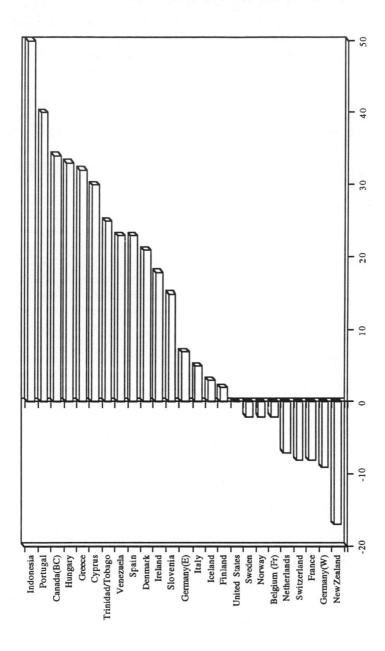

Figure 4.5: Achievement Score Differences Between Urban and Rural School
Areas: Population A (Positive Value Favors Urban Schools)

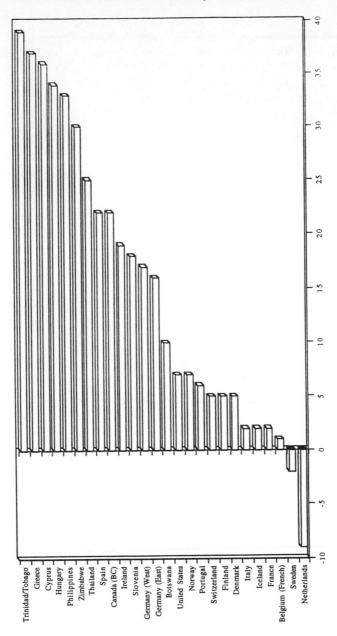

Figure 4.6: Differences in Overall Reading Achievement Between Urban and
Rural Schools: Population B (Positive Score Indicates Urban Advantage)

Figure 4.6 gives the parallel information for Population B (Hong Kong, New Zealand, Singapore, and Venezuela are excluded because of the small number of rural students). Only the Netherlands shows a clear advantage for the rural student. For Sweden, Belgium (French), France, Iceland, Italy, Denmark, Finland, and Switzerland, the differences are negligible, and nearly so for Portugal, Norway, and the United States. For the rest of the countries, it seems that the traditional view of urban advantage remains a strong hypothesis.

Self-Ratings in Reading

Country Patterns

In order to investigate cultural and gender differences in self-ratings in reading, all students were asked to rate their own reading ability on a four-point scale, ranging from Very Good through Good and Average to Not Very Good. Table 4.9 presents the results for Population A, arranged in order of country means on the Narrative scale. This table shows that 27.7% of 9-year-old students regard themselves as Very Good and another 34.1% as Good. In other words, 61.8% are above Average, and only 11.8% below Average.

National differences in modesty are also apparent. Less than 12% of students in Finland, Hong Kong, and Hungary regarded themselves as Very Good, yet these countries have large numbers of excellent readers. By contrast, over half the students of Cyprus and Greece perceived themselves as Very Good, while 47% of American and 44% of Canada (BC) students rated themselves at this level. Such confident self-assessments may well be warranted in the case of the United States. At the other end of the scale, students of Singapore and Hungary showed the most modesty, with 30% and 27% respectively rating themselves Not Very Good. When the ratings were averaged across the four categories, on the four-point scale, the highest countries were Cyprus, Greece, Canada (BC), the United States, and Ireland. The lowest were Hong Kong, Hungary, Singapore, and Indonesia.

It is clear that students have some difficulty in making realistic estimates of their ability on an international scale. The correlation between actual achievement and rated achievement, between countries, was only .19.

Table 4.9

Student Self-Ratings of Reading Ability Given in Percents and the
Correlation with Achievement: Population A

Country	Not very good	Average	Good	Very good	Mean	r with Narrative score
Finland	9	37	44	10	2.6	.27
United States	3	17	33	47	3.2	.27
Sweden	4	19	50	27	3.0	.34
France	15	29	35	21	2.6	.35
Italy	8	33	36	23	2.7	.25
New Zealand	8	23	35	33	2.9	.37
Norway	8	28	37	26	2.8	.34
Iceland	8	23	38	31	2.9	.33
Hong Kong	13	65	15	6	2.1	.18
Singapore	30	28	27	15	2.3	.25
Switzerland	8	30	38	23	2.8	.44
Ireland	9	16	34	41	3.1	.34
Belgium/Fr	9	25	36	29	2.9	.37
Greece	4	16	26	53	3.3	.26
Spain	15	34	28	23	2.6	.30
Germany/W	12	18	46	23	2.8	.41
Canada/BC	7	14	36	44	3.2	.35
Germany/E	16	19	38	26	2.7	.53
Hungary	27	26	36	11	2.3	.38
Slovenia	17	12	43	28	2.8	.42
Netherlands	8	24	34	33	2.9	.25
Cyprus	4	11	32	53	3.3	.29
Portugal	8	41	30	21	2.6	.28
Denmark	7	34	32	27	2.8	.48
Trinidad/Tobago	17	12	33	38	2.9	.33
Indonesia	11	45	27	14	2.4	-.01
Venezuela	17	34	21	23	2.5	.05
Mean (Median)	11.8	26.4	34.1	27.7	2.8	(.33)

Within-Country Patterns

Within countries, however, the relationships are clearer. In most countries students are able to assess their own ability reasonably well, with correlations as high as .53. In Germany (East) (.53), Denmark (.48), Switzerland (.44), Slovenia (.42), and Germany (West) (.41) they rated themselves more accurately; in Indonesia (-.01), Venezuela (.05), and Hong Kong (.18) they had more difficulty. The median correlation was .33 for the 27 countries.

For Population B the trends were almost identical, so no table is given here. Again, the highest self-ratings were shown by Cyprus and Greece (Mean 3.2) and the lowest by Hong Kong (2.1) and Singapore (2.2). The correlation between the two sets of self-rating means for Populations A and B was a high .84. The only discrepancies of any magnitude were shown by the United States, Ireland, Canada (BC), and Portugal, all of which dropped their mean ratings by 0.3, while students of Hungary and Germany (East) raised theirs by the same margin. In 19 of the 26 countries which gathered data for both populations, the two sets of mean self-rating were within 0.1 of each other. The tendency to rate one's ability high or low seems then to be more influenced by cultural norms than by students' relative performance on an international scale. Students are certainly not aware of their comparative status across countries.

A further analysis of gender differences in the self-ratings of students was attempted for Population A in order to compare, first, the absolute differences between boys and girls and second, the relative accuracy of their judgments. Other studies have suggested that girls have lower self-concept than boys in many societies, so it would be expected that they might rate themselves lower than would boys (Wellesley, 1992). For the first comparison (see Table 4.10), mean self-assessments for girls were slightly higher than those for boys in all countries except Finland, Hong Kong, the Netherlands, Singapore, and Sweden (mean difference = .10, favoring girls). The girls' mean achievement levels were also higher than those of the boys, so it is not surprising that they would estimate their ability highly.

The second question was approached by comparing the overall standard score differences between boys and girls on the self-rating measure with the comparable standard score differences on total achievement. For instance, in Belgium (French), the boys' self rating was 2.75 and their mean achievement was 503, while for the girls the numbers are 2.97 and 512. When converted into standard score form (for both genders), boys were found to rate themselves as below average (-0.13), yet they scored above average (0.06); girls rated themselves above average (0.60) and their achievement was also above average, but by a smaller margin (0.29). It can be inferred that the boys in that country rated themselves lower than their achievement level warranted and the girls rated themselves higher. The boys rated themselves too low in 14 countries; the girls did so in 12 countries. As the mean discrepancies between self-rating and achievement were almost identical between genders, one can only conclude that there is no systematic gender difference in the accuracy of students' perceptions of their own abilities at age nine. The mean ratings and the correlations with achievement rise and fall together by country, and the gender differences are negligible.

Table 4.10

Student Self-Ratings of Reading Ability and Reading Achievement by Gender: Population A

Country	Boys			Girls		
	Self-Rating	Achieve-ment	Correla-tion	Self-Rating	Achieve-ment	Correla-tion
Belgium/French	2.75	503	.42	2.97	512	.35
Botswana	--	--	--	--	--	--
Canada/BC	3.13	495	.40	3.20	506	.39
Cyprus	3.30	479	.37	3.40	484	.29
Denmark	2.75	463	.53	2.88	489	.49
Finland	2.58	564	.27	2.53	575	.40
France	2.54	530	.41	2.69	533	.40
Germany/East	2.60	490	.56	2.87	509	.52
Germany/West	2.74	501	.45	2.89	508	.43
Greece	3.21	499	.28	3.37	510	.27
Hong Kong	2.15	512	.21	2.14	524	.16
Hungary	2.22	495	.41	2.40	504	.47
Iceland	2.90	508	.39	2.96	528	.34
Indonesia	2.43	394	-.03	2.46	397	-.04
Ireland	3.02	502	.32	3.13	517	.38
Italy	2.67	525	.28	2.81	537	.24
Netherlands	2.92	483	.24	2.91	488	.28
New Zealand	2.84	519	.45	3.05	539	.36
Nigeria	--	--	--	--	--	--
Norway	2.78	517	.39	2.85	533	.37
Philippines	--	--	--	--	--	--
Portugal	2.55	474	.32	2.75	483	.29
Singapore	2.27	510	.27	2.26	521	.26
Slovenia	2.72	491	.49	2.94	506	.52
Spain	2.60	500	.36	2.60	508	.31
Sweden	3.01	533	.37	2.98	546	.41
Switzerland	2.73	507	.46	2.81	517	.49
Thailand	--	--	--	--	--	--
Trinidad/Tobago	2.80	443	.37	3.03	460	.34
United States	3.20	543	.31	3.28	552	.32
Venezuela	2.45	379	.07	2.61	392	.04
Zimbabwe	--	--	--	--	--	--
Mean	2.74	494.8		2.84	506.6	
SD	0.29	39.0		0.31	39.4	

Table 4.11

Student Self-Ratings of Reading Ability and Reading Achievement
by Gender: Population B

Country	Boys			Girls		
	Self-Rating	Achieve-ment	Correla-tion	Self-Rating	Achieve-ment	Correla-tion
Belgium/French	2.80	480	.28	2.84	486	.32
Botswana	2.80	327	.14	2.91	333	.19
Canada/BC	2.79	513	.39	2.96	534	.42
Cyprus	3.11	493	.46	3.36	501	.42
Denmark	2.76	523	.50	2.86	527	.50
Finland	2.50	554	.29	2.65	568	.35
France	2.65	553	.33	2.78	549	.33
Germany/East	2.77	523	.32	3.14	530	.33
Germany/West	2.56	522	.49	2.77	526	.47
Greece	3.17	509	.39	3.22	510	.41
Hong Kong	2.08	533	.23	2.03	538	.26
Hungary	2.35	528	.44	2.77	542	.42
Iceland	2.96	530	.41	3.03	543	.41
Indonesia	--	--		--	--	
Ireland	2.76	502	.39	2.88	525	.33
Italy	2.63	511	.36	2.87	520	.32
Netherlands	2.72	511	.24	2.79	520	.36
New Zealand	2.79	544	.49	2.89	549	.41
Nigeria	--	--		--	--	
Norway	2.85	516	.33	2.87	520	.37
Philippines	2.81	427	-.03	2.87	432	-.02
Portugal	2.20	528	.26	2.31	520	.30
Singapore	2.19	534	.31	2.15	534	.33
Slovenia	2.77	529	.42	3.06	534	.38
Spain	2.39	488	.39	2.39	492	.32
Sweden	2.84	540	.40	2.92	555	.38
Switzerland	2.61	535	.33	2.74	538	.32
Thailand	2.19	464	.07	2.21	488	.02
Trinidad/Tobago	2.74	466	.39	3.17	492	.28
United States	2.76	530	.43	2.94	543	.38
Venezuela	2.41	419	.22	2.53	421	.29
Zimbabwe	2.51	380	.18	2.62	363	.09
Mean	2.65	500.4		2.78	507.8	
SD	0.26	51.2		0.31	53.3	

Does this pattern of gender differences in self-rating continue on to the 14-year-old level? Table 4.11 shows once again that, on average, girls rate themselves better readers than boys in all countries except Hong Kong, Spain, and Singapore. The standard errors are all approximately 0.02. In Cyprus, Germany (East), Hungary, Italy, Slovenia, and Trinidad and Tobago, girls were especially more confident in their self-ratings. Indeed, the girls in Population B do achieve better than boys in most countries, but internationally the mean standard score difference between the actual achievement of boys and girls (0.14) is not as great as the difference in self-ratings (0.23). In most countries then, girls perceive themselves as better readers than boys by a slightly greater margin than their achievement level would warrant. There is no evidence in either population to suggest that girls are either more modest or more accurate than boys in assessing their reading ability. The finding is somewhat surprising, considering what has been stated regarding girls' self-concept, and the reasons for this phenomenon should probably be sought in the culture of the classroom in many countries as well as in the culture of the home.

The Metacognitive Views of Students

In addition to estimating their own ability in reading, the students in Population A were asked to select, from a list of eleven common views about ways to become a good reader, the three that they thought were most important. This task seeks to determine the importance of those views about reading (often called metacognitive beliefs in that they are above the act of reading itself) in promoting successful performance. It was anticipated that these beliefs would vary somewhat between countries and provide an indirect indicator of the priorities of the students' own teachers in reading instruction. The beliefs were drawn from a review of teaching practices as well as from earlier studies of metacognition.

Table 4.12 shows the 11 options from which the students chose, in each population, arranged in order of popularity for Population A. The percentages given for each population were calculated by averaging the percentages of students in each country who chose each option. All countries were given equal weight in this analysis.

Inspection of this table reveals a similar pattern of popularity for both age groups. Most students give priority to liking it, having lots of time for reading, and concentrating well. The older students give more weight to vocabulary expansion and having many more good books available than the younger ones did, and understandably less to sounding out the words, a skill hopefully learned at an earlier age. Few students see much virtue, in any country, in written exercises, in reading homework, or in being told how to do it. Most seem to support the view that one improves one's reading with regular, interesting, concentrated reading.

Table 4.12

Percentages of Students Choosing Each Strategy for Becoming a
Good Reader: Population A and B

	Pop B	Pop A
1. Liking it	58	69
2. Having lots of time to read	37	33
3. Being able to concentrate well	36	48
4. Knowing how to sound out words	34	24
5. Learning the meaning of lots of words	25	35
6. Having many good books around	20	27
7. Lots of drill at the hard things	18	18
8. Having lots of reading for homework	15	9
9. Having a lively imagination	13	15
10. Having lots of written exercises	8	6
11. Being told how to do it	8	9

Country Differences

An examination of the patterns of responses for each country was not immediately fruitful, as the similarities were more apparent than the differences. It is possible that many of the less able 9-year-olds were unable to respond with adequate insight to produce meaningful results. Therefore, an analysis was undertaken of the highest scoring 20% of Population A students in each country (by average score). Differences in priorities between countries were immediately more apparent, so the analysis was taken further. The mean percentages of students choosing each way for each school system were converted to standard scores and comparisons were made between the views of the students in the ten highest achieving countries and those of the ten lowest achieving countries. The difference in standard scores represents an indication of the extent to which the views held by the best students are reflected in the achievement levels of the whole sample of 9-year-olds.

Table 4.13 shows the mean z-score, on each of the 11 options, for the ten high scoring and low scoring countries, with the differences in the standard scores given in the right-hand column.

Table 4.13

Views of Top 20% of Students on How to Become a Good Reader
(mean z-scores)

	10 High achieving countries	10 low achieving countries	Difference
Ways to become a Good Reader			
Like reading	0.10	0.07	0.03
Lots of time reading	0.08	-0.03	0.11
Can concentrate well	0.17	-0.06	0.23
Can sound out words	-0.73	0.41	1.22
Learn many word meanings	0.32	-0.39	0.69
Have many good books	0.33	-0.40	0.72
Have lively imagination	0.23	-0.49	0.72
Do lots of homework	0.02	0.37	0.35
Drill at hard things	-0.14	0.32	0.46
Do many written exercises	0.06	0.04	0.02
Be told how to do it	-0.01	-0.01	0.00

A study of the profile for the high achieving countries shows that their students gave relatively more priority to "Having many good books around" (.33), "Learning many new word meanings" (.32), and "Having a lively imagination" (.23). They gave least priority to "Being able to sound out the words" (-.73) and "Having lots of drill at the hard things" (-.14). By contrast, the students in countries which had many poor readers gave heavy emphasis to "Sounding out the words" (.41), "Doing lots of homework" (.37), and "Drilling the hard things" (.32). They saw relatively little value in using their imagination, having many books, or learning many words. The right-hand column of Table 4.13 shows that the largest difference between high and low scoring countries was found in sounding out the words, which was a common view of good readers in low scoring countries, and in the availability of good books and exercising one's imagination, which were prevailing views in the high scoring countries. The contrast in philosophies implied by these three choice patterns deserves further investigation. One explanation of the contrast is that the views of these good readers are conditioned by those of their teachers and the fact that many students failed to learn to read in school systems where the best students believed that reading is a skill building process, requiring much deliberate practice, provides some evidence that students would be better employed reading good books for enjoyment and imagination. There may be other explanations.

Within Country Patterns

In order to examine within countries the effects of these student views about good reading, correlations were calculated between student achievement and the belief statements chosen by students in each country in Population A, and broken down by gender. Most correlations were low and only 2% reached .20. The variation within countries was smaller and less revealing than that between countries.

A count of the positive correlations showed that students of both sexes who scored highest tended to give priority to liking reading, concentrating hard, sounding out the words, and using one's imagination; the low scorers gave more weight to doing lots of reading homework, being told how to do it, and having lots of time available for reading. There were many exceptions to these trends however, and the correlations were not substantial.

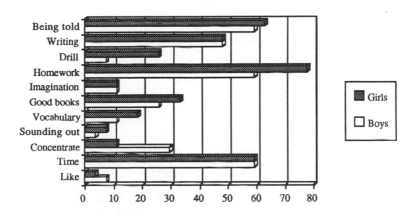

Figure 4.7: Percentage of Countries Reporting Negative Correlation of
Metacognitive Categories with Achievement: Population A

There are some gender differences that are worthy of note (see Figures 4.7. and 4.8). The main difference is that in more countries successful boys believe that drills are a source of their strength in reading, but the belief is held by unsuccessful girls in many more countries than it is by unsuccessful boys. Beliefs in the importance of imagination and in sounding out the words are held more often by higher achieving girls than boys, and belief in the importance of homework is held by unsuccessful girls in more countries than by boys. These differences, particularly those concerning drill and imagination, may say something about gender and role expectation, and are worthy of further exploration in several countries.

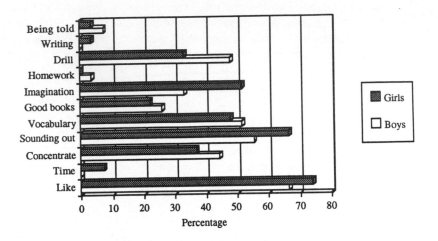

Figure 4.8: Percentage of Countries Reporting Positive Correlations of
Metacognitive Categories with Achievement: Population A

Summary

Building as it does on earlier studies of reading and the relationship between achievement and various home and personal factors, the IEA Reading Literacy study extends our knowledge to a wider range of countries and adds some nuances to what has been known, but does not radically change the picture. It is still true in all countries that girls read better than boys, and that students in homes that have plenty of books will read better than will students from homes with fewer books. Girls also seem to have a high degree of self-confidence in their ability to read. High achieving children, however, are no longer necessarily members of the social group that one thinks of as "middle class" in terms of possessions, but the families tend to live in those regions that one considers more affluent, the town or the suburban areas of the city. It is clear that the students' home language has a major effect on their reading ability and that countries vary considerably in the proportion of students who do not speak, at home, the language of the school. This survey also suggests that modest amounts of television watching may not have the deleterious effect that has been argued from research in individual countries. There is evidence, also, that the personal beliefs of students about how to improve one's reading do differ across countries and cultures and that they are associated with differences in achievement. The international trends that have emerged in this chapter must be tempered by close examination of the situation in individual countries and even communities within countries. These data can suggest areas for further exploration using more detailed analyses or ethnographic methods.

5

Differences Among Countries in School Resources and Achievement

KENNETH N. ROSS AND T. NEVILLE POSTLETHWAITE

Chapter 4 examined the indicators of home circumstances and their association with reading literacy performance. The aim of this chapter is to examine school resources and their relationship to performance.

In order to develop reading skills, schools require a range of resources such as books, libraries, instructional time, and good teachers. The national or regional ministries of education are usually responsible for the allocation of resources to schools. These resources may or may not be equally distributed, and they may or may not influence learning outcomes. Educational policy-makers and planners must have knowledge of the amount and distribution of resources as well as the relationship of school resources to school learning outcomes. Only with such knowledge can they have a firm basis for arriving at informed decisions about appropriate resource levels and suitable patterns of resource allocation.

The first part of this chapter presents information on variations in the provision of resources among systems of education. It also examines the relationship between national provision and national reading performance. The second section compares the relationships, among and within countries, between school provisions and average school performance.

The overall scores on the Reading Literacy tests were presented in Chapter 2. Wealthier countries normally have more resources than poorer countries; wealthier schools normally have more resources than poorer schools. The reason for examining the relationship between resources and reading performance between countries and between schools within countries is that more meaningful generalizations can be made if the relationships are consistent at both levels.

Resources in this study include teachers, the organization of the school, books, and special reading programs. It must be remembered that the data presented in this chapter were collected by means of questionnaires. The limitations of questionnaire procedures for obtaining information about students, teachers, and schools must be acknowledged. There are at least four serious limitations. First, the responses may not be accurate. Despite the careful work undertaken to ensure that values for open-ended questions were within the ranges specified by each country as reasonable for that country, there can still be errors within those ranges and in closed question responses. Second, there is the problem of the "compliance effect" or "socially desirable" responses. In many countries the administration of the questionnaires was conducted under the auspices of the Ministry of Education; thus teachers and school principals could well have given answers based on what they thought they should answer rather than based on the real situation. Third, any item of information collected may provide only an incomplete and often indirect indication of the phenomenon in which one is interested. Finally, questionnaires may be completed in a careless fashion (especially by young children) with resultant increases in errors of measurement (Wolf, 1993). The figures in all tables in this chapter are based on replies from teachers and school principals. (In the case of Switzerland, the principal's questionnaire was completed by teachers as there are no primary school principals in that country.)

The values in the following tables are either means and standard deviations, or percentages for "students" as the unit of reporting. A mean value indicates that the average student in a country was exposed to a particular condition. Thus, in Table 5.1, the 2.8 for Belgium (French) for *public library* means that the average Belgian student had a score of 2.8 on a scale that rated whether he/she lived in an area where a public library was: 1 = not readily available; 2 = available in a neighboring town or city (less than 2 hr of normal one-way travel time); and 3 = available locally (within 30 min of normal one-way travel time). A percentage value represents the percentage of students who are exposed to a particular condition. Thus, it was 97.3% of all students in the francophone schools of Belgium (French) who had teachers whose mother tongue was French (the same language as the test) while 73.7% of students in the sample were taught by women teachers (see Table 5.2). The *s.e.* stands for the standard error of sampling, which provides an indication of the probable accuracy of the sample estimate of the population value. In the case of Belgium (French) it simply means that 95% of the time one can expect the population value to lie between plus and minus two standard errors from this estimate of 97.3% (that is, between 95.3 and 99.3%). In short, the sample in Belgium (French) produced accurate estimates. It will be seen that the estimates are, in general, very good. In some tables only minimum, average, and maximum standard errors are given at the foot of the table because it would have required too much space to give the separate standard errors for each country. At the very bottom of the columns the correlation with the overall mean achievement score for each school system is presented.

Variation Among Systems of Education: Population A

School Community Resources

Each school is located in a geographical area which can be characterized in terms of its reading resources. The school principal for each school involved in the study was asked to indicate whether a public library and bookstore were:
1   not readily available
2   available in a neighboring town or city (less than 2 hr of normal one-way travel time) or
3   available locally (within 30 min of normal one-way travel time).

Table 5.1

Available School Community Resources and Parental Cooperation:
Population A

Country	Public library		Bookstore		Parental cooperation	
	Mean	SD	Mean	SD	Mean	SD
Belgium/French	2.8	.53	2.8	.49	3.1	.79
Canada/BC	3.0	.22	2.8	.46	3.6	.90
Cyprus	2.8	.43	2.9	.28	4.0	.96
Denmark	3.0	.20	2.9	.39	3.4	.60
Finland	2.9	.36	2.9	.43	3.4	.64
France	2.7	.58	2.7	.52	3.0	.95
Germany/East	3.0	.23	2.8	.39	3.1	.41
Germany/West	2.9	.33	2.8	.48	3.2	.68
Greece	2.7	.62	2.9	.34	3.8	.99
Hong Kong	2.9	.45	2.8	.58	4.1	.83
Hungary	3.0	.19	2.9	.30	3.2	.41
Iceland	2.9	.33	2.8	.48	3.0	.77
Indonesia	1.7	.84	2.2	.81	2.9	.57
Ireland	2.9	.39	2.7	.56	3.4	.72
Italy	2.7	.65	2.8	.50	2.9	.75
Netherlands	3.0	—	3.0	—	3.2	.59
New Zealand	2.9	.37	2.9	.35	3.4	.97
Norway	3.0	.21	2.9	.42	3.3	.70
Portugal	2.4	.85	2.3	.82	3.3	.80
Singapore	3.0	–	3.0	–	3.5	.70
Slovenia	2.9	.32	2.8	.45	3.1	.43
Spain	2.8	.58	2.6	.68	3.2	.78
Sweden	3.0	.32	2.8	.42	3.0	.54
Switzerland	3.0	–	3.0	–	3.0	.55
Trinidad/Tobago	2.5	.74	2.7	.52	2.9	.93
United States	3.0	.23	2.9	.35	3.6	.92
Venezuela	2.4	.81	2.6	.72	2.7	.93
Minimum s.e.	0.00		0.00		0.00	
Average s.e.	0.01		0.01		0.02	
Maximum s.e.	0.03		0.03		0.04	
Correlation	.72		.57		.33	

The school principal was also asked to report on a five-point scale (1 = much below average, to 5 = much above average), the extent to which the school received parental support for the educational principles or goals of the school. This rating was made on the basis of "how this school compared with other schools" that he or she knew.

The first two indicators in Table 5.1 represent community reading resources, and the third represents general community support for the school. It will be seen that in the Netherlands, Singapore, and Switzerland all schools are in communities with public libraries and bookstores that are locally available, whereas this is not always the case in Indonesia, Portugal, Trinidad and Tobago, and Venezuela. The between-country correlations with achievement are .72 and .57 respectively for these two indicators, showing that countries where more of these community resources are locally available tend to have higher reading scores.

The between-country correlations of parental cooperation with reading scores is .33, also indicating that where a country's school principals perceive the parents to be supporting the school, there is a tendency for the country to have higher reading scores. Although parental cooperation may, in part, be a function of the educational level or socioeconomic level of the homes, it can also be partially a function of the school's efforts to involve parents.

Teachers

Teachers are a major resource. Among other things, 70–90% of a country's educational budget is spent on teachers' salaries. Although it is often the case that teachers' qualifications (Ross & Postlethwaite, 1992) and their subject matter knowledge (Ross & Postlethwaite, 1989) are strong predictors of student achievement, no measures of these indicators were available in this study. However, measures were available on whether the mother tongue of the teacher was the same language as the test (which was the language of instruction in the schools), the gender of the teacher, the number of female special reading teachers, the extent to which the teacher had attended an in-service training course in the last year, and on some conditions of the school in which he or she taught. These latter indicators included hours per year the school was open, instructional time per week, school size, class size, and pupil/teacher ratio. Tables 5.2 to 5.4 present information on these indicators for all countries.

In nearly all systems of education, well over 90% of students are taught by teachers with the same mother tongue as the medium of instruction in the schools. The major exceptions in Population A are Indonesia and Singapore. In Indonesia the national language is Bahasa Indonesia, but in many parts of Indonesia other languages are used for daily communication. In most cases, it is in third grade that the medium of instruction changes from the local language to Bahasa Indonesia. Nevertheless, the radio and TV and several daily newspapers are presented in Bahasa Indonesia. In Singapore the medium of instruction is English, but most of the population speaks Malay, Tamil, or one of three major Chinese languages. The correlation of .32, given at the foot of the table, indicates that systems where more students are taught by teachers with the language of the test as their mother tongue are more likely to have higher national achievement scores.

Table 5.2

Percent Students with Teachers Having the Same Mother Tongue as the Test Language, the Percentage of Female Teachers (Classroom and Special), and the Number of In-Service Reading Courses Teachers Attended in the Last Three Years: Population A

Country	Same language		Female class-room teachers		Female special teachers			Number of in-service courses		
	Percent	(s.e.)	Percent	(s.e.)	Mean	SD	(s.e.)	Mean	SD	(s.e.)
Belgium/French	97.3	(1)	73.7	(.02)	.62	.83	(.03)	0.38	0.87	(.03)
Canada/BC	89.4	(1)	90.7	(.01)	2.01	1.64	(.07)	3.10	1.16	(.05)
Cyprus	99.5	(0)	56.9	(.01)	.19	.45	(.01)	1.72	1.46	(.04)
Denmark	99.0	(0)	79.1	(.01)	3.68	4.23	(.12)	1.62	1.47	(.04)
Finland	98.0	(0)	65.6	(.02)	.97	.92	(.03)	0.41	0.89	(.03)
France	92.7	(1)	57.0	(.02)	.27	.61	(.03)	0.45	0.92	(.04)
Germany/East	98.8	(0)	98.3	(.01)	.62	.38	(.06)	2.31	1.23	(.05)
Germany/West	98.7	(0)	80.1	(.01)	.70	.46	(.04)	1.07	1.20	(.03)
Greece	98.3	(0)	51.3	(.02)	.14	.57	(.02)	1.71	1.57	(.06)
Hong Kong	97.0	(1)	69.8	(.01)	1.00	2.85	(.09)	0.51	0.80	(.03)
Hungary	100.0	--	98.4	(.00)	.29	.94	(.03)	1.86	1.53	(.05)
Iceland	99.5	(0)	84.2	(.01)	2.52	2.19	--	0.59	1.00	(.02)
Indonesia	20.8	(1)	46.3	(.02)	--	--	--	0.92	1.41	(.05)
Ireland	95.0	(1)	69.2	(.02)	.59	.66	(.03)	0.29	0.61	(.03)
Italy	99.2	(0)	94.0	(.01)	3.67	2.96	(.12)	1.14	1.12	(.04)
Netherlands	95.4	(1)	39.2	(.02)	.61	1.43	(.06)	0.88	0.87	(.04)
New Zealand	96.1	(1)	76.0	(.01)	.78	.98	(.03)	1.56	1.45	(.04)
Norway	98.4	(0)	80.4	(.01)	1.42	1.49	(.05)	1.33	1.25	(.04)
Portugal	100.0	--	91.8	(.01)	1.36	1.80	(.07)	1.20	1.25	(.05)
Singapore	15.3	(0)	88.4	(.00)	.02	.14	(.00)	0.99	1.17	(.01)
Slovenia	99.2	(0)	98.6	(.00)	1.73	1.42	(.04)	1.84	1.34	(.04)
Spain	87.8	(1)	75.9	(.01)	1.10	1.24	(.03)	0.94	1.08	(.03)
Sweden	98.8	(0)	97.0	(.00)	2.40	1.56	(.05)	1.90	1.54	(.05)
Switzerland	97.4	(0)	63.9	(.01)	1.98	2.72	(.08)	0.68	0.77	(.02)
Trinidad/Tobago	91.6	(1)	70.2	(.02)	.09	.55	(.02)	0.92	0.72	(.02)
United States	98.3	(0)	84.0	(.01)	1.41	1.42	(.04)	2.13	1.40	(.04)
Venezuela	98.5	(0)	85.8	(.01)	1.42	2.92	(.10)	0.74	1.10	(.04)
Correlation	0.32		0.18		0.17			0.05		

The percentage of students taught by female teachers ranges from 39.2% in the Netherlands to 98.6% in Slovenia. In general, most systems have many more female than male teachers at the primary school level. The correlation with national achievement is, however, not large for this population.

The average number of special reading teachers (female) in the school is an indicator of the effort (or policy) of a country to supply special reading teachers. The variation of the average number of special teachers per school is large, ranging from very low (Singapore, Trinidad and Tobago, and Cyprus) to high (Denmark, Iceland, Sweden, and Italy). The correlation with achievement is .17.

The last item of data is the number of times a teacher attended an in- or on-service teacher training course in reading in the last three years. This is a tricky indicator because in some systems in-service training is compulsory every year or two and in other systems it is optional. When this training is optional, general experience shows that it is the better teachers who attend. There is a further complication, namely, that some teachers reported attendance at in-service courses for general mother tongue. The responses indicate that the range was from an average of 0.29 (Ireland) to 3.10 (Canada/BC). The correlation between educational system achievement and the average number of times teachers had attended an in-service course was near zero.

Table 5.3 presents some general data on the conditions of the school. The first indicator of conditions is the number of hours a school is open per year for instructional purposes. School principals were asked to state how many instructional hours and minutes their school offered per week (excluding breaks). They were also asked how many weeks per year the school was open. The number of hours the school is open per year is the product of these two items of information. The actual range of the number of hours was from 585 (Iceland) to 1017 (Indonesia). The standard deviation was also large, ranging from 24 hr in Finland to 316 hr in Venezuela. The second indicator in Table 5.3 is the average number of hours of instruction per week received by the students, as reported by teachers. It will be seen that the lowest values are for Denmark, Iceland, Norway, and Slovenia (about 16 hr per week), whereas the highest values are for Indonesia, Italy, the Netherlands, and the United States (more than 25 hr per week). The variation within countries was particularly high in Ireland, Switzerland, Trinidad and Tobago, the United States, and Venezuela. However, it will be noted that among countries there was no significant relationship between the students' time in class and achievement. The third indicator is school size. Most countries had average school sizes between 200 and 500 pupils. The exceptions were schools in Hong Kong, Singapore, Slovenia, Spain, and Venezuela, which were considerably larger. Some countries also had large standard deviations in this variable.

Table 5.3

School Conditions Indicators: Hours of Instruction, School and
Class Size, Pupil/Teacher Ratio: Population A

Country	Hours per year		Hrs Instruc. per week		School size		Class size		Pupil/teacher ratio	
	Mean	SD	Mean	SD	Mean	SD	Mean	SD	Mean	SD
Belgium/French	900	67	24.1	1.5	244	136	20.3	4.6	16.9	4.3
Canada/BC	936	121	24.3	1.8	333	144	23.3	3.1	21.1	9.1
Cyprus	731	111	20.3	3.0	241	112	25.3	5.8	21.2	3.5
Denmark	662	40	16.5	1.0	391	197	17.2	4.5	14.9	17.9
Finland	705	24	18.3	0.5	273	145	24.6	5.0	19.6	2.6
France	878	53	24.2	1.8	160	85	23.5	5.5	21.9	4.0
Germany/East	679	55	18.5	1.3	432	159	20.8	3.4	13.9	9.8
Germany/West	663	64	17.7	1.6	281	129	22.5	4.1	22.0	4.2
Greece	691	84	19.7	2.1	241	168	23.4	6.1	21.5	4.5
Hong Kong	1012	152	23.8	2.7	700	358	36.4	6.0	27.3	8.3
Hungary	699	83	19.0	2.3	546	254	23.4	4.7	16.0	3.1
Iceland	585	104	16.4	2.5	463	305	20.1	5.2	17.6	8.7
Indonesia	1017	94	25.2	0.9	204	94	32.5	16.5	34.2	18.7
Ireland	709	--	21.5	6.4	333	219	31.0	7.8	30.6	3.8
Italy	912	152	25.6	3.5	464	284	16.0	5.4	16.8	17.3
Netherlands	1009	84	25.4	2.0	200	74	25.7	5.7	22.5	4.3
New Zealand	963	41	23.4	1.6	287	135	29.7	7.1	24.3	3.9
Norway	615	100	16.0	1.5	202	129	17.7	5.8	12.1	3.7
Portugal	930	200	22.9	1.3	168	161	20.7	5.4	17.7	3.9
Singapore	966	16	24.2	0.4	1457	427	38.4	3.9	25.8	4.0
Slovenia	596	79	15.9	1.6	705	366	24.6	3.9	19.5	14.1
Spain	907	118	23.7	2.7	657	462	28.8	6.4	24.5	6.5
Sweden	800	--	20.0	--	244	163	20.1	3.9	13.1	3.1
Switzerland	870	152	21.7	4.3	259	290	19.6	3.8	14.5	6.1
Trinidad/Tobago	910	271	21.4	7.9	450	235	28.0	6.7	27.2	4.6
United States	1007	116	26.4	4.3	527	274	24.6	5.0	20.6	11.4
Venezuela	766	316	18.0	8.5	762	449	32.7	8.0	38.4	31.7
Minimum s.e.	0.0		0.00		2.91		0.046		0.05	
Mean s.e.	2.0		0.05		6.75		0.104		0.27	
Maximum s.e.	6.2		0.10		15.05		0.294		1.06	
Correlation	-0.09		0.05		-0.06		-0.31		-0.61	

The fourth indicator in Table 5.3 is class size. In Hong Kong, Indonesia, Ireland, Singapore, and Venezuela it can be seen that the class sizes are large (over 30 students per class), whereas in Denmark, Italy, Norway, and Switzerland they are under 20. The most striking standard deviation is for Indonesia (16.5), indicating that the range of class sizes is high. Indeed, the smallest class size in Indonesia was 3 and the largest was 104. It is also of interest to note that the correlation of class size and achievement between countries was -.31, indicating that, in general, those countries with smaller class sizes (mainly wealthier countries) had students with higher achievement.

The fifth indicator is pupil/teacher ratio which, it will be noted, is always lower than class size with the exception of Indonesia, Italy, and Venezuela. The pupil/teacher ratio is the total enrollment of students in the school divided by the number of full-time (and full-time equivalent) teachers in the school. In a sense, it is an indicator of the wealth of schools in terms of teacher supply relative to the number of students. Thus, for Belgium (French), there is one full-time teacher for 16.9 students. Other countries with one full-time teacher for 17 or fewer students were Denmark, Germany (East), Hungary, Italy, Norway, Sweden, and Switzerland. Those countries with 25 or more students per full-time teacher were Hong Kong, Indonesia, Ireland, Singapore, Trinidad and Tobago, and Venezuela. The correlation between each country's average pupil/teacher ratio and national achievement scores was -.61. This means that the greater the number of teachers per student in a country, the higher the achievement tended to be. This finding is clearly linked to the amount of money allocated to the staffing of schools.

Books as Resources

It is often maintained that a plentiful supply of books is a prerequisite for students to be able to read and improve their reading comprehension. Furthermore, it is often suggested that it is the efforts and the initiative of the school principal and teaching staff that produce better readers. This is often reflected in such indicators as the existence of a school reading room or such ventures as a student or school newspaper or magazine. Tables 5.4 and 5.5 review the extent to which books are made available in classrooms and schools.

Table 5.4 presents data on the provision of a classroom library and a school library. It will be seen that in most countries some 80 or 90% of students are in classrooms with classroom libraries, although Greece, Indonesia, Trinidad and Tobago, and Venezuela have relatively low provision. The school principals were asked about whether there was a school library. It can also be seen that some systems have high provision for both classroom and school libraries, but in other systems provision is more in the classroom (e.g., Cyprus and Hong Kong) or more in the school library (e.g., Slovenia). The correlations indicate that those systems which provide more libraries in schools and classes have higher reading performance; this is particularly the case for classroom libraries.

The percentage of schools having a special reading room for students is low in Cyprus, Greece, Ireland, and Portugal and high in Denmark, Iceland, Hungary, the Netherlands, Spain, and Sweden. The percentage of schools having a student/school newspaper or magazine is low in Cyprus, the two Germanys, Ireland, New Zealand, Sweden, and Trinidad and Tobago, but very high in Denmark, the Netherlands, Singapore, and Slovenia. With the exception of Cyprus and Portugal, many primary schools have a teacher library. There is a correlation of .54 between the percentage of schools having a teacher library and student reading achievement, and a correlation of .23 for the possession of a reading room for students.

Table 5.4

Percent of Students in Schools with Class Library, School Library, Student Reading Room, Student Newspaper and Teacher Professional Library: Population A

Country	Class library	School library	Reading room	Student newspaper	Teacher library
Belgium/French	83	72	20	32	60
Canada/BC	99	99	22	28	81
Cyprus	99	0	0	1	2
Denmark	72	99	68	83	96
Finland	57	83	52	21	97
France	83	82	52	31	33
Germany/East	40	50	14	10	48
Germany/West	86	78	13	12	77
Greece	51	71	8	22	75
Hong Kong	97	56	39	70	30
Hungary	80	96	59	29	89
Iceland	57	94	52	35	64
Indonesia	52	99	34	70	14
Ireland	97	84	10	14	30
Italy	62	92	30	21	88
Netherlands	86	96	53	98	99
New Zealand	97	99	19	17	75
Norway	78	100	33	31	96
Portugal	64	93	10	34	5
Singapore	93	100	49	94	87
Slovenia	70	100	39	86	97
Spain	87	99	58	38	61
Sweden	87	96	65	14	82
Switzerland	88	87	24	33	81
Trinidad/Tobago	51	68	19	9	15
United States	96	97	35	52	75
Venezuela	30	66	23	20	21
Minimum s.e.	0	0	0	0	0
Mean s.e.	1	1	1	1	1
Maximum s.e.	2	2	2	2	2
Correlation	0.49	0.17	.23	-.11	.54

Table 5.5 provides information on the average number of textbooks per student in class, the number of books per student in the classroom library, the number of magazines or newspapers per student in the classroom library, the number of books per student in the school library, the number of books per student added to the school library in recent years, and a composite indicator labeled school reading resources. This construct includes the existence of a school library, a reading room for students, a school newspaper or magazine, and a professional library for teachers.

Table 5.5

School Reading Resources (Average Number per Student):
Population A

Country	Textbooks in class Mean SD	Books in class library Mean SD	Magazines Mean SD	Books in school library Mean SD	Books added to library Mean SD	School reading resources Mean SD
Belgium/Fr	3.8 1.4	3.1 2.0	0.30 0.34	3.5 5.5	0.42 1.0	1.82 1.1
Canada/BC	4.0 1.5	3.3 1.7	0.19 0.21	23.6 11.7	1.74 1.5	2.27 0.8
Cyprus	4.9 0.8	2.1 1.6	0.11 0.20	-- --	-- --	0.03 0.3
Denmark	5.0 0.8	2.5 2.5	0.16 0.36	33.1 17.5	1.54 1.7	3.41 0.7
Finland	4.2 0.7	1.8 1.2	0.09 0.17	7.9 5.9	0.38 0.5	2.49 0.8
France	4.5 1.2	3.5 2.6	0.24 0.32	5.3 4.7	0.67 1.2	1.84 1.2
Germany/E	4.9 0.7	1.1 0.8	0.08 0.14	1.2 1.3	0.12 0.4	1.22 0.9
Germany/W	4.4 0.7	2.2 1.3	0.05 0.09	3.0 2.7	0.21 0.3	1.80 0.9
Greece	4.8 0.6	2.2 4.3	0.14 0.30	1.9 2.5	0.23 0.4	1.73 1.0
Hong Kong	4.3 1.4	2.8 0.8	0.03 0.08	5.0 4.2	0.47 0.6	1.72 1.2
Hungary	4.9 0.8	1.2 0.8	0.04 0.08	13.6 12.1	0.71 0.8	2.69 0.9
Iceland	4.7 1.0	2.0 2.0	0.08 0.20	10.7 10.2	0.77 0.8	2.35 1.0
Indonesia	3.1 1.3	2.0 2.3	0.25 0.31	4.0 3.9	1.19 1.9	2.15 0.8
Ireland	4.2 0.7	2.6 3.0	0.15 0.48	3.4 2.8	0.43 0.5	1.36 0.8
Italy	3.9 1.1	2.9 3.6	0.13 0.28	2.5 2.8	0.35 0.6	2.13 0.8
Netherlands	4.7 0.9	3.5 8.7	0.17 0.34	2.8 4.0	0.13 0.2	3.43 0.7
New Zealand	4.4 1.2	2.1 1.0	0.13 0.17	17.8 11.3	1.43 1.1	2.06 0.8
Norway	4.7 0.9	3.8 7.9	0.07 0.29	16.8 14.3	1.01 1.7	2.47 0.7
Portugal	4.2 0.9	2.6 2.2	0.27 0.40	2.2 2.9	0.09 0.2	1.35 0.7
Singapore	4.3 0.6	2.0 0.8	0.07 0.13	6.8 3.9	0.50 0.6	3.29 0.7
Slovenia	4.8 0.8	1.5 1.4	0.17 0.19	13.3 9.5	0.44 0.4	3.21 0.7
Spain	4.7 0.9	1.4 1.0	0.12 0.21	4.4 3.1	0.37 0.5	2.56 1.0
Sweden	5.0 1.0	3.1 2.0	0.05 0.09	16.1 11.4	0.80 0.9	2.43 0.9
Switzerland	5.0 0.8	3.5 2.3	0.22 0.33	9.2 10.2	1.19 2.5	2.14 0.9
Trinidad/Tobago	3.9 0.6	1.3 1.0	0.12 0.15	1.0 1.5	0.23 0.4	1.06 0.8
United States	5.3 1.0	3.1 1.6	0.13 0.20	15.8 10.4	0.92 1.4	2.54 1.0
Venezuela	3.1 1.2	1.6 4.6	0.37 0.94	1.5 1.7	0.21 0.6	1.18 1.0
Minimum s.e.	0.01	0.01	0.00	0.05	0.01	0.01
Mean s.e.	0.03	0.08	0.01	0.21	0.03	0.03
Maximum s.e.	0.06	0.39	0.03	0.53	0.08	0.06
Correlation	0.60	0.32	-0.55	0.23	0.07	0.27

The average number of textbooks per student in class ranges from 3.1 in Indonesia and Venezuela to 5.3 in the United States. Most countries have between 2 and 3.5 books per student in the classroom library, but Finland, Germany (East), Hungary, Slovenia, Spain, Trinidad and Tobago, and Venezuela have fewer. The average number of textbooks per student correlates .60 with reading achievement between countries, while the correlation is .32 for the number of books per student in the classroom library.

In comparison to book provisions, the average number of magazines or newspapers per student in the classroom library is low, particularly in Finland, the two Germanys, Hong Kong, Hungary, Iceland, Norway, Singapore, and Sweden. The simple correlation of -.55 indicates that those countries that provide more magazines and newspapers (i.e., Indonesia, Portugal, and Venezuela) have lower achievement scores. It is tempting to speculate that either it is much more useful for students to have books rather than magazines to read, the quality of the texts in magazines is not particularly helpful for students' reading, or poorer countries can afford magazines more readily than books. The range of the number of books per student in the school library is very large: from one book per student in Trinidad and Tobago to 33 books per student in Denmark. The number of books per student added to the school library during the last year varies from 0.09 in Portugal to 1.74 in Canada (BC). This variable is not an effective indicator for the purposes of this analysis. The supposition was that many books added within the last year would be an indicator of the effort a school or country puts into the supply of reading materials. However, the standard deviations indicate considerable variance among schools within countries, suggesting that the purchasing policies for schools in any one country for a given year are not uniform. Finally, the level of school reading resources (calculated as the sum of the existence of a school library, reading room for students, school newspaper or magazine, and a teacher library for professional reading) shows a large variation from 0.03 in Cyprus to over 3.4 in Denmark and the Netherlands. The correlation of .27 lends some support to the hypothesis that countries with more school reading resources, as defined above, tend to achieve better in reading literacy.

School Initiatives in Reading

Table 5.6 presents data on special initiatives in reading in schools. The first column presents the percentage of students in schools with a special reading program. The range was from 35% in Italy to 100% in Hong Kong. The correlation with national mean scores was .20. The programs that were offered took the form of extra class lessons (column 2), individual instruction (column 3), special remedial reading courses (column 4), the sponsoring of informal initiatives to encourage reading (e.g., book club) (column 5), and the provision of a special program for the improvement of reading instruction (column 6).

Table 5.6

Percent of Schools Offering Special Reading Programs

	Offer special program	Extra class lessons	Extra Individual instruction	Special remedial reading course	Sponsor reading activities	Program improve instruction
Belgium/French	76	17	33	56	50	38
Canada/BC	93	54	82	62	92	56
Cyprus	46	60	55	80	77	66
Denmark	98	10	86	82	21	71
Finland	94	20	95	3	53	49
France	51	16	31	54	40	38
Germany/East	53	5	57	50	30	16
Germany/West	50	8	24	71	17	7
Greece	37	20	32	45	43	26
Hong Kong	100	47	24	37	71	90
Hungary	96	57	98	21	22	74
Iceland	76	34	86	42	32	33
Indonesia	80	64	5	79	26	90
Ireland	62	28	45	67	49	46
Italy	35	10	40	18	18	24
Netherlands	48	52	13	100	74	41
New Zealand	89	26	83	72	95	81
Norway	93	8	91	48	51	77
Portugal	48	23	83	28	39	15
Singapore	45	70	77	55	78	75
Slovenia	93	23	51	91	99	48
Spain	66	72	34	58	54	45
Sweden	96	43	18	90	67	61
Switzerland	67	24	35	65	14	7
Trinidad/Tobago	77	53	73	30	51	80
United States	91	33	25	65	97	72
Venezuela	50	50	25	47	30	68
Minimum s.e.	0	1	0	0	0	0
Mean s.e.	1	1	1	1	1	1
Maximum s.e.	2	2	2	2	2	2
Correlation	.20	-.37	.24	-.18	.29	-.23

Within countries it may well be the case that those schools undertaking such initiatives are those where the students are experiencing difficulties in learning to read, and therefore need such programs. For each indicator there is wide variation in provision among countries. Only the provision of special programs, individual instruction, and the sponsoring of reading activities have positive correlations with reading achievement between countries.

Variation Among Systems of Education: Population B

The form of the presentation of resources for Population B is similar to that for Population A.

School Community Resources

Table 5.7

Available School Community Resources and Parental Cooperation:
Population B

Country	Public library		Bookstore		Parental cooperation	
	Mean	SD	Mean	SD	Mean	SD
Belgium/French	2.8	0.5	2.9	0.3	2.7	1.0
Botswana	2.1	0.9	1.9	0.9	2.6	0.9
Canada/BC	3.0	0.0	2.9	0.4	3.6	0.8
Cyprus	2.9	0.3	3.0	0.0	4.2	1.2
Denmark	3.0	0.0	2.8	0.4	3.4	0.6
Finland	3.0	0.0	2.9	0.3	3.4	0.5
France	2.8	0.5	2.8	0.5	3.2	1.0
Germany/East	2.9	0.4	2.8	0.5	3.0	0.2
Germany/West	3.0	1.1	2.9	0.3	3.1	0.8
Greece	2.8	0.6	3.0	0.0	3.4	1.1
Hong Kong	2.9	0.4	2.9	0.5	3.8	1.9
Hungary	3.0	0.0	2.9	0.3	3.2	1.4
Iceland	3.0	0.0	2.9	0.4	2.9	0.9
Ireland	2.9	0.4	2.7	0.5	3.5	0.8
Italy	2.6	0.7	2.7	0.6	2.9	0.8
Netherlands	3.0	0.0	3.0	0.0	3.2	0.6
New Zealand	3.0	0.0	3.0	0.0	3.7	0.9
Norway	3.0	0.0	2.8	0.5	3.2	0.6
Philippines	2.4	0.8	2.3	0.8	3.6	0.9
Portugal	2.7	0.7	2.7	0.7	3.5	0.9
Singapore	3.0	0.0	3.0	0.0	3.4	0.8
Slovenia	2.9	0.3	2.8	0.4	3.1	0.4
Spain	2.8	0.5	2.7	0.6	3.3	0.9
Sweden	2.9	0.5	2.8	0.6	3.1	0.6
Switzerland	3.0	0.0	3.0	0.0	2.9	0.6
Thailand	2.6	0.7	2.6	0.8	3.5	0.8
Trinidad/Tobago	2.7	0.5	2.9	0.3	3.2	1.0
United States	2.9	0.3	2.8	0.5	3.5	0.9
Venezuela	2.7	0.7	2.8	0.5	2.9	0.9
Zimbabwe	1.6	0.9	2.0	0.9	3.1	1.1
Minimum s.e.	0.00		0.00		0.01	
Mean s.e.	0.01		0.01		0.03	
Maximum s.e.	0.04		0.04		0.05	
Correlation	0.86		0.82		0.31	

As can be seen from Table 5.7, in nearly all countries the average student was in a school with a public library and bookstore either locally available or within two hours' travel. The notable exceptions were Botswana, the

Philippines, and Zimbabwe. The perceived degree of parental cooperation was correlated .31 with achievement at the between-country level, whereas the community resource indicators had correlations in excess of .80.

Teachers

Table 5.8 indicates that for most countries close to 100% of the mother tongue language class teachers have the same home language as the language of the test. The exceptions are Botswana, the Philippines, Singapore, Thailand, and Zimbabwe. Given that these countries include some of the lowest scoring countries, it is not surprising that the correlation (.64) is so high. The percentage of female classroom teachers is less than at the Population A level. Mother tongue teaching is the domain of females in Finland, Germany (East), Hungary, Italy, the Philippines, Singapore, Slovenia, Thailand, and Trinidad and Tobago, but very much a male profession in the Netherlands, Switzerland, and Zimbabwe. However, the percentage of male or female mother tongue teachers in different countries has only a small correlation with the countries' reading performance in Population B.

Conditions of the School

Table 5.9 presents indicators on the number of instructional hours per year, the average number of hours of instruction per week for students (as reported by teachers and then by school principals), school size, class size, pupil/teacher ratio, pupil/special reading teacher ratio, and the average percentage of students in the classes tested who did not have the same mother tongue as the language of the test.

The correlation of .17 between the average instructional hours per year in countries and their reading performance, although positive, is not significant. The standard deviation within countries is very different. Cyprus clearly entered the official number of hours instead of asking the schools, but all other countries asked the schools. The (stated) variation among schools in Botswana, Ireland, Portugal, Thailand, Trinidad and Tobago, Venezuela, and Zimbabwe is clearly high. In Finland and Sweden there is little variation. The large standard deviations in some countries raise questions about the accuracy of school principal responses. There is much debate on how many days there should be in the school year. Perhaps it is more important to think in terms of the number of instructional hours. It would be even more appropriate to examine the amount and frequency of actual instruction in any given day or week and how the school day is organized (see Stevenson & Stiegler, 1992). This topic is worthy of much more intensive research effort.

The total number of hours of instruction per week is less than 23 hr in Botswana, Denmark, Finland, Greece, Hungary, Slovenia, Trinidad and Tobago, and Zimbabwe. It is 30 hr or more per week in Italy, the Netherlands, the Philippines and Thailand. The variation is high in Botswana, Ireland, Trinidad and Tobago, Venezuela and Zimbabwe. Either there is no uniform policy, or there must be some doubt about the responses given by the school principals in those countries. The correlation of weekly hours of instruction with achievement is a low value of .02.

Table 5.8

Percent of Students Having Teachers with the Same Mother Tongue as the Test Language and the Proportion of Female Teachers: Population B

Country	Same language		Female classroom teachers	
	Percent	(s.e.)	Percent	(s.e.)
Belgium/French	98	(1)	60	(2)
Botswana	47	(2)	55	(2)
Canada/BC	92	(1)	51	(1)
Cyprus	99	(0)	66	(1)
Denmark	100	(0)	66	(1)
Finland	100	(0)	83	(1)
France	98	(0)	66	(2)
Germany/East	100	(0)	84	(1)
Germany/West	99	(0)	51	(2)
Greece	100	(0)	77	(1)
Hong Kong	98	(1)	60	(2)
Hungary	100	(0)	92	(1)
Iceland	99	(0)	46	(1)
Ireland	99	(0)	60	(2)
Italy	100	(0)	82	(1)
Netherlands	99	(0)	27	(2)
New Zealand	94	(1)	61	(2)
Norway	98	(0)	58	(1)
Philippines	34	(1)	92	(1)
Portugal	98	(0)	73	(1)
Singapore	25	(1)	81	(1)
Slovenia	99	(0)	98	(0)
Spain	86	(1)	57	(1)
Sweden	99	(0)	69	(1)
Switzerland	92	(1)	21	(1)
Thailand	53	(3)	87	(2)
Trinidad/Tobago	97	(0)	86	(1)
United States	99	(0)	73	(2)
Venezuela	98	(0)	78	(2)
Zimbabwe	4	(1)	35	(2)
Correlation	0.64		0.10	

School size is larger in Population B than for Population A. Most average school sizes are between 500 and 1000. For Finland, Greece, Italy, Norway, and Switzerland, mean school sizes are below 400, and for the Philippines, Portugal, and Thailand, above 1500. In general, countries with larger school sizes appear to perform less well (-.20), but it should be noted that, in general, it is in the poorer countries that there are larger school sizes.

Table 5.9

Conditions of Schools as Expressed in Hours of Instruction, School and Class Size, Pupil/Teacher Ratio, and Percent of Class Speaking a Language Other Than the Test Language: Population B

Country	Hours of instruction Per year Mean	SD	Per week Mean	SD	School size Mean	SD	Class size Mean	SD	Pupil/ teacher ratio Mean	SD	Pupil/ special teacher ratio Mean	SD	Pupil Non-school lang. Percent
Belgium/French	1090	103	28.5	2.2	538	255	19.8	4.9	8.8	2.6	101	199	14
Botswana	663	390	22.6	7.9	630	253	35.7	7.2	34.0	6.5	70	181	39
Canada/BC	999	109	25.4	3.0	712	375	25.0	4.8	17.1	3.1	135	76	11
Cyprus	891	0	27.0	0.0	566	182	29.8	3.1	15.8	4.3	344	288	0
Denmark	903	63	22.6	1.6	456	161	19.1	3.4	14.5	15.8	99	53	4
Finland	857	11	22.5	0.2	356	131	18.6	4.3	11.1	1.8	213	147	0
France	1047	85	29.4	2.2	601	214	24.5	3.7	14.8	1.6	41	124	8
Germany/East	878	50	23.4	1.1	444	143	20.8	3.6	13.3	3.0	141	211	0
Germany/West	870	63	23.0	1.5	576	295	24.7	3.9	15.5	3.8	131	210	12
Greece	743	73	22.3	1.6	328	143	27.4	5.0	16.5	3.4	--	--	2
Hong Kong	1067	192	28.3	3.7	1037	343	38.1	4.1	21.5	2.9	118	228	0
Hungary	798	57	21.8	1.3	549	252	25.0	5.4	16.0	3.2	91	227	0
Iceland	794	78	23.0	2.3	447	307	20.9	5.5	15.9	3.6	151	107	1
Ireland	870	267	25.6	7.3	552	217	25.6	5.7	17.6	2.4	262	180	7
Italy	1050	117	30.3	2.7	372	221	18.8	4.7	12.6	15.0	110	95	1
Netherlands	1197	129	30.2	3.2	772	449	24.2	4.4	18.2	16.0	209	394	7
New Zealand	982	63	25.2	1.8	900	372	26.4	4.6	16.5	2.0	275	161	5
Norway	857	114	23.2	3.1	266	101	22.3	6.0	10.0	1.8	103	77	2
Philippines	1201	162	30.3	3.5	1833	--	47.2	8.2	36.9	12.4	411	645	36
Portugal	1158	288	27.8	2.9	1565	712	26.8	3.4	13.3	3.4	765	897	1
Singapore	993	43	24.9	1.0	1280	388	35.1	4.7	20.8	3.0	133	408	82
Slovenia	722	89	20.6	1.5	703	370	24.3	3.6	18.4	6.9	420	241	6
Spain	926	133	24.4	2.4	605	393	29.7	7.1	24.4	8.1	269	260	8
Sweden	932	24	23.3	0.6	448	245	25.1	3.8	11.2	3.9	126	75	6
Switzerland	1108	149	28.6	3.6	331	268	17.4	5.4	13.5	4.1	96	151	16
Thailand	1200	294	30.0*	4.1	1691	1013	45.8	14.9	17.2	3.6	412	708	36
Trinidad/Tobago	769	345	20.1	8.8	1106	532	33.1	7.1	23.4	6.8	285	522	0
United States	1032	127	28.5	3.5	988	657	23.9	6.1	20.9	26.6	293	197	3
Venezuela	1073	530	26.7	13.3	839	463	29.7	9.4	52.3	41.0	327	419	0
Zimbabwe	800*	330	22.5	8.9	629	406	39.9	11.8	29.4	4.1	--	--	59
Minimum s.e.	0.00		0.00		2.85		0.07		0.04		1.23		0.00
Mean s.e.	5.11		0.11		12.98		0.19		0.24		8.44		0.01
Maximum s.e.	19.27		0.48		52.35		0.76		1.49		36.14		0.03
Correlation	0.17		.02		-0.20		-0.58		-0.72		0.00		-0.47

*These figures were supplied by the NRCs from different sources.

Average class size varies from 17.4 in Switzerland to 46 and 47 in Thailand and the Philippines. As can be seen from the correlation of -.58, the lower scoring countries tend to have larger class sizes. The pupil/teacher ratio, which is an indicator for the "teacher wealth" of the schools, tends to be very low (i.e., few students per teacher) in general and in Belgium (French), Finland, Norway, and Sweden in particular. It is high (over 30) in Botswana, the Philippines, and Venezuela. The correlation of -.72 indicates that the more teacher provision that is made in a country the higher will be that country's reading performance level. It will be remembered that pupils per teacher per school is correlated with school mean achievement scores. However, more pupils per teacher per school is a sign of "less teacher wealth" of the school. Hence, a negative correlation means that "fewer pupils per teacher" is associated with higher mean school achievement scores.

The number of pupils per special reading teacher varies widely, but the correlation with reading achievement is zero.

Finally, the average percentage of students in the classes tested not having the same mother tongue as the test varies from zero in some countries to 82 and 59% in Singapore and Zimbabwe respectively. Again, there was a tendency for countries with classes having more non-national language (language of test) students enrolled to have lower scores. However, there are three categories. The first category comprises countries where it is common to speak the national language(s) at home and have a different language of instruction at school. These include Botswana (where many speak Setswana at home), the Philippines (many not speaking Tagalog at home), Singapore (where the test was in English but most speak one of the Chinese languages or Bahasa Malaya or Tamil at home), Thailand (where 36% do not speak central Thai at home), and Zimbabwe (where more than half speak Ndebele or Nshona at home). The second category comprises countries with many guest workers or new immigrants who speak their own national language(s) at home, but where the language of instruction at school is that of the host country. Of these Switzerland, Belgium (French), and Germany (West) have the highest percentages. Italy represents a third category where many students speak a dialect at home but use the same written language form.

Book and Reading Resources

Table 5.10 presents information on the percentage of students in schools with a school library, a student reading room, a student magazine or newspaper, and a teacher reading room. Also included are the average number of textbooks per student, school library books per student, the library books per student added in the last year, and a composite indicator labeled school reading resources. In all but three countries (Botswana, Germany (East), and Zimbabwe), over 75% of students were in schools with a school library. In 10 of the 30 systems of education 100% of students were in such schools. The extent of national provision of school libraries and national reading performance were significantly correlated (.55). The composite of school reading resources consisted of school library, reading room for students, student newspaper, teacher (professional) library, drama club, debating club, literature club, and writing club. All of the indicators in this group were positively correlated with reading literacy performance among countries, as were the indicators of textbooks per student and library books per student.

Table 5.10

Book and Reading Resources in School (Percentage of Students in Schools with Selected Resources and Number per Student): Population B

Country	School library	Read- ing room	Student news- paper	Teacher Reading room	Textbooks in class		Library books		Library books added		School resources	
	%	%	%	%	Mean	SD	Mean	SD	Mean	SD	Mean	SD
Belgium/French	82	59	25	78	1.4	1.1	6.5	9.7	0.25	0.37	2.9	1.3
Botswana	44	21	33	9	1.9	1.2	0.3	1.7	0.03	0.05	1.2	1.2
Canada/BC	99	40	57	73	1.7	1.1	20.3	11.3	1.04	0.77	4.2	1.5
Cyprus	100	37	74	58	1.6	1.2	10.7	11.5	0.40	0.38	4.0	1.6
Denmark	99	76	85	96	2.3	1.1	28.9	14.0	1.35	1.42	4.4	1.1
Finland	83	47	44	96	1.7	1.2	6.4	8.1	0.22	0.19	3.1	1.2
France	99	89	35	64	1.4	0.8	4.6	2.9	0.34	0.29	3.5	1.2
Germany/East	40	9	17	44	1.6	0.9	0.5	1.0	0.09	0.16	1.5	1.0
Germany/West	78	43	66	84	2.0	0.9	2.4	3.4	0.18	0.21	3.8	1.4
Greece	86	8	14	62	1.1	1.0	2.1	4.2	0.16	0.28	1.9	1.2
Hong Kong	100	76	96	51	1.5	1.2	5.4	3.3	0.41	0.60	4.7	1.7
Hungary	96	58	29	90	2.0	0.0	12.8	11.6	0.71	0.74	3.9	1.3
Iceland	96	71	67	73	2.3	1.2	14.2	15.2	1.08	1.24	3.8	1.6
Ireland	84	33	50	21	1.5	0.9	3.7	3.8	0.26	0.33	2.9	1.6
Italy	88	32	29	87	1.2	0.9	4.5	4.5	0.18	0.27	2.4	1.0
Netherlands	93	67	79	98	1.6	1.3	3.4	4.2	0.19	0.33	4.0	1.3
New Zealand	100	52	88	68	1.3	0.8	13.4	11.0	0.73	0.43	4.9	1.4
Norway	98	39	47	97	1.8	1.1	13.8	10.4	0.59	0.49	2.9	0.9
Philippines	100	51	80	41	0.8	0.8	2.9	5.3	0.28	0.62	4.5	2.2
Portugal	100	58	78	36	0.9	0.4	3.1	3.2	0.14	0.18	3.1	1.2
Singapore	100	52	90	78	1.1	0.4	10.2	5.4	0.77	0.70	5.3	1.5
Slovenia	100	45	88	98	1.4	1.0	12.9	9.5	0.39	0.27	5.6	1.1
Spain	97	53	40	58	1.9	1.2	4.5	3.8	0.40	0.45	2.9	1.4
Sweden	97	77	37	82	1.8	1.1	17.6	16.4	0.84	1.44	3.2	1.0
Switzerland	92	53	29	92	2.5	1.2	13.6	13.4	0.92	1.09	3.1	1.2
Thailand	100	86	96	84	1.0	0.7	7.6	6.1	0.50	0.49	4.5	1.8
Trinidad/Tobago	100	30	41	34	0.7	0.6	2.9	2.8	0.14	0.17	2.6	1.4
United States	100	52	85	67	2.2	1.1	19.0	13.7	1.01	2.55	4.6	1.6
Venezuela	85	35	35	29	0.8	1.0	1.5	2.9	0.24	0.93	1.5	1.0
Zimbabwe	49	27	31	16	0.7	0.5	1.8	4.5	0.18	0.20	3.3	1.6
Minimum se	0	1	0	0	0.00		0.03		0.00		0.02	
Mean se	1	1	1	1	0.03		0.23		0.02		0.04	
Maximum se	2	2	2	2	0.05		0.62		0.11		0.09	
Correlation	0.55	0.39	0.22	0.67	0.38		0.46		0.43		0.42	

School Clubs Involving Reading and Language

At the Population B level, information was given by school principals on whether or not the school had a drama club, a debating club, a literature club, and a writing club. The percentage of students attending schools having such clubs is given in Table 5.11. There is considerable variation across countries; however, none of the correlations with achievement between countries were large in magnitude.

Table 5.11

Percent of Schools with Clubs Involving Reading: Population B

Country	Drama	Debating	Literature	Writing
Belgium/French	39	4	1	4
Botswana	25	9	2	2
Canada/BC	85	31	11	35
Cyprus	42	9	44	38
Denmark	74	5	9	3
Finland	35	3	1	8
France	65	5	18	13
Germany/East	11	4	27	1
Germany/West	72	2	21	9
Greece	14	3	4	2
Hong Kong	61	52	77	29
Hungary	43	5	59	13
Iceland	59	33	1	4
Ireland	40	66	6	12
Italy	13	5	1	2
Netherlands	47	6	7	7
New Zealand	76	90	6	19
Norway	10	0	8	5
Philippines	58	32	40	51
Portugal	39	9	14	3
Singapore	82	68	36	22
Slovenia	83	2	79	75
Spain	25	4	8	6
Sweden	21	5	6	12
Switzerland	37	5	3	3
Thailand	30	22	27	26
Trinidad/Tobago	41	25	8	4
United States	70	42	18	25
Venezuela	0	--	--	--
Zimbabwe	90	78	13	34
Minimum se	0	0	0	0
Mean se	1	1	1	1
Maximum se	2	2	2	2
Correlation	0.15	-0.13	0.11	-0.01

Table 5.12

Percent of Schools Reporting Special Reading Initiatives and
Programs: Population B

Country	Sponsor initiatives	Extra class lessons	Individual instruction	Special reading programs	Insufficient special staff	No special programs	Program improvement of reading instruction
Belgium/French	39	22	72	87	32	75	21
Botswana	26	75	32	34	63	2	46
Canada/BC	46	34	69	49	48	0	41
Cyprus	73	30	50	26	24	0	29
Denmark	22	42	95	92	3	3	76
Finland	67	7	83	6	22	23	23
France	68	22	10	65	43	21	63
Germany/East	19	4	49	40	0	55	12
Germany/West	15	5	18	53	4	74	6
Greece	44	46	15	10	18	78	12
Hong Kong	89	15	16	40	38	0	82
Hungary	22	57	98	21	16	4	74
Iceland	28	22	87	21	46	28	20
Ireland	35	60	78	91	71	58	26
Italy	17	20	42	6	36	35	33
Netherlands	31	15	12	--	20	21	34
New Zealand	74	52	82	87	58	0	71
Norway	23	9	89	50	51	14	51
Philippines	72	33	69	42	54	63	76
Portugal	55	78	47	31	53	15	44
Singapore	59	55	64	38	57	65	73
Slovenia	98	19	62	86	36	9	36
Spain	60	60	43	65	22	26	46
Sweden	44	40	28	96	25	6	46
Switzerland	25	15	33	48	11	2	7
Thailand	97	65	48	76	33	50	76
Trinidad/Tobago	46	30	34	43	82	3	34
United States	47	34	26	46	45	34	45
Venezuela	36	39	31	35	40	61	40
Zimbabwe	30	48	40	13	30	36	30
Minimum se	0	1	0	1	0	0	0
Mean se	1	1	1	1	1	1	1
Maximum se	2	2	3	2	2	2	2
Correlation	0.13	-0.39	0.17	0.20	-0.38	-0.16	0.00

Special Reading Programs and Initiatives

Table 5.12 presents results on the extent to which schools in each country
sponsor initiatives in reading, such as having extra class lessons, individual
tuition, and special programs of reading. It also presents the percentage of
students in schools reporting that they have insufficient specialized staff, offer

no special programs, and have programs for the improvement of reading instruction. It is interesting to note that Finland, which was the highest scoring country, tended to have schools sponsoring the initiatives of individual instruction but not extra classes or special reading courses. On the other hand, France, which was another high scoring country, preferred sponsoring special reading courses. Countries reporting higher percentages of students in schools with insufficient specialized staff and with no special reading programs tended to have lower achievement levels. It is also of interest to note that countries reporting a higher percentage of insufficient specialized staff and of extra class lessons had lower achievement levels.

Consistency of Relationships Between and Within Countries

The patterns of between-country correlations can be confounded by the wealth of each country. Richer countries can afford more resources than poorer countries. It is of interest, therefore, to discover if the same relationship holds within countries as between countries. If the relationship is consistent then there are better grounds for generalization.

Tables 5.13 and 5.14 summarize the correlations for each population. Only those variables that were available for both populations have been listed. First the *Correlation among countries* for each indicator is presented. Then the average of all *Correlations among schools within countries* is presented with the number of the correlations that had a negative sign and the number that had a positive sign. The final column simply states *yes* or *no* for each variable, indicating whether the pattern of correlations among schools within countries is consistent with the correlation among countries. A "yes" is given in the final column for each indicator if at least 18 countries have within-country correlations that have the same sign as the among-country correlation. The cut-off figure of 18 countries represented two-thirds of the countries for Population A and slightly less than two-thirds for Population B.

For example, consider the first indicator, *Availability of Public Libraries*, listed for Population A in Table 5.13. The among-country correlation for this indicator was .72 and the average of the within-country correlations was .07. There were 19 of the 27 countries in Population A where the within-country correlation had the same sign as the among-country correlation and therefore a "yes" is registered in the final column of Table 5.13.

From Table 5.13 and 5.14 it may be seen that at the Population A level there were 7 indicators that featured a "consistent" relationship with reading performance, while at the Population B level there were 12 consistent indicators. There were five indicators that proved to be consistent in both Population A and Population B: *Availability of Public Libraries, Availability of Bookstores, Textbooks per Student, Teacher's Library,* and *Parental Cooperation.*

144   *Kenneth N. Ross and T. Neville Postlethwaite*

Table 5.13

Correlations with Reading Scores Among Countries and Among
Schools within Countries and the Consistency between the Two
Levels of Analysis: Population A

Indicators	Correlation among countries	Correlation among schools within countries			Consis-tency of analysis yes/no
		Average correlation	Consistency of sign -	+	
Availability public libraries	.72	.07	8	19	yes
Availability bookstore	.57	.09	4	23	yes
Hours of instruction per year	-.09	.05	7	20	no
Instruction time per week	.05	.05	10	17	no
Size of school	-.06	.14	3	24	no
Size of class	-.31	.14	5	22	no
Teacher gender (female)	.18	.08	6	21	yes
Teacher MT same as test	.32	.05	6	19	yes
Pupil-teacher ratio	-.61	.12	8	19	no
Textbooks per student	.32	.07	8	19	yes
School library books per student	.23	.04	12	14	no
School library books added	.07	-.02	17	9	no
School resources: school libr.	.17	.04	8	17	no
School resources: read. room	.23	.00	12	14	no
School resources: stud. news.	-.11	.03	8	19	no
School resources: teach.'s lib.	.54	.07	8	19	yes
School reading resources (comp)	.27	.05	10	17	no
No special program in school	-.20	-.03	17	9	no
Special program - extra lessons	-.37	-.01	12	15	no
Special program - ind. instr.	.24	.00	10	17	no
Reading courses	-.18	-.01	14	12	no
Project improv. reading instr.	-.23	.06	9	18	no
Sponsor reading initiatives	.24	.05	11	16	no
Parental cooperation	.33	.23	3	24	yes

The "survival" of these five consistent indicators provides a useful summary message for the educational planner. This message is that differences in reading performances, among and within countries, are consistently associated with the availability of books in the community (public libraries and bookstores), the availability of books in schools (students textbooks and teacher libraries), and the level of parental cooperation with schools.

As mentioned above, this message needs to be interpreted along with some knowledge of the socioeconomic context of different countries. That is, it is instructive to examine the strength of the relationships upon which the message is based after having taken some account of differences in the wealth of nations.

Table 5.14

Correlations with Reading Scores Among Countries and Among
Schools within Countries and the Consistency between the Two
Levels of Analysis: Population B

| Indicators | Correlation among countries | Correlation among schools within countries | | | Consistency of analysis |
| | | Average correlation | Consistency of sign | | yes/no |
			-	+	
Availability public libraries	.86	.08	10	20	yes
Availability bookstore	.82	.09	10	20	yes
Hours of instruction per year	.17	.06	10	20	yes
Instruction time per week	.18	.05	11	19	yes
Size of school	-.20	.15	5	25	no
Size of class	-.58	.21	3	27	no
Teacher gender (female)	.10	.04	12	18	no
Teacher MT same as test	.64	.05	10	14	no
Pupil-teacher ratio	-.72	.02	12	18	no
Textbooks per student	.38	.07	10	19	yes
School library books per student	.46	.08	13	17	no
School library books added	.43	.04	10	20	yes
School resources: school libr.	.55	.07	6	16	no
School resources: read. room	.39	.09	7	23	yes
School resources: student news	.22	.12	5	25	yes
School resources: teach.'s lib.	.67	.08	7	23	yes
School reading resources (comp)	.42	.18	5	25	yes
No special programs in school	-.16	-.01	13	13	no
Special program - extra lessons	-.39	.02	14	16	no
Special program - ind. instr.	.17	-.01	14	16	no
Reading courses	.20	-.01	17	12	no
Project improv. reading instr.	.00	.00	15	15	no
Sponsor reading initiatives	.13	.03	11	19	yes
Parental cooperation	.31	.25	2	28	yes

It was therefore decided to partition the strength of the among-country relationships between books in the community, books in schools, parental cooperation, and reading performance by conducting a commonality analysis that included an allowance for national wealth. The books in the community measure was formed as a principal component score from the two variables describing availability of public libraries and availability of a bookstore. The books in school measure was formed as a principal component score from the two variables describing textbooks per student and the existence of a teacher's library. The measure of national wealth was taken as the Composite Development Index (CDI) described earlier in this book. The results of this commonality analysis have been presented in Table 5.15.

Table 5.15

Commonality Analysis for Books in the Community, Books in
Schools, Parental Cooperation, and National Wealth

Source of Variance Explanation	Population	
	A	B
Variance Related to National Wealth		
a) Unique to National Wealth	9.43	3.43
b) Shared with National Wealth	41.00	50.66
Subtotal Related to National Wealth	50.43	54.09
Variance not Related to National Wealth		
a) Unique to Other Factors		
Books in the Community	0.62	10.50
Books in Schools	7.43	0.11
Parental Cooperation with Schools	2.66	3.09
b) Shared among Other Factors	0.82	12.30
Subtotal not Related to National Wealth	11.53	26.00
Total Variance Related to All Factors	61.96	80.09

From Table 5.15 it can be seen that the total amount of variance in
reading scores among countries that was explained by the four factors
(national wealth, books in the community, books in school, and parental
cooperation) was 62% for Population A and 80% for Population B. Most of
this variance, for both populations, was related to variance either unique to
national wealth or shared with national wealth. The term "shared" in this
instance refers to variance related to the other three variables but whose
source could not be disentangled from national wealth. These shared
components were fairly large, being 41% for Population A and 51% for
Population B.

In the lower half of Table 5.15, the variance of reading achievement
among nations accounted for by sources not related to national wealth have
been listed. For Population A this was only 12% and for Population B this was
much larger at 26%.

It is interesting to note the pattern of unique contributions of sources
other than national wealth. Parental cooperation accounted for about 3% in
each of the populations, whereas books in the community was negligible for
Population A, but accounted for over 10% of total variance at the Population B
level. On the other hand, books in the school was negligible at the Population
B level, but accounted for over 7% at the Population A level. The shared

contribution among these three factors also differed, being 1% at the Population A level and 12% at the Population B level.

Although, among the countries considered, national wealth accounted for much of the variation in reading achievement, it was clear that there are certain things over and above wealth that are important. At the Population A level these are books in the school and parental cooperation. At the Population B level these are books in the community, parental cooperation, and the 12% "shared," which is predominantly associated with an interaction of books in the community with parental cooperation.

Conclusion

This chapter has presented a descriptive account of the level of school resources and their relationship to reading achievement in the countries participating in the study. The descriptive accounts considered clusters of variables of school community resources, teachers, books as resources, and school initiatives in reading for both Populations A and B. Each cluster considered the mean value for each variable across countries and its correlation with reading achievement.

In the last part of the chapter the linkage between the variables in all clusters and reading achievement were examined at both the between and within country levels of analysis. Where variables were "consistent," that is, consistent for both among and within country relationships, these variables were selected for further analyses. These analyses involved the conduct of a commonality analysis that sought to establish whether the variables could account for variance in reading achievement among countries in a manner that was independent of national wealth. The results of the analyses showed that this was indeed the case and that at the Population A level books in school and parental cooperation with school each had unique effects, while at the Population B level, books in the community and parental cooperation with school had both unique and shared effects.

It would appear that the general message is that books (more in school for younger children and more in the community for older children) are essential no matter how rich or poor a nation is. Parental cooperation with schools is also of crucial value.

This chapter has dealt with common factors for all countries at the same time. It might be that any individual country could find other important resource variables, but this will emerge from the various national analyses that countries undertake themselves.

6

The Teaching of Reading

INGVAR LUNDBERG

In this chapter the main concern is the topology of reading instruction or, in other words, how reading is taught in different countries. First, the similarities and differences in teacher characteristics and in the nature of teaching reading in many countries will be described. Second, the result of this descriptive inquiry will be used to identify those teaching behaviors and attitudes that are associated with higher reading achievement among students. Whenever such behaviors can be identified they might be used to improve teaching practices and student learning in the participating countries. The relationships between instructional factors and student achievement will be examined within a multivariate framework, where several controlling factors are introduced to adjust for differences in home and school resources.

As a background for interpreting and discussing the results to be presented, it is useful to provide a brief outline of some of the current issues and controversies concerning reading and reading instruction.

Is There Any Best Method of Teaching Reading?

From the debate on methods of instruction in the early grades, it might seem as if the most crucial factor in the acquisition process is related to a teaching method such as phonics or to a meaning-based approach. Yet, a major finding from program comparison studies (Stahl & Miller, 1989) is that there is great variation in effectiveness within any particular instructional method. It is highly unlikely that a universally best method for teaching reading can be defined. The effectiveness of a method depends much on the details of its implementation, its materials, its teachers, its students, its cultural context, and the compatibility of each with the other. According to Lohnes and Gray (1972), not more than 3% of the variance in students' reading achievement can actually be accounted for by method alone. Other instructional conditions, such as time for reading instruction (Rosenshine & Stevens, 1984) have been found to account for substantially more variance.

The issue of the best method should also be seen in the light of the considerable variation of informal literacy socialization that takes place outside the context of formal reading instruction in school. Many children may have a very limited amount of exposure to print and very few opportunities to interact with text under the supervision of encouraging and interested adults, whereas others have had daily experience of storybook reading and thousands of hours of playful and active involvement in text and print over the preschool years. In fact, such initial differences between children even tend to increase over the years in a snowballing process recently come to be known as the Matthew Effect in educational development (Stanovich, 1986).

How can teachers cope with such differences, given only 200 hr or so per year devoted to literacy instruction in the early years? Children with rich stimulation at home and in preschool settings are frequently successful in school no matter how badly the initial instruction is organized; the poorer group rarely recovers from the disadvantages they arrive with. Since factors in home background seem to play such a crucial role and the variations in home conditions tend to be wide, it has been difficult to demonstrate clear effects of variations in teaching practices.

In an international study including many different countries with many different teaching traditions and many different practices of early informal literacy socialization, one may expect a wider spectrum of influential factors in the total set of countries than within any single educational system. Thus, given the high variance across countries, it might be possible to detect signals of teaching practices that have an influence on students' reading achievement as well as reading activities and thereby demonstrate that teaching, after all, can compensate for initial disadvantage.

As will be seen, most of the analyses presented in this chapter are based on questionnaire responses from the teachers involved in the study. The limitations of questionnaire data in this context have been discussed earlier (in Chapters 1, 3, and 5). In many questions on instructional practices and attitudes there are high risks of compliance effects or socially desirable responses being made. Many teachers might want to portray themselves as more sophisticated and more advanced than they actually are in their daily teaching under stressful and noisy conditions and with all the practical duties they have to perform. With regard to these limitations, some important dimensions of teaching, such as the teachers' ability to interact and cooperate, their commitment, enthusiasm, responsibility, time management ability, evaluative skills, etc., cannot easily be captured by the questionnaire.

An analysis of the materials teachers use for reading instruction and the instruments they use to assess their students' reading achievement would probably have yielded a more concrete and perhaps more valid notion of the belief systems of reading teachers or the "teaching culture" around the world. In a survey of this size, however, it was not possible to undertake such analyses within the prevailing limitations of time and resources. An even deeper understanding of the teaching processes would, of course, have been obtained with direct classroom observations and in-depth interviews of the teachers. Such qualitative studies will be undertaken in several participating countries, where a small number of distinctive classrooms (e.g., over-achieving and under-achieving classrooms) will be selected on the basis of the quantitative data collected in the main survey.

Reading and the teaching of reading are to a large extent cognitive–linguistic acts which are situated in social and cultural contexts. This implies that it is not often possible to take a successful approach to reading instruction from one country and expect that it will work equally successfully in another cultural setting. "The process of moving a program from one place to another requires care, adaptation and sensitivity to the mores of the new cultural context" (Stahl, 1992). Although this relativistic and contextual perspective is well taken, it should not prevent us from recognizing the invariance of successful teaching practices across many countries and sharing this knowledge in a sensible way.

The Teacher Questionnaires

The main focus of the teacher questionnaire was on the teaching environment and instructional orientation. The teacher questionnaire for Population A included a total of 46 main questions, several of them divided into many subquestions, making up a total of some 160 variables (see Appendix D). For the purpose of analysis, the variables were categorized into four main groups:

1.   Teaching conditions: class size, instructional time, language background, grouping, remedial needs, parental involvement, classroom resources, organization.
2.   Teacher characteristics: gender, training, experience, reading habits, and attitudes to reading and reading instruction.
3.   Instructional strategies: activities and methods.
4.   Assessment: forms and aspects covered.

Most of the 9-year-olds had spent only a few years in school. In the questionnaire, therefore, many items concerned instructional procedures relevant to the beginning stages of teaching. Great care was taken to cover issues related to code and skill emphasis and to comprehension or meaning-oriented teaching.

For Population B (14-year-olds) the teacher questionnaire was considerably reduced for two reasons. First, it was considered that in most cases the teachers at that age level were exerting a less powerful influence on the students' achievement and reading habits. After all, the students had a school history of more than seven or eight years with many different teachers influencing their abilities, as well as a life outside school with a multitude of factors operating on their reading development. Thus, the impact of the eighth or ninth grade teacher who filled in the questionnaire was expected to be rather limited. Secondly, due to limited resources a decision had to be taken to perform a multivariate analysis only for Population A. This priority was motivated by the expectation that factors influencing students' achievement would be more easily identified at the lower age level. Thus, the short-term policy implications of the study were expected to be stronger for the younger children. For the older age group, a more descriptive and comparative analysis of the results was judged to be adequate. Such an analysis could be useful for generating more explanatory hypotheses about teaching and teaching conditions which could be tested in further investigations.

The teacher questionnaire for Population B, like that for Population A, was concerned with training, experience, and reading habits. Issues about instructional strategies and classroom resources were also covered. A total of 28 questions were included, covering 88 variables which could be categorized in the same way as for Population A. The main emphasis was on instructional orientations for promoting reading comprehension and voluntary reading. In addition, 29 questions on the quality of school climate (Williams & Batten, 1981) were included for Population B only, and are therefore not referred to in the analysis of Population A data below.

Teacher Characteristics

What kind of teachers are responsible for reading instruction around the world? How do they vary across countries in terms of education, experience, gender, reading habits, and attitudes to the aims of instruction? Is there any simple and direct relationship between certain teacher characteristics and student achievement? For example, does the teacher's gender have any influence on student achievement? Is it better for boys to have male teachers and girls to have female teachers, or does a mismatch between teacher sex and student sex cause better results? Is there any relationship between teachers' attitudes towards educational aims and how they respond to the questions on how they teach? These are examples of the questions to be answered in this section.

Education

The pattern of teacher education varies considerably across countries. In some cases, teacher education is an integral part of post-secondary education, either at universities or at special teachers' colleges. In other countries, university studies oriented towards specific disciplines precede the teacher training proper. Still, the total post-secondary study period is regarded as a preparation for the teaching profession.

The varying patterns and the varying interpretations of the concept of teacher education make it difficult to compare the length of education across countries. In addition, basic changes of teacher education have taken place in several countries over the past few decades, and the teachers involved in the present study vary considerably in years of experience. Thus, teacher education and teacher experience may be expected to show a strong covariation in many places. Older teachers had a different form of training from their younger colleagues. Therefore, with references to the problems raised here, it was decided not to report further details on teacher education in this chapter.

Experience

Teaching is certainly a most demanding profession, involving skill in management and fast decision making, independent judgment, patience, empathy, communication skills, careful planning, stress tolerance, deep subject knowledge, and psychological insight. A high level of teaching expertise can certainly not be acquired within only a few years of practical teaching experience. One would then expect a relationship between experience and student achievement.

Table 6.1 presents the average number of years of teaching experience reported by the teachers in each country. As can be seen, high scoring countries were found at all levels of experience (e.g., in Sweden and France in the upper half of both populations, and the United States, New Zealand, and Iceland in the lower half). Within countries, however, some significant positive correlations between teaching experience and achievement could be found (e.g., in Canada (BC), Greece, Indonesia, Norway, Portugal, Sweden, and the United States in Population A, and Belgium (French), Greece, Norway, and Zimbabwe in Population B). No significant negative correlations were found. Thus, more experienced teachers are associated with higher student achievement levels in many countries. Further examination of the impact of teacher experience on student achievement will be presented in the last section of this chapter.

Gender Differences

As pointed out in Chapter 5, countries varied in the proportion of female teachers in their schools. Almost all Population A teachers were female in Slovenia, Sweden, Hungary, Germany (East), Italy, and Portugal, whereas less than half of the teachers in Indonesia and the Netherlands were female at the same level. In Population B there was still a strong predominance of female teachers in Slovenia and Hungary. However, less than half of the teachers were female in Switzerland, the Netherlands, Zimbabwe, Iceland, and Canada (BC). The female dominance decreased somewhat from Population A to Population B. Table 6.2 presents the proportion of female teachers for each country, as reported by teachers in the sample.

Are Female Teachers Better at Reading Instruction Than Male Teachers?

There was a weak tendency showing that higher average reading scores were obtained in education systems with a high proportion of female teachers. When the whole pooled international data set was analyzed, a significant difference in student achievement associated with the gender of teachers was obtained in both populations.

Table 6.1

Average Number of Years' Teaching Experience

Population A			Population B		
Country	Years Teaching	S.D.	Country	Years Teaching	S.D.
Portugal	22.8	9.6	Belgium/French	20.2	8.8
Italy	21.6	9.0	France	18.7	8.3
Sweden	21.4	9.1	Germany/E	18.7	10.5
France	21.2	8.6	Italy	18.7	7.2
Germany/E	20.3	9.8	Cyprus	18.4	7.4
Germany/W	19.6	8.2	Denmark	17.8	7.9
Slovenia	19.3	9.4	Spain	17.8	8.7
Ireland	19.0	10.9	Norway	17.6	8.6
Singapore	18.9	11.2	Switzerland	17.6	9.9
Denmark	18.3	7.5	Hungary	16.9	10.1
Spain	18.2	8.4	Netherlands	16.9	8.2
Belgium/French	17.6	8.4	Germany/W	16.7	7.5
Cyprus	17.4	12.3	Sweden	16.6	9.4
Hungary	17.0	10.7	Ireland	16.5	8.7
Netherlands	16.7	6.9	Slovenia	16.3	7.9
Trinidad/Tobago	16.7	9.4	Finland	15.2	10.2
Norway	16.4	8.2	Iceland	14.8	9.7
Hong Kong	16.0	10.7	Trinidad/Tobago	14.8	9.2
Finland	15.3	11.2	Singapore	14.5	10.8
United States	14.9	8.9	Canada/BC	13.9	9.0
Switzerland	14.5	10.1	Thailand	13.6	6.5
New Zealand	14.0	9.6	United States	13.5	8.4
Greece	13.4	9.6	New Zealand	12.6	8.5
Canada/BC	13.3	9.5	Greece	12.4	6.4
Venezuela	12.5	7.2	Venezuela	11.9	7.4
Iceland	12.1	8.8	Philippines	11.0	8.2
Indonesia	11.5	7.5	Botswana	10.5	7.7
			Hong Kong	10.1	9.0
			Nigeria	9.5	6.1
			Portugal	9.1	6.9
			Zimbabwe	5.9	6.5

At the within-country level, female teachers had students with significantly higher scores than male teachers in several countries. In Population A there were 10 countries with strongly significant differences ($p < .001$) between female and male teachers, with regard to how well their students performed on the reading tests when examined in multiple regression, with gender as dummy variables (Canada (BC), Cyprus, Greece, Hong Kong, Iceland, Indonesia, Spain, Sweden, Trinidad and Tobago, and Venezuela). In all cases, female teachers had better students. In Population B significant differences were obtained in 8 countries. Female teacher superiority was observed in Hong Kong, the Netherlands, Singapore, Spain, Switzerland, and Zimbabwe, whereas male teacher superiority was found only in Greece and New Zealand.

Table 6.2

Percentage of Female Teachers

Population A		Population B	
Country	% female teachers	Country	% female teachers
Slovenia	98.6	Slovenia	97.9
Germany/E	98.4	Hungary	92.4
Hungary	98.4	Philippines	91.8
Sweden	97.0	Thailand	86.8
Italy	93.4	Trinidad/Tobago	86.0
Portugal	90.3	Germany/E	83.2
Canada/BC	89.8	Finland	83.0
Singapore	88.3	Italy	82.2
Venezuela	85.6	Singapore	80.5
Iceland	84.2	Venezuela	77.6
United States	83.9	Greece	76.2
Germany/W	79.8	United States	73.1
Denmark	79.1	Portugal	72.5
Norway	78.9	Sweden	68.7
New Zealand	75.9	France	65.6
Spain	75.6	Nigeria	65.6
Belgium/Fr	73.7	Cyprus	65.5
Trinidad/Tobago	70.2	Denmark	65.4
Hong Kong	69.6	New Zealand	61.3
Ireland	69.2	Hong Kong	60.3
Finland	65.7	Ireland	60.3
Switzerland	63.1	Belgium/Fr	59.9
Cyprus	57.0	Norway	57.4
France	56.7	Spain	57.1
Greece	51.3	Botswana	52.6
Indonesia	45.7	Germany/W	50.7
Netherlands	39.4	Canada/BC	48.4
		Iceland	45.5
		Zimbabwe	34.3
		Netherlands	27.9
		Switzerland	20.8

Thus, in many countries women appeared to be better teachers than men, especially at lower grade levels. No simple explanation of this difference can be offered here. In each country possible differences in recruitment to the profession and other differences related to tradition and sex roles warrant further exploration.

Gender Match Between Students and Teachers

An interesting question is whether a gender match between teacher and student is better than a mismatch. Is there an advantage for boys to have male teachers or for girls to have female teachers?

When the whole international data set was analyzed together in a multiple regression, with gender as a dummy variable, a significant interaction was obtained, indicating a weak gender match advantage. However, even very small tendencies become statistically significant when they are based on an enormously large number of observations.

At the country level, significant interactions were absent in a majority of cases. In Population A, a significant interaction was observed only in three countries (Ireland, Singapore, and Spain). Figure 6.1 summarizes the average result in these three countries and shows that girls had a higher performance when they had a female teacher, whereas boys tended to do better with male teachers.

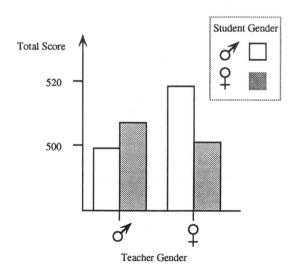

Figure 6.1: The Average Reading Achievement of Boys and Girls as Related to the Teacher's Gender in Three Countries (Ireland, Singapore, Spain) with a Significant Interaction Between Student Gender and Teacher Gender (Population A)

In Population B significant gender interactions were obtained in five countries (Canada, Ireland, New Zealand, Trinidad and Tobago, and Spain). Figure 6.2 presents the average results for these countries. Four of the five countries with significant gender match had their education systems established within the British tradition, and they all have an early school start.

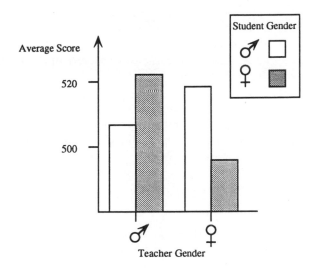

Figure 6.2: The Average Reading Achievement of Boys and Girls as Related to the Teacher's Gender in Five Countries (Canada (BC), Ireland, New Zealand, Trinidad and Tobago, Spain) with a Significant Interaction Between Student Gender and Teacher Gender (Population B)

How can the gender-match effect be explained? A popular hypothesis is generated from dynamic psychology referring to the process of identification. Young boys, then, need a male identification object from which values and ideals are incorporated. Boys who meet male adults who seem to enjoy and value reading will be more ready to embark on the important journey into literacy. In a corresponding way, girls will profit more from female teachers. However, it should be noted that this hypothesis was not supported in a majority of countries.

Teacher Readership

The amount of reading reported by the teachers can be expected to be related to the way they teach and to their attitudes towards reading and reading instruction. A reasonable assumption is that the teachers' reading pattern will affect their students' reading. For example, a teacher with strong interests in literature will probably try to develop similar interests among her/his students. Another reasonable assumption is that a high level of readership reflects high intellectual aspirations among the teachers. Those who expand their knowledge by extensive reading would be expected to increase their competence as teachers.

The teachers' reading habits were assessed by questions on how often they read various kinds of materials. Three main areas were covered: professional reading (articles on teaching, articles on reading), expository reading (books on history or politics, books on the arts, books on science), and literature reading (novels or short stories, poems, plays, children's literature (Population A); articles on literature (Population B)). A principal component analysis of the Population A data yielded the three factors listed above, with reasonably high consistency in most countries.

The average reported frequency of reading varied considerably across countries. The strong compliance effect involved in questions asked about highly valued habits made it difficult to interpret the between-country variation. The social desirability factor probably operates differently in different countries. A closer look at the within-country results might be more revealing.

Are the Reading Habits of Teachers Related to their Instructional Practices and Attitudes?

In a number of countries significant correlations were found between the teachers' personal readership and some of the instructional strategies reported. Table 6.3 presents the statements on instructional practices where significant correlations were found in a large number of countries in Population A. The figures in the table refer to the number of countries with significant correlations (> .20). The correlations seldom exceeded .35. For example, "learning library skills" was significantly correlated with teachers' professional reading in seven countries, with expository reading in 11 countries, and with literature reading in 13 countries.

With few exceptions, the correlations were similar across the three domains of teachers' readership. In a majority of countries, teachers who reported frequent reading in any area tended to have discussions about books with their students. They also tended to have their students study the style and structure of texts and compare pictures and text in stories. Teachers with a high level of readership tended to use self-prepared teaching materials more often. In assessment they focused more on the amount of reading and on students' interests. Most of these teaching behaviors seem to reflect a view of reading where the constructive and active nature of the reading process is recognized. A student-oriented style of teaching was also indicated.

Not surprisingly, there were some significant correlations which were more concentrated on a specific domain of readership. Thus, for example, having the students read plays and dramas was more often correlated with the teachers' reading of literature than with any other domain of readership. This also held for having students learn library skills, assessing their literary appreciation, and having them dramatize stories. Clearly, these practices reflected the teachers' literature orientation both in their own reading and in their teaching practice.

Table 6.3

The Number of Countries with Significant Correlations Between Teacher Readership and Instructional Practices in Population A

	Teacher readership		
Instructional Practice	Professional	Expository	Literature
Discussion of books	16	16	17
Reading plays or dramas	9	12	17
Learning library skills	7	11	13
Playing reading games	8	13	12
Dramatizing stories	11	13	16
Reading students' writing	12	13	12
Making predictions	14	8	9
Diagramming content	11	12	8
Compare stories	8	15	15
Use self-prepared materials	16	14	11
Know students' reading interests	11	13	13
Interviews for assessment	15	16	14
Literary appreciation	9	13	12
Students' interests	19	16	18
Generalization and inference	12	11	8
Frequency teaching exposition	10	16	12
Frequency teaching documents	12	14	11

The amount of professional reading, on the other hand, showed a more frequent relationship with having the students make predictions, diagram content, and make generalizations and inferences from the text. To some extent, such practices may reflect a more instrumental and achievement-oriented attitude of reading instruction. The teaching methods are also in line with current research on the teaching of text comprehension (Pearson & Fielding, 1991).

To summarize, it was observed that the relationship between the teachers' own reading and their instructional practices were similar across many countries in Population A. This tendency provides some support for an internal validation of the questionnaire.

In Population B, many consistent correlations between teacher readership and instructional practices were also observed. The main results of this correlation analysis are summarized in Table 6.4, which is the same format as Table 6.3 above. Thus, the numbers in the table refer to the number of countries where significant correlations were found. First, it should be noted that the frequency with which various types of reading were taught correlated significantly with teacher readership in many countries. The frequency of teaching expository reading correlated significantly with teachers' professional reading and expository reading in 20 countries. There was also an expected imbalance between the readership domains. Thus, the frequency of teaching document reading was not correlated with teachers' frequency of reading literature as often as with expository and professional readership.

Table 6.4

The Number of Countries with Significant Correlations Between
Teacher Readership and Instructional Practices in Population B

Instructional practice	Teacher readership		
	Professional	Expository	Literature
Discussion of books	14	10	16
Reading plays or dramas	4	5	10
Relate to own experience	11	10	15
Study style and structure	11	8	16
Use illustrations	7	15	5
Talk to somebody else	11	9	12
Frequency teaching narrative	12	6	9
Frequency teaching expository	20	20	11
Frequency teaching documents	13	17	5

Teacher readership also correlated significantly with a number of activities in which students may be involved. Teachers who reported extensive personal reading of literature seemed to have students who were often involved in a discussion of books, and who often read plays or dramas, or studied style and structure of texts. Teachers who reported extensive reading of expository text seemed to have their students learn how to use illustrations (graphs, diagrams, tables) to understand texts. Teachers with a high level of readership also reported that they taught students to increase their comprehension by comparing what they read with experiences they have had. The students were also taught to talk to somebody else about what they had read or they wrote something of their own on what they had read. Thus, as in Population A, teachers who read frequently tended to have a more modern view about reading in which the active, constructive and social character of reading is emphasized.

*Is There Any Relationship Between Teacher Readership and
Student Achievement?*

Contrary to expectation, no clear relationships were found between teachers' reading habits and student reading achievement. Within the pooled international data set including all teachers in Population A, the only significant relationship with achievement was observed in exposition readership, where the correlation with the total achievement score was negative (-.12).

Teacher Readership and Student Voluntary Reading

One would expect that teachers who have a well-developed reading habit would inspire students' reading interest to a greater extent than teachers with less developed reading habits. It is both a question of acting as a role model and more deliberately encouraging students to read. However, with rather few exceptions, most of the correlations between teacher readership and student voluntary reading were small and statistically insignificant, suggesting that factors outside school are more powerful determinants of student voluntary reading habits, in particular the cultural capital of the homes. Among 9-year-olds, the extent to which reading skills have become fully automatized and effortless is certainly also important.

Teacher Views on Reading Instruction and Teaching Aims

Teacher characteristics also involve teachers' general conception of the aims of teaching reading and their belief systems or views on reading instruction. The teacher questionnaire for Population A included a set of 26 statements related to reading instruction, such as, "Children should always understand what they read" or "Every mistake a student makes when reading aloud should immediately be corrected". For each of the statements, the teachers had to express the extent to which they agreed or disagreed with the statement, using a five-point bipolar scale, where 1 indicated strong disagreement and 5 strong agreement. Some of the statements expressed a view of reading instruction where accuracy and careful sequencing were emphasized. Other statements expressed a more student-oriented or comprehension-oriented view of reading instruction. Another task in the questionnaire involved the ranking of the importance of aims for reading instruction. The aim ratings will be discussed first.

Teacher Ratings of Aims (Population A)

Twelve different aims were presented to teachers in Population A who had to select the five most important aims and rank them by importance. Examples of such aims were: "developing a lasting interest in reading;" "developing students' critical thinking;" and "increasing speed of reading." By having teachers make a selection of aims and rank them it was, to some extent, possible to avoid compliance effects, which would have occurred if the teacher had to consider each aim separately and give a rating of its importance.

There was a surprising conformity of the rankings across countries. The highest average rank was given to the aim of "improving students' reading comprehension skills," which had the first rank in 12 countries and the second in six countries. Almost equally high ranking was given to the aim of "developing a lasting reading interest," which was given the highest rank in 15 countries. High average rankings were also given to the aim of "making reading enjoyable;" ten countries had this aim as the second most important. The least important aims were to "deepen the emotional involvement," "developing skills in reading aloud," and "develop word attack skills."

The Population A countries were divided into three subgroups of nine countries in each: High achieving (Finland, the United States, Sweden, New Zealand, Italy, France, Norway, Iceland, and Singapore); middle achieving (Ireland, Spain, Greece, Canada (BC), Belgium (French), Switzerland, Hong Kong, Germany (West), and Germany (East); and low achieving (Venezuela, Indonesia, Trinidad and Tobago, Portugal, Denmark, the Netherlands, Cyprus, Slovenia, and Hungary). The ranked aims were subdivided into two main groups, one indicating emphasis on skills and the other indicating emphasis on encouragement and development of reading interests. The first group contained the following five aims:
1.   developing skills in reading aloud
2.   improving students' reading comprehension
3.   extending students' vocabulary
4.   improving word-attack skills
5.   increasing speed of reading.

The encouragement–interest group contained:
1.   developing a lasting interest in reading
2.   developing students' research and study skills
3.   developing students' critical thinking
4.   expanding students' world views
5.   making reading enjoyable.

These two groups of aims were compared across the three groups of countries. The results are presented in Figure 6.3. The encouragement–interest factor was, on the average, given a higher rank than the skills factor, regardless of achievement level. However, the high achieving countries had a wider gap between the two sets of aims than the low achieving countries.

In some countries there was a large difference between the average rankings of the two types of aims. In Finland, Sweden, Norway, Denmark, Germany (West), Germany (East), Switzerland, New Zealand, and Canada (BC) the teachers gave a much higher priority to aims related to encouragement and development of reading interests than to the skills-oriented aims. In Venezuela, Indonesia, Hungary, the Netherlands, and Ireland skills aims were considered more important than interest aims.

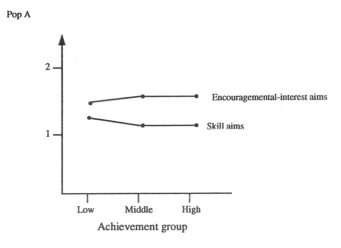

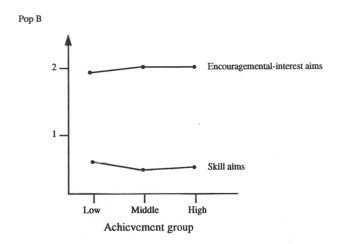

Figure 6.3: The Average Difference Between Teacher Ratings of Encouragement–Interest Aims and Skill Aims for Countries with Low, Middle and High Average Achievement Level

The relative emphasis on skills aims in the low achieving countries might reflect an experienced necessity to pay attention to developing the basic elements of reading, whereas this stage of acquisition is already passed by a majority of children in the high achieving countries. An alternative interpretation would be that skills emphasis inhibits students from a natural literacy acquisition process.

Some Concluding Comments on Aims

The invariance across countries in the ranking of teaching aims is certainly a remarkable finding. Obviously, the reading task must have inherent demand characteristics which invoke almost universal agreement on what is important to teach. Most national teaching cultures seem to value highly the aims of developing students' own strategic thinking and their lasting interest and enjoyment of reading and literature. Functional, everyday literacy is not generally valued as a focus for teaching. It may be that instrumental literacy is assumed by the teachers to be developed in other subject areas or through environmental reading outside school.

The valued aims are often at variance with instructional reality where several restrictions are imposed, such as management and discipline problems, big classes with students varying widely in ability and interests, limitations on materials, classroom environment, and time constraints. In the next section the relationship between aims and actions will be further explored.

Is There Any Relationship Between Teachers' Aims in Reading Instruction and How They Teach?

As described above, the aims of reading instruction presented to the Population A teachers could be divided into two subgroups: where the skill aspect of reading was emphasized, and where thinking, enjoyment, and reading interests were more in focus.

Do these different orientations of attitudes towards reading instruction correlate differently with various indicators of teaching behavior? The answer is, only to a limited degree. Only in a few countries were significant correlations found. For instance, one question concerned to what degree the teachers have their students involved in discussions of books. In Denmark, Greece, the Netherlands, and Portugal there was an expected positive correlation with the sum of the enjoyment–interest items and a negative correlation with the sum of the skills items. In a sense this finding is a partial validation of the questionnaire items involved, or at least it demonstrates an internal consistency in the response patterns in these countries.

Likewise, there was a positive correlation in four countries between the enjoyment–interest factor and encouragement of parental involvement in their children's reading. The skills factor was negatively related to parental encouragement. In six countries there were significant correlations with some items about teachers' views. "When my pupils read to me I expect them to read every word accurately" correlated positively with the skills aims and negatively with the enjoyment–interest aims. The same expected pattern was observed for "every mistake a child makes in reading aloud should be corrected at once." The reverse pattern was obtained in five countries with "all children should enjoy reading." The frequency with which the teacher assesses the amount of reading done by the students also correlated significantly with the aim factors in many countries. However, the sign pattern of the correlations was very inconsistent across countries.

Although there were some positive findings, there was no really convincing evidence of a strong and consistent relationship across countries between the aims preferred by the teachers and the way they report that they teach. Closer analyses at the within-country level might reveal clearer results. However, the basic limitation of questionnaire data should be recognized. It is interesting to note that Fishbein and Ajzen (1975) also demonstrated the lack of correspondence between attitudes or beliefs on the one hand and actual behavior on the other.

Is There Any Relationship Between Teachers' Views About Reading
Instruction and Their Students' Achievement on the Reading Tests?

When single questions in the questionnaire are correlated with specific outcome variables, such as the students' performance on the expository texts, one would normally not expect many significant correlations. One reason for that is the lack of reliability when a single item is used. Poor reliability of the measures often prevents a true relationship from being seen, because it is attenuated by the measurement error. When like items are combined in a scale, however, it might be possible to reveal an underlying relationship. Here one simple example will be given. In further reports of multivariate analyses of the data from this study, more complicated cases will be presented.

Teachers are believed to vary in terms of the degree to which they emphasize accuracy, order, and careful sequencing in their reading instruction of young children. Out of the 26 statements given to the Population A teachers, the following statements were particularly formulated with the intention of capturing this attitude about reading instruction:
1.   "When my pupils read to me, I expect them to read every word accurately."
2.   "Every mistake a child makes in reading aloud should be corrected at once."
3.   "All children's comprehension assignments should be marked carefully to provide them with feedback."
4.   "Children should learn most of their new words from lessons designed to enhance their vocabulary."
5.   "Reading learning materials should be carefully sequenced in terms of language structure and vocabulary."

It was assumed that these five items were all indicators of an underlying or latent trait or attitude. Of course, each item captures something which is specific to that very item, but also something which is more general and which the item has in common with some other items. In a similar way, the outcome or achievement factor can be constructed by an analysis of what narrative, expository, and document reading have in common. If this underlying or latent general reading ability is correlated with the latent accuracy–order factor, in a sense the measurement errors which attenuated the correlation between single items and single measures of achievement have been removed. A more "true" relationship can then be revealed. Figure 6.4 presents the results of a LISREL analysis of this simple model of the relationship between teacher attitude and student achievement. The analysis is based on the pooled data set of all classes in Population A.

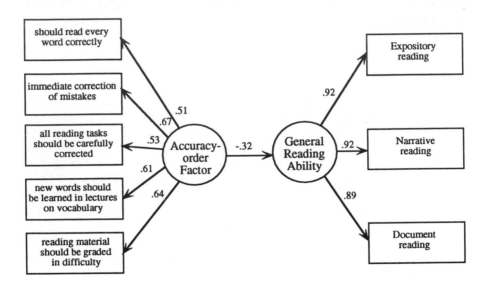

Figure 6.4: The Relationship Between Two Latent Factors: A Teaching View
Emphasizing Accuracy and Order (Five Indicators) and Student Reading Ability
(Three Factors)

The relationship between the factors is expressed by the number -.32, which tells us that if we increase the factor of accuracy–order–sequencing emphasis by one standard deviation unit, the average reading ability of the students will decrease by one third of a standard deviation unit. In other words, the more emphasis the teacher places on accuracy, order, and sequencing, the poorer is the average reading achievement of the students.

Even though the method used in this analysis is sometimes named causal analysis, one cannot immediately make a causal inference from the finding. Only correlational data were obtained in this cross-sectional survey and causal interpretations are not justified. It might seem reasonable to assume that a too strict regimen in teaching can be harmful to students and reduce the possibility of skill development according to their potential. On the other hand, a logical and, perhaps in some cases, plausible alternative could be that teachers who are confronted with poorly achieving students might be forced to change their teaching strategies and put more emphasis on accuracy and order. It requires longitudinal studies with careful direct classroom observations to clarify the causal issue.

In any case, the model given as an example here had a very good fit, i.e., the original relationships between the manifest variables could be reproduced with high accuracy from the model (AGFI = .9). The model was based on the pooled international data set. The next step is to investigate how this model works at the national level. In forthcoming reports more examples of this kind of modeling will be given. Obviously, such procedures have the power of revealing relationships which are normally obscured by unreliable manifest variables.

Instructional Practices

In this section a descriptive overview is given of how the instructional practices varied across countries. The next section will deal with the relationship between instructional practices and student achievement.

Time Allocation on Various Reading Domains

A first obvious question to ask is how frequently teachers dealt with each of the three domains of reading: Narrative, Expository, and Documents. The frequency with which they taught students to understand these types of materials was rated on a five-point scale (almost never, three or four times a year, about once a month, at least once a week, nearly every day).

In Population A, narration was on the average taught with the highest frequency (3.5 times per week). Exposition teaching had a mean rating of 3.15 and teaching about documents had 2.6. Table 6.5 displays the distribution of ratings across countries for the three domains. Narration was taught with particularly high frequency in Portugal, Denmark, and Hungary. Low narrative ratings were given by teachers in Sweden, Norway, Venezuela, and Indonesia. For exposition, high ratings were found in Italy, Portugal, and Hungary, and low ratings in Denmark and Hong Kong. High frequency of document teaching was reported in Italy and the United States, whereas Denmark and Hong Kong gave low ratings.

In Population B the pattern was rather similar. Narration was taught with an average frequency rating of 3.6 across all 31 countries, exposition with an average of 3.3, and documents with an average of only 2.3. If the comparisons are restricted to the ten western countries with relatively similar economic development, the similarities in time allocation are high. Narration was taught with the highest frequency in Denmark, whereas Finland, Sweden, and the Netherlands had the lowest frequency. In Exposition Germany (West) took the lead, but the variation between countries was very small indeed for this genre of reading. More attention to documents was paid by teachers in Germany (West) and Switzerland, as compared with the other countries in the subgroup.

Table 6.5

Between-Country Variation in Time Per Week Allocated to
Teaching of Various Reading Domains in Population A

Country	Narrative	Expository	Document
Belgium/Fr	3.8	3.6	3.5
Canada/BC	4.2	3.7	3.3
Cyprus	3.8	3.6	3.2
Denmark	4.4	2.8	1.7
Finland	3.7	3.7	3.0
France	3.8	3.4	3.5
Germany/E	4.1	3.6	2.8
Germany/W	4.1	3.7	2.9
Greece	3.8	3.6	3.3
Hong Kong	3.7	2.8	1.9
Hungary	4.4	3.9	2.9
Iceland	4.2	3.4	2.6
Indonesia	3.3	3.1	2.8
Ireland	4.1	3.6	3.0
Italy	4.1	4.1	3.7
Netherlands	4.0	3.6	2.6
New Zealand	4.1	3.6	3.1
Norway	3.3	3.1	2.5
Portugal	4.6	4.1	3.3
Singapore	4.2	3.1	2.7
Slovenia	3.7	3.7	3.0
Spain	3.9	3.7	2.9
Sweden	3.1	3.4	2.8
Switzerland	3.9	3.4	2.5
Trinidad/Tobago	3.8	3.6	3.5
United States	4.1	3.7	3.6
Venezuela	3.1	3.0	2.3

The ratio between document teaching and narration is an indication of the relative stress teachers put on document teaching, regardless of their general frequency bias. Across all countries this ratio was .75 in Population A and .64 in Population B, suggesting that document teaching had a somewhat stronger position in the lower grades. A notable exception was Denmark, where the ratio was only .39. In developing countries in Population B, the ratio was closer to 1.0, which could indicate either a response bias in the direction of giving a relatively high rating to everything, regardless of the content, or a true difference in teaching pattern, with far more emphasis on document teaching than in more developed countries. However, it is clear that reading teachers generally give more emphasis to narration in most countries.

Grouping Students for Reading Instruction

According to a review of research literature on grouping (Barr & Dreeben, 1991), the practice of grouping students within classes on the basis of ability is pervasive in American schools. Despite extensive research on the effects of ability grouping on student achievement, no convincing evidence for the advantage of ability-grouped reading instruction within classes has so far been presented. In this study, the teachers of Population A marked the most common type of grouping that was used in reading instruction. The alternatives were: no grouping at all, age grouping, ability grouping, grouping by students' interests, and other types of grouping.

Some kind of grouping was used by almost all teachers in all countries. By far the most common type of grouping was ability grouping. The only exceptions were Finland and Italy. In Finland, 40% of the teachers reported interest grouping as the most frequent type of grouping and only 36% marked ability grouping. Corresponding figures in Italy were 41 and 38%. Countries with a very high proportion of ability grouping were the Netherlands (94%), Ireland (89%), New Zealand (89%), Hungary (84%), Singapore (80%), and Iceland (80%). Countries with a relatively low proportion of teachers practicing ability grouping were Norway (21%), Venezuela (24%), and Switzerland (28%).

The practice of ability grouping can be regarded as a management technique which is presumed to facilitate teaching. However, on the between-country level there was no clear relationship of ability grouping with student achievement. On the other hand, there was a slight correlation between ability grouping and average class size (.28). In countries with relatively poor economic development, large classes are mainly a reflection of limited resources. When the eight countries with the lowest CDI were excluded from the analysis, the correlation between the practice of ability grouping and average class size increased to .59, which indicates a recognition that large classes require some management measures, such as ability grouping.

Age grouping was a very rare practice, except in the United States where this kind of grouping was reported by 17% of the teachers as the most common grouping. More frequent is interest grouping. As mentioned above, Finland and Italy took the lead here. Other countries with relatively high proportions in this category were Portugal (36%), Belgium (29%), and Greece (28%).

The relatively high variance of grouping patterns within many countries makes it possible to explore the determinants and the effects of grouping more thoroughly at the within-country level. Such analyses are expected to be included in some national reports.

Homework Assignment

Like many other skills, reading requires thousands of hours of practice before it is fully automatized and can proceed with the same facility and speed as normal listening to speech. A simple assumption, then, is that the more opportunities given to practice the skill the faster and better the skill will develop. The teachers in Population A were asked if they assigned homework in reading to their students, and if they did, how frequently homework was given. They were also asked how many minutes they expected an average student to spend on the assigned homework each time it was given. It is assumed that this expectation reflects the amount of homework assigned to students each time.

Table 6.6

Time (Minutes) Teachers Expect Students to Spend on Reading
Homework Each Time it is Assigned (Population A)

United States	51.25
Iceland	28.35
Greece	26.79
Indonesia	24.42
Trinidad/Tobago	24.37
Cyprus	24.21
Italy	23.38
Hungary	22.06
Singapore	21.83
Venezuela	21.50
Hong Kong	20.09
Sweden	19.66
Portugal	19.65
Spain	19.08
Slovenia	17.13
Netherlands	16.35
Canada/BC	15.73
France	15.32
New Zealand	14.98
Finland	14.42
Belgium/Fr	14.29
Denmark	13.76
Norway	13.40
Germany/E	13.29
Germany/W	12.10
Switzerland	10.28
Ireland	10.23

Across countries the teachers' expectations of the time spent on homework vary considerably, as can be seen in Table 6.6. In the United States the average teacher expects the students to work for more than 50 min, whereas the Irish and Swiss teachers think that 10 min is enough. Relatively high expectations (more than 20 min) are found among teachers in Cyprus, Greece, Hong Kong, Hungary, Iceland, Indonesia, Italy, Singapore, Trinidad and Tobago, and Venezuela. In fact, there is no relationship between the average expected time for homework and the reading achievement of the countries. However, the variation within many countries is substantial, with standard deviations of about 10 min. Given the substantial variation, the impact of homework should be explored further within countries.

In Population A, the teachers were asked about the frequency with which students read at home as a part of the reading/language program. Wide variations between countries were also observed here. More than three times per week was reported in Cyprus, Hungary, Italy, Portugal, Ireland, Iceland, and Norway. Only once per week or less was reported in the Netherlands, Hong Kong, Belgium (French), and Switzerland.

In Population B, the frequency of homework assignment in reading was estimated by the students. High frequency, or more than two times per week, was reported in Indonesia, Venezuela, Trinidad and Tobago, the United States, Hong Kong, Italy, and Cyprus. Countries with low frequency of homework were the Netherlands, Iceland, Sweden, Norway, and Finland. Thus, high achieving and low achieving countries were found in both extreme groups. Neither the student data from Population B nor the teacher data from Population A supported the hypothesis that the amount and the frequency of homework is a powerful determinant of reading achievement across countries. Within-country analyses might, however, yield a different picture.

International Constructs of Teaching Behavior

The term "construct" is used here to refer to a measure of something that is not directly observable, but is literally constructed by the researcher to summarize or account for the regularity or relationships found in the questionnaire responses. By establishing a limited number of constructs, the large data set (more than 100 questions on instruction in Population A) can also be reduced to a more manageable number. The accuracy–order factor discussed above is an example of a construct. Another example could be "comprehension emphasis," which is a teaching strategy constructed from many questions related to comprehension. The construct analysis was restricted to Population A, where most questions on teaching were given (see Table 1.9 for the original construct list).

The establishment of international constructs for Population A is based on a pooled data set from all of the 27 countries involved. Groups of questions which were intended to be conceptually related were subjected to a principal component analysis. The obtained constructs or factors were checked in each country. In most cases the internationally-based constructs also seemed to be applicable to the individual countries; they explain about the same amount of variance, they are about equally reliable, and the questions have about the same factor loadings in each country. (For a more technical description of how the constructs were formed, see Beaton (1993).)

By using internationally defined constructs, certainly some information is lost in each individual country. Several questions which might be useful in one country had to be dropped at the international level. That is the price to be paid in order to conduct an international analysis. Within a given country, a different set of constructs might actually "explain" more or take care of the variables in a better way.

The international perspective meant that the full range of variation between countries was utilized. This implies, at least in principle, that the chances of detecting potent determinants of differences in achievement increase. For example, within one country, the variation of a specific instructional method might be extremely small (i.e., most teachers in a country show similar trends), whereas across all countries the variation might be considerable. This is one of the main justifications of an international study.

The internationally defined constructs facilitate the description of what is going on in the classrooms of the different countries. With a limited set of constructs, where each construct means much the same across countries, comparative analyses will be much simpler than if all 110 variables had to be considered. Moreover, the reliability of the comparisons is much higher than if responses to individual items are used, i.e., measurement error is reduced.

The following constructs on teaching were finally established for Population A (they overlap with those listed in Table 1.9, but are not identified):

1.   *Comprehension instruction* was derived from ten questions or items in the teachers' questionnaire, concerning the students' activities during reading instruction.

	International factor loadings
Dramatizing stories	.62
Orally summarizing their reading	.61
Relating experiences to reading	.70
Making predictions during reading	.63
Diagramming story content	.64
Looking for the theme or message	.77
Making generalizations and inferences	.78
Studying the style or structure of a text	.73
Comparing pictures and stories	.63

Student leading discussion about passage	.64
Variance explained	*.46*
Reliability	*.87*

2.   *Emphasis on phonics* built on three items, two related to students' activities and one to assessment.

Learning letter–sound relationships	.85
Word-attack skills (e.g., prediction)	.80
Frequent assessment of phonics skills	.77
Variance explained	*.65*
Reliability	*.73*

3.   *General emphasis on assessment* built on five items, one related to student activities, two to finding out what students need, and two to methods of assessment.

Answering reading comprehension exercises in writing	.65
Use exercises in workbooks and text books to discover students' needs	.61
Ue tests in workbooks and textbooks	.69
Use multiple-choice questions	.66
Use written open-ended questions on material read	.60
Variance explained	*.41*
Reliability	*.64*

4.   *Assessment of low order skills* built on seven items related to assessment of different aspects of reading ability.

Students' word-recognition ability	.73
Students' vocabulary	.75
Use of background knowledge	.73
Sentence understanding	.75
Reading study skills	.71
Amount of reading	.60
Decoding	.65
Variance explained	*.50*
Reliability	*.83*

5.   *Encouragement to read* built on two items related to strategies of teaching.

Encourage children to read more	.87
Encourage children to use the library more	.87
Variance explained	*.76*
Reliability	*.68*

6.   *Taking students' interests into account* built on four items, one related to assessment methods, three related to methods of discovering students' needs.

Records of student interests	.59
Knowledge of students' reading interests	.74
Informal observation	.56
Interviews	.73
Variance explained	*.44*
Reliability	*.57*

These were the main factors on instruction and assessment which emerged from the international analysis. In this first step a number of items did not fit into any of the constructs. They were used in a second round, in which some additional factors were extracted.

7.   *Student-oriented reading* built on eight items, seven related to students' activities and one to teachers' stimulation of reading interests.

Independent, silent reading in a library	.56
Discussion of books read by students	.70
Learning library skills	.65
Reading plays or dramas	.57
Reading other students' writing	.58
Listening to students reading to small groups or pairs	.55
Reading in other subject areas	.34
Hold discussions about books	.43
Variance explained	*.31*
Reliability	*.68*

8.   *Teacher-centered instruction* was based on nine items, five related to teaching strategies, two to assessment methods, one to assessment aspects, and one to students' activities.

Introduce the background of a passage before reading it	.64
Ask children to describe their strategy for understanding	.35
Show children how to understand a text	.59
Compare stories, poems, fables and tales	.61
Use materials you have prepared yourself	.62
Use teacher-made vocabulary tests	.77
Use standardized or formal tests of comprehension	.50
Assess literary appreciation	.57
Learning new vocabulary systematically	.59
Variance	*.53*
Reliability	*.68*

9.   *Reading aloud to students* built on five items, one related to student activities, one to teaching strategies, two to views on teaching, and one to teacher stimulation.

Students listening to teachers reading stories aloud	.77
Teacher reads aloud to children	.54
Every day children should be read to by the teacher from a storybook	.75
Children should be encouraged to read texts they have written	.69
Teacher reads attractive stories to students to encourage them to read outside school	.40
Variance	*.42*
Reliability	*.65*

Differences Between Countries in Teaching Strategies and Assessment Emphasis

In this section the variation across education systems of each of the nine constructs defined above is described. Table 6.7 presents the average factor score means and standard deviations for each country (Population A). The scale for each construct has an international mean of 0 and a standard deviation of 1.0. Across all constructs one would then expect a grand mean close to zero in each country. However, this was not the case in several

Table 6.7

Mean Factor Scores and Standard Deviations of Teaching Constructs: Population A

Country	N	Comprehension mean	Comprehension SD	Phonics mean	Phonics SD	Gen. assessment mean	Gen. assessment SD	Assess. of low order mean	Assess. of low order SD	Encouragement mean	Encouragement SD	Students' interest mean	Students' interest SD	Student-oriented mean	Student-oriented SD	Teacher-oriented mean	Teacher-oriented SD	Reading aloud mean	Reading aloud SD
Belgium/Fr	146	-.40	.31	-.23	.41	.05	.34	-.07	.38	-.02	.45	-.16	.48	-.21	.39	-.17	.32	-.16	.41
Canada/BC	145	.23	.35	.16	.37	-.62	.48	.06	.36	.20	.30	.27	.31	.48	.37	.18	.32	.50	.24
Cyprus	303	.51	.29	.31	.50	.19	.29	.20	.25	.25	.28	-.08	.41	.08	.37	.30	.31	-.09	.29
Denmark	202	-.27	.28	.04	.32	-.25	.41	-.05	.38	-.16	.38	.25	.33	-.33	.32	-.24	.31	.06	.34
Finland	70	-.14	.30	-.11	.29	-.11	.27	-.20	.33	-.08	.43	.24	.29	-.02	.34	-.21	.31	.06	.40
France	129	-.43	.28	-.35	.45	.06	.31	-.18	.43	-.03	.46	-.25	.44	-.16	.36	-.13	.35	-.50	.41
Germany/E	99	.02	.24	.16	.27	-.26	.36	-.06	.34	-.32	.45	-.01	.36	-.20	.32	-.06	.36	-.26	.39
Germany/W	145	-.17	.26	.00	.31	-.41	.37	-.15	.43	-.43	.45	-.10	.36	-.29	.33	-.29	.27	-.28	.36
Greece	174	.44	.36	.14	.47	.23	.31	.27	.21	.13	.36	-.09	.44	-.19	.39	.38	.32	-.08	.31
Hong Kong	156	-.21	.32	.22	.33	-.02	.29	-.04	.35	-.20	.46	-.20	.44	-.20	.36	-.08	.38	-.27	.35
Hungary	142	.47	.26	.07	.39	.31	.19	.08	.31	.10	.34	.33	.21	-.01	.30	.14	.27	-.35	.36
Iceland	272	-.49	.31	-.36	.46	-.18	.33	-.10	.40	-.02	.41	-.01	.44	-.13	.40	-.47	.36	.26	.33
Indonesia	170	.06	.32	.27	.20	.20	.27	.29	.20	.17	.32	.20	.32	.43	.43	.35	.26	-.17	.32
Ireland	118	-.18	.39	.23	.30	.19	.33	-.05	.35	.10	.39	-.27	.42	-.12	.33	-.11	.40	-.02	.44
Italy	146	.36	.38	.13	.37	.27	.27	.21	.27	.07	.36	.26	.28	-.24	.26	.28	.36	-.08	.32
Netherlands	96	-.29	.30	-.21	.45	-.28	.35	-.49	.40	-.17	.46	-.24	.45	-.02	.32	-.47	.29	-.09	.39
New Zealand	175	.10	.36	.06	.39	-.40	.52	-.17	.42	.11	.34	.13	.34	.52	.32	-.02	.36	.45	.25
Norway	177	-.13	.34	-.19	.46	.09	.34	-.15	.40	-.18	.40	.03	.34	-.10	.32	-.26	.31	.39	.28
Portugal	144	.33	.33	.14	.22	.42	.21	.35	.19	.12	.37	.05	.41	.06	.47	.45	.31	.17	.31
Singapore	204	-.01	.37	.20	.25	.18	.25	-.02	.37	.21	.33	-.18	.43	.14	.37	.09	.36	.08	.36
Slovenia	136	.17	.22	.14	.24	.20	.24	.28	.17	.10	.37	.26	.27	.15	.29	.18	.27	-.09	.31
Spain	299	-.11	.39	.14	.33	.15	.33	.15	.29	.17	.35	-.08	.42	.01	.41	-.05	.39	.07	.40
Sweden	227	-.18	.33	-.49	.40	-.25	.45	-.64	.63	-.02	.37	-.16	.34	.11	.34	-.35	.36	.37	.30
Switzerland	224	-.20	.28	-.22	.37	-.28	.36	-.40	.47	-.38	.41	-.24	.38	-.27	.35	-.30	.31	-.11	.33
Trinidad/Tobago	210	.09	.36	.35	.22	.24	.29	.34	.18	.11	.37	.05	.41	.07	.37	.64	.31	-.13	.32
United States	298	.15	.35	.14	.40	.15	.33	.27	.24	.16	.33	.02	.41	.25	.36	.23	.31	.34	.35
Venezuela	126	.16	.43	.09	.38	.13	.39	.16	.34	.09	.41	.01	.51	.12	.46	.30	.42	-.02	.31

countries. Grand means greater than +.10 were observed in Portugal, Indonesia, the United States, Canada (BC), Trinidad and Tobago, Slovenia, Italy, Cyprus, Hungary, Greece, and Venezuela. Most of these countries are non-European or Mediterranean countries. Negative grand means were observed in all Nordic and West European countries.

If a country mean clearly deviates from zero, the teachers of that country report an activity level which is either higher or lower than the international mean level. A high positive grand mean might indicate a general response bias or compliance effect over and above a generally high activity level, reflecting culturally based attitudes. When country means for each teaching construct are compared, such tendencies should be taken into account.

Comprehension Instruction

Most of the activities covered by this construct are regarded by reading specialists as highly desirable practices in reading instruction. They conform well to schema theory and similar views of the reading process where the active, constructive nature of reading comprehension is emphasized. Questions involved in this construct are thus vulnerable to influences by social desirability or compliance on the part of teachers.

Countries with a high reported frequency of activities related to comprehension instruction were Cyprus, Greece, Hungary, Italy, Slovenia, Portugal, and Venezuela. The United States, Canada (BC), and New Zealand also seemed to have a comparatively strong emphasis on comprehension instruction. Within the ten West European countries the comprehension emphasis was generally weaker. The rank order was: Norway, Finland, Germany (West), Sweden, Switzerland, Denmark, the Netherlands, Belgium (French), France, and Iceland. The similarities between these countries were strikingly high.

High variation between teachers was found in Venezuela. In Slovenia, by contrast, there was a strong uniformity in the teachers' responses on the questions related to comprehension instruction.

Emphasis on Phonics

The majority of the students involved in this study (in Population A) were in Grade 4, by which point in a student's school career most of the beginning instruction is over. Hence, one would not expect much emphasis on letter–sound relationship, blending and decoding skills among the teachers. Surprisingly enough, however, the average teacher in most countries reported a rather frequent (almost once per month) assessment of the ability to segment and blend sounds in words. They also generally expressed a favorable attitude towards phonics elements in teaching.

Countries with high factor scores were Trinidad and Tobago, Cyprus, Hong Kong, Indonesia, Ireland, and Singapore. The high score in Hong Kong was somewhat surprising, considering that the Chinese script is basically nonphonemic, although the importance of phonological demands in reading Chinese is often underestimated.

The Anglo-Saxon countries had an intermediate position with the highest score in Canada (BC). All of the ten West European countries had lower scores than New Zealand. The rank order was: Denmark, Germany (West), Finland, Norway, the Netherlands, Switzerland, Belgium (French), France, Iceland, and Sweden. In this field of teaching, Sweden was obviously an outlier, with the lowest average score of all countries involved in the study. The highest standard deviations were found in Cyprus and Greece, whereas the Indonesian teachers responded with the highest uniformity.

General Emphasis on Assessment

Emphasis on assessment in reading instruction might be interpreted in different ways. One possibility is that such emphasis reflects care, good planning, and systematic management. Another alternative interpretation is that emphasis on assessment is typical of highly centralized educational systems, where accurate records of the students' progress and standardized testing are required by the ministry of education. A third alternative is that extensive testing reflects fragmentation and compartmentalization of the reading curriculum, where subskills are emphasized rather than a more unified language arts curriculum. Whatever the background is, the variation across countries was quite clear.

High emphasis on assessment was found in Portugal, Hungary, Italy, Trinidad and Tobago, Greece, Indonesia, Slovenia, and Cyprus. Some of these countries had strongly centralized school systems at the time of testing (Greece, Cyprus, Hungary, and Slovenia). Among the Anglo-Saxon countries, Canada (BC) and New Zealand seemed to be very reluctant to make regular assessments of reading, as indicated by their low position in the rank order of countries, whereas the United States was closer to an intermediate position. Most west European countries showed low emphasis on assessment.

The standard deviations varied from .52 in New Zealand to .19 in Hungary.

Assessment of Low-Order Skills

This construct is more specific than the general assessment factor. The focus on low-order skills reflects a more restricted, skills-oriented view of reading. A correlation between this construct and the accuracy–order–sequencing factor would be expected. The pooled international data set actually yielded a correlation of .32, which is significant but not very high.

Again, the leading countries were Portugal, Trinidad and Tobago, Indonesia, Slovenia, Greece, Cyprus, and Italy. However, the teachers of the United States also gave high ratings here. All the west European countries had negative means, with Sweden as the clear outlier again.

Slovenian teachers gave the most uniform responses, and the most variation was found in Sweden.

Encouragement to Read

This construct is built on only two items in the questionnaire. It worked well across countries and had a satisfactory reliability. Encouraging students to read more and use the library more is certainly recognized by most teachers as a highly desirable practice, although it might be easy to forget it in the course of daily schoolwork.

Not unexpectedly, the high scoring countries were Cyprus, Singapore, Indonesia, Greece, Trinidad and Tobago, and Spain. High ranks were also occupied by the United States, Canada (BC), and New Zealand. Perhaps encouragement is a more important element in the teaching culture in these countries than in the west European countries, particularly in both Germanys and Switzerland, where encouragement seemed to have a very low priority in the repertoires of instructional practices.

Taking Students' Interests into Account

This construct also involves risks for compliance, and one might expect the same rank order amongst countries as before. The data did not confirm this expectation. Among the leading countries, Denmark and Finland entered the scene. No simple explanation of this change of pattern can be offered here.

Student-Oriented Reading

Although this construct emerged in the secondary analysis and was rather difficult to label, it is more focused on reading activity than the taking into account of students' interests and may be somewhat less vulnerable to compliance. Many of the items involved in this construct indicate a "modern" approach to teaching, where the students' active interaction with texts is particularly emphasized. Countries with frontier positions in reading research and with a well-educated teaching force would then be expected to have high mean scores on this construct. This expectation was partly met. New Zealand, Canada (BC), and the United States all had high ranks on this construct. Somewhat surprising was the low position of Denmark, where the reading debate by tradition has been very lively.

Teacher-Centered Instruction

This construct has many similarities with construct (1) on comprehension instruction. Here, the active role of the teacher is more emphasized.

The leading countries on "teacher-centered instruction" were those with low ranks on the achievement scale: Indonesia, Venezuela, Trinidad and Tobago, Portugal, Greece, and Cyprus. The teaching practices covered by this construct do not seem to be harmful to reading development. On the contrary, they conform quite well to modern conceptions of good teaching. Thus, an element of compliance might be suspected here.

Reading Aloud to Children

In recent years reading specialists have become increasingly aware of the educational power involved in the practice of reading aloud to children (e.g., Wells, 1986). By listening to a story which is read well, students are exposed to a rich variety of vocabulary and to the specific linguistic forms which are typical of written language as opposed to oral language. They also get used to the typical structure of written discourse (story grammar). By being exposed to good literature at an early age, they also have the chance of gradually recognizing the enjoyment of reading and of developing a lasting interest in literature. Although such benefits are well recognized by reading specialists, it is not necessarily common knowledge among teachers around the world. Some teachers may regard reading aloud to students as a kind of entertainment which can be offered as a reward for good behavior, rather than as a powerful instructional method.

High emphasis on reading aloud to children was found in the United States, Canada (BC), New Zealand, Norway, Sweden, and Iceland. The high score in Canada (BC) might partly be related to the fact that the students there were younger than in most other countries. One would expect that younger students more often than older students enjoy the benefit of being read to by the teacher, more as a compensatory measure than as a deliberate instructional strategy. However, the students of the other high scoring countries on this construct were of average or above average age. Here, a more modern teaching orientation is reflected rather than an age adaptation.

Concluding Comments on Teaching Patterns

To summarize the results reported in this section, there was a certain invariance in the response pattern across countries in Population A. In one set of countries, the reported level of activity in almost every aspect of teaching and assessment was high. It is unlikely that this response pattern actually mirrors what takes place in many of these classrooms. In any case, it did not show up in the achievement of the students, as can be seen in the next section.

Another recurring pattern was that the teachers in the United States, Canada (BC), and New Zealand, in that order, generally reported higher activity levels than the teachers of west European and Nordic countries at the same level of economic development. No simple explanation for this fact can be offered. One might speculate on the role of the English language as a more difficult written form to cope with in the first stages of reading acquisition, which in turn might have increased the awareness of instructional issues among educators. But it should also be remembered that the available time for reading instruction is generally greater in the Anglo-Saxon countries. Thus, an elevated frequency level can be expected.

Teaching Practices and Students' Achievement

This section is devoted to an analysis of the data from Population A, in order to investigate whether the teaching factors involved in this study had an influence on students' reading achievement. If anything emerges from such an analysis, guidelines could be provided for the improvement of teaching and teaching conditions. The earlier IEA study on reading comprehension reported by Thorndike (1973) gave no grounds for optimism on this point. The somewhat disheartening conclusion from that study was that very little evidence could be detected to illustrate the impact of school and teaching factors on students' reading achievement. Nevertheless, the richness of data in the present study, together with new approaches and more refined analytical tools, might have made it possible to disentangle the complicated network of interacting and interrelated variables and throw more light on which factors are important in reading instruction.

Analysis of the Pooled Data Set for Population A

In this step of the analysis of the impact of teaching on reading achievement, the responses of all 4800 teachers in Population A were pooled in a common international data set. One reason for doing this was to obtain a sufficiently large data basis for testing an international model. Class achievement means were taken as the outcome variable. When looking at all of these classes, each with its specific teaching conditions and instructional practices, things rapidly become very complicated. It is not easy to tease out one factor and examine its influence on another factor. All sorts of confounding influences can obscure the picture and make interpretations difficult. For example, the classes vary considerably in socioeconomic background. Classroom conditions and teacher characteristics and, indirectly, teaching practices can be expected to covary with such background factors. And it is also known that student achievement is, to a large extent, associated with socioeconomic factors (see Chapter 4). When an association between teaching and achievement is found, it is then difficult to know whether it is teaching *per se* that is important or whether it is just a reflection of differences in socioeconomic factors.

If the socioeconomic background of the classes accounts for most of the variation in achievement, there is not much left for the teaching factors to explain. However, with the teaching dimension in focus, as in this chapter, it is still important to find out what there is in teaching that makes a difference over and above background resources. The best procedure then is to control for socioeconomic background, i.e., keep such factors constant when investigating the association between teaching and achievement. It should be noted, however, that this step might involve aggregation bias, leading to an overcorrection for background factors. (In secondary analyses of data from this study, various hierarchical techniques will be explored.)

The strength of the direct and indirect relationships between various teaching components was estimated by path analysis. The structural relationships were specified as if there were causal relationships between the components, and the quantitative implications of such a causal structure were estimated with a LISREL-program.

Table 6.8

The Direct Associations (Path Coefficients) Between Background Variables and Factors in the Model (Only Significant Coefficients Are Specified, $t > 4.0$; $p < .01$)

	Community type	Community resources	Books at home
Teacher condition			
class size	.27	–	-.24
instruction time	–	.07	-.14
prop. stud. other language	.11	–	-.22
prop. stud. need help	–	–	-.10
time teaching class	-.05	-.05	.11
Teacher characteristics			
education	.11	–	.11
experience	–	–	–
sex	.11	–	.09
accuracy-order view	.05	-.12	-.38
Instructional behaviour			
comprehension teaching	–	.10	-.14
phonics teaching	–	–	-.09
general assessment emphasis	–	–	-.08
assessment of low-order skills	–	–	-.10
student-oriented reading	–	-.05	.07
Reading achievement			
documents	.10	.09	.32
expository	.05	.09	.39
narrative	.06	.10	.38
voluntary reading	–	–	.27

In the path model presented in Figure 6.5, three controlling factors were introduced:
1.   "type of community," which indicated one of the following categories: (a) village or rural community; (b) small town community; (c) large town community; and (d) city of 1 million or more, or any equivalent extreme category of relevance in a particular country. (It was assumed that teaching conditions, teachers, and instructional practices are on the average different in rural areas from those existing in highly urbanized areas.)

2. "Community resources," which indicated whether the school was located in a community where there is access to one or more of the following literacy-related facilities: public library, bookstore, secondary level schools, higher education institution. (It is assumed that the more of these things that are accessible the more stimulating is the environment which, in turn, will have an impact on the teaching environment as well as student achievement.)

3. Finally, the students were asked to estimate the number of books at home. The following choices were presented: none, 1–10, 11–50, 51–100, 101–200, and more than 200. A reasonable assumption (see Chapter 4) is that the more books found in a student's home, the richer literacy stimulation is provided in the home. It also reflects the general socioeconomic standard of the home. Thus, this factor was expected to have a strong influence on student achievement and on student voluntary reading. Teaching conditions, teachers, and teaching practices are also assumed to be related to the socioeconomic standard of the home.

Table 6.8 presents the path coefficients. Thus, the direct relationships between the three background variables and each of the factors specified in the model are presented.

Number of books at home evidently had a clear direct impact on many variables, especially on achievement. The negative relationship with class size and the proportion of students speaking a language other than the test language is notable. It indicates that schools where the students come from homes with high socioeconomic levels have smaller classes and fewer immigrant students. An opposite influence on class size is exerted by community type. Obviously, rural communities tend to have smaller classes.

The question then arises as to whether there is any potential variance for the teacher and teaching factor to explain once the background variables have had a chance to exert their influence. In Figure 6.5, only the path coefficients related to the outcome factors and only coefficients greater than .10 have been included. The meaning of a path of that size is that if the value of an antecedent factor is increased by the size of one standard deviation unit, the outcome variable will be increased by 10% of a standard deviation unit.

As can be seen, there are no large effects left after the introduction of the control variables. Nevertheless, there are some notable effects. Although they may be small, they are at least pure in the sense that they are not confounded with background factors.

Class size had a negative effect on expository reading. This is the direction that teachers would expect (i.e., that small classes go with higher achievement), although it has been hard to demonstrate this within more restricted data analyses. Likewise, instructional time now appears to exert a demonstrable positive effect on achievement.

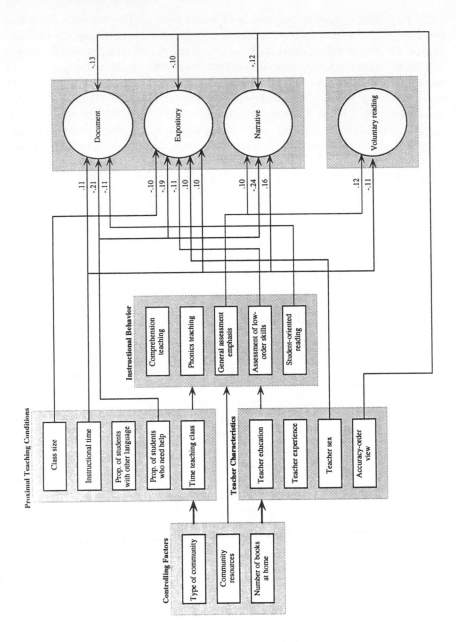

Figure 6.5: A Path Model of the Relationship Between Teaching Factors and
Reading Achievement. Only Path Coefficients Greater Than .10 Are Indicated

The proportion of students needing remedial help had the expected negative association with the outcome variables and was not moderated to any noticeable extent by the introduction of controlling variables. After all, the teachers' judgment of poor achievement among the students might best be regarded as an outcome variable.

The positive coefficient for teacher gender once again confirms the slight superiority of female teachers discussed earlier. The negative effects of accuracy–order views, assessment of low-order skills, and student-oriented reading are not readily interpretable. They may be related to the compliance effect that seems to emerge in different ways. Negative coefficients would be obtained if teachers of poorly achieving students had a stronger tendency to give high-frequency responses to the items on teaching in the teacher questionnaire, as a more or less unconscious defense or compensation for an uneasy suspicion of being a poor teacher. Or the poorer students may be seen to be at a stage where they require help with those skills which better readers acquired earlier. Thus, the high ratings given by teachers of low-achieving students might reflect an adaptation to the students' needs. However, it should be stressed that there is no independent evidence supporting these hypotheses or speculations.

The conclusion to be drawn from the information presented in Figure 6.5 is that factors related to teaching conditions, teacher characteristics, and teacher behavior as measured in this study have a rather small impact on student achievement, when factors related to home and community resources are partialled out. The fact that some explanatory power is left for teaching, over and above home and community background, indicates that variations in schooling do, after all, make some difference. In countries with relatively small variations in socioeconomic conditions, it may well be the case that teaching factors will prove to be more powerful determinants of reading achievement.

Country Control

As a final step in the path-analyses, countries were introduced as controlling factors on the far left of the structural model. Technically speaking, the countries were treated as "dummy" variables. The question was how much the teaching factors contributed to explain variation in achievement between all classes when country-specific factors had also been partialled out. In other words, are there any invariant factors related to teaching over and above country variation as well as home and community variation? In an international study of this kind, such a question has a status of critical importance. The search for invariance is, after all, at the heart of all scientific endeavors.

When the country control was introduced, very little variance was left to be explained by the factors in the model. Inspection of the total effects on achievement (i.e., both the direct arrows and the indirect paths through intermediate constructs or factors), a fair picture is given of what is left. None of the constructs related to teaching practices had any significant effect on achievement. Among the teacher characteristics, teacher gender still had a total effect that was significant. The proportion of students needing remedial help was the only factor among the teaching conditions that survived the country control and still yielded a significant effect (-.20) on achievement. The strongest factor of all was number of books at home. Here the total effect (or correlation) on achievement was close to .40 and the direct path has a size of about .30. This is, indeed, a remarkable finding. Regardless of country, language, culture, wealth, and teaching resources, the single most critical factor in the development of literacy is the literate environment in the home. The absence of significant universal teaching effects indicates that teaching and teaching conditions, to a large extent, are best understood as situated or embedded in the specific cultural configuration characterizing a given country. It may, of course, also be the case that the critical factors in teaching behavior were not captured in this study.

Within-Country Correlations

Although it has been difficult to demonstrate clear international effects of teaching practices on achievement at the level of pooled data, it was hoped that there might still be a chance to find effects within countries, especially in egalitarian societies with wide variations in teaching practices. However, only a few significant correlations between teaching constructs and achievement in Population A were found when the analysis was made on the data from each country separately.

Comprehension instruction correlated significantly with achievement only in Greece (.23), Iceland (.18) and Sweden (.17).

Phonics emphasis was negatively correlated with achievement in Switzerland (-.24) and the United States (-.21), and positively in Indonesia (.22).

General assessment emphasis correlated positively with achievement in two countries, Greece (.20) and Iceland (.17), and negatively in one country, Slovenia (-.21).

Assessment of low-order skills produced a very mixed pattern. It showed a positive correlation in Canada (BC) (.17), Trinidad and Tobago (.21), and Venezuela (.18), and a negative correlation in Germany (East) (-.20), the Netherlands (-.24), and Switzerland (-.19). Negative, but only marginally significant correlations were also found in Sweden (-.12), the United States (-.13), and Slovenia (-.16).

Encouragement to read showed one positive correlation, in Ireland (+.22).

Taking students' interests into account did not correlate with achievement in any country.

Student-oriented reading correlated positively in Denmark (.17), Finland (.24), France (.16), Italy (.20), Sweden (.25), and Trinidad and Tobago (.17), and negatively only in Germany (East) (-.22).

Teacher-centered instruction had the highest correlation in Hong Kong (.18). No other significant correlations were found.

Reading aloud to students produced a negative correlation with achievement in Germany (East) (-.24). Remaining correlations were not significant.

Thus, the significant correlations between teaching constructs and achievement are also few at the between-class, within-country level and are generally rather low. The most promising construct seems to be student-oriented reading. The next question is: do these correlations remain when adjustments for various teaching conditions are made? This question requires country-specific path-models of the kind represented by Figure 6.5. In further analyses of the data from this study, country structures will be compared with the full international model (see Chapter 7). In each specific country, significant deviations from the international model can be identified and interpreted. In general, a deviation is a signal of an interaction between a specific factor and the country under consideration. It indicates that this variable has a specific meaning and impact in this country, as compared with other countries.

From the above, it is clear that separate national data analyses should be undertaken, since configurations of variables and constructs may well be different from what has been used in these international analyses. After all, an international study should look for diversity as well as unity, even though diversity does not always permit simple comparisons along common scales. It is reassuring that each participating education system will be conducting and reporting national analyses of this kind.

More Effective and Less Effective Classrooms

The last step in the analysis of teaching data in this section involves a closer look at extreme groups of classes in each country. Postlethwaite and Ross (1992) developed a procedure for identifying the 20 most effective classes and the 20 least effective classes in each country in Population A. Being effective in their sense meant that the achievement was higher than expected, given the homes from which the students in the class came, whereas less effective meant the opposite.

The classes were selected by a statistical technique, where the average reading achievement levels of the classrooms in each country were related to a composite measure of home resources (such as number of books, home possessions, meals per week, and use of the test language at home). There was, of course, a significant correlation between student home background and reading achievement, which meant that it was possible to predict with some accuracy the expected achievement for a class, given a certain level of average home resources. However, the prediction was far from perfect. Some classes, in fact, showed a far higher achievement than expected, and other classes had an achievement level which was far below what was expected. In each country, the 20 classes with the most pronounced over-achievement (more effective classrooms) and the 20 classes with the most pronounced under-achievement (less effective classrooms) were selected for further study. It should be noted that with this definition of effectiveness it was possible for either a relatively high or a relatively low scoring class to be described as effective, because its reading scores were far above what could be expected from a knowledge of the home background of its students. Likewise, it was possible for either a high scoring class or a low scoring class to be described as less effective.

The critical issue was the identification of the factors that most clearly discriminate these two extreme groups of classrooms from one another. With the focus of the present chapter, it is most natural to ask whether there were any clear differences between effective and less effective classrooms in terms of teaching conditions, teacher characteristics, and teaching strategies. If consistent differences in some respects were to be found across many countries, some important signals would have been discovered which might have been masked by many interfering factors operating when the full set of data was analyzed.

Table 6.9

Number of Countries Where Teaching Factors Discriminated
Significantly Between Effective and Less Effective Classes

Variables	Number of countries
Proximal teaching conditions	
Class size	11
Time teaching this class	9
Instructional time	6
Teacher characteristics	
Teacher readership	17
Teacher sex	14
Teacher experience	11
Teacher views: accuracy, order	8
Teacher education	0
Teaching practices	
Assessment of low-order skills	11
General assessment emphasis	10
Comprehension teaching	9
Student-centered reading	9
Phonics emphasis	6
Encouragement to read	6
Taking student interests into account	5
Teacher-centered reading	0

Postlethwaite and Ross (1992) used a large number of indicators to identify which had the most discriminating power in each country. Here, the focus is restricted to the teaching factors investigated in this report. They are listed in Table 6.9. Each factor is accompanied by a number indicating in how many countries of Population A clear difference was found between more effective and less effective classes.

In some countries, very few teaching-related factors discriminated between more effective and less effective classrooms (e.g., Canada (BC), New Zealand, the United States, Portugal, the Netherlands, Belgium (French), and Germany (East and West)). Instead, factors related to community and school resources were more powerful. In other countries several teaching factors appeared in the list of the top indicators (e.g., Greece, Hong Kong, Italy, and Switzerland). Further details of these country findings are found in Postlethwaite and Ross (1992).

Among the proximal teaching conditions, class size was the most frequently occurring discriminator. In 11 countries, the more effective classes were larger than the less effective. One possible interpretation is that in some countries smaller classes are arranged when there are many poorly performing students. Another interpretation is found in urban–rural contrasts. Rural schools tend to have smaller classes and lower achievement levels. However, most of these nations are highly urbanized. Thus, there may be other reasons.

The variable with the next highest frequency as a potent discriminator was the time the teacher has taught the class. Evidently, there is an advantage in having the opportunity to get to know the children and follow their progress over a longer period of time. On the other hand, this finding may represent only high turnover rate of teachers, as well as students, in less stable areas.

Finally, in this group of variables, instructional time is slightly longer in the more effective classes in at least six countries, which was not unexpected. It may seem surprising that the relatively powerful factors related to the proportion of students with another home language and students in need of remedial help did not show up as discriminators. However, it should be recognized that all factors related to home resources have already been removed in the process of identifying the extreme group of classes.

As for teacher characteristics, several rather strong findings were observed. Most notable is perhaps teacher readership, which was an important discriminator in 17 countries with all three domains of readership: professional reading, expository reading, and literature reading, all equally represented. Although this factor disappeared from the overall international model because of insignificant relationships with achievement, it reappeared when only the extreme classes were considered, country by country. Obviously, teacher readership reflects the level of intellectual and professional aspiration among the teachers and indirectly may be an indication of higher commitment to good teaching, at least when the compliance effect is kept to a minimum, as is the case in this analysis at the country level.

Again, teacher gender played a more significant role, as the female teachers were more commonly found in the more effective classrooms than in the less effective ones. Teachers in the more effective classrooms also had longer experience than teachers in less effective classrooms, at least in 11 of the countries. It seems as if the attitude towards instruction, where order and accuracy are emphasized, was a good discriminator in eight countries. Teachers of more effective classes in these countries valued accuracy and order more than teachers in less effective classrooms. This is not easily interpreted, in view of the findings presented earlier where a negative relationship with achievement was reported. However, the present analysis is made within countries and with home background controlled, and a relatively small group of classes have been examined. Another interesting observation in this new analysis is that the education level of the teachers was not a discriminator in any country. It might well be the case that the variation in educational level within a given country in Population A is too small for this factor to emerge.

Do teachers in more effective classrooms teach in a different way compared with teachers in less effective classrooms? This is certainly a crucial question, with implications for teacher training and in-service training. Among the factors related to teaching practices, the following appear as significant discriminators in some ten countries: general emphasis on assessment, assessment of low-order skills, and student-oriented reading and comprehension instruction. In five or six countries, encouragement to read, taking students' interest into account, and phonics emphasis had discriminatory power. However, there was no consistent pattern across countries, where a given set of factors went together in several countries. They are rather spread out in different directions. Nevertheless, it should be noted that student-oriented reading and comprehension instruction went together in six countries (Finland, Greece, Hungary, Italy, Sweden, and Switzerland), and phonics emphasis and assessment of low-order skills went together in six countries (Finland, France, Hong Kong, Indonesia, Italy, and Norway). Thus, it would appear that in some countries teaching does make a difference. Nevertheless, as Postlethwaite and Ross (1992) pointed out, the use of extreme groups was for generating likely indicators to be used in further national analyses with full data sets.

A Portrait of a Good Reading Teacher

Is there sufficient information to make generalizations leading up to a composite of features characterizing the best possible teacher of reading, working in any country, under optimal conditions? Certainly not. As has been repeatedly emphasized, teaching is necessarily bound to unique configurations of cultural and historical conditions. It is not often possible to take successful practices in reading instruction from one country and expect that they will work equally successfully in another cultural setting. There is also a fallacy of using correlational studies to prescribe teaching practices. When a successful teaching practice appears in many countries and when certain teaching conditions turn out to be favorable in many countries, there is then a basis for some generalization, although even this must be done with great care and sensitivity. With these reservations in mind, it might be worthwhile to attempt a brief summary statement by drawing a picture of a successful teacher, even though the painting is done with a very broad brush.

A good reading teacher for 9-year-olds in this international sense is usually a female teacher. The good teacher has many years of teaching experience. Outside of school, the good teacher reads a lot, both professionally about education and also literature. She or he has stayed with the class long enough to get to know the children well, and has followed their progress carefully by informal as well as more formal assessment methods. The good teacher gives the students many opportunities to do independent, silent reading in a library which is richly stocked, and she or he often holds discussions with the students about the books they have read. The children of the good teacher are encouraged to read outside school and to use the library often. During reading lessons, the children are guided to interact actively with the text by relating their own experiences to what is read, by making predictions of upcoming events during reading, and by making generalizations and inferences. The good reading teacher also takes the students' interests into account when selecting reading materials. The student-oriented approach with a clear focus on strategies for understanding does not prevent the good teacher from using phonics elements now and then in her teaching to meet particular students' needs or when unknown long words, like names, are encountered.

Concluding Comment

A good teacher is, of course, much more than has been captured in this brief sketch, which has been limited by the kind of data provided in this study. Direct classroom observations and in-depth interviews with many teachers and an analysis of the materials they use for reading instruction might have provided sufficiently rich information for painting a more detailed, vivid and accurate portrait.

It is inevitable that this international perspective has highlighted unity as well as diversity, thereby clarifying, or at least contributing to the insight of the complexity of instructional effectiveness in teaching reading. Simple prescriptions or technical specifications of optimal teaching conditions and instructional strategies are not the main keys for raising the literacy levels around the world. The question on how in the world reading is taught has been given one answer here. However, the empirical data provided by the Reading

Literacy study might also serve as a departure for further reflections on the relativity of teaching rather than as fuel for the debate on the best method for teaching reading. There is certainly still much to examine regarding the teaching of reading.

7

Multivariate Analyses of Data From Population A

INGRID MUNCK AND INGVAR LUNDBERG

The analyses presented so far in this volume have, with few exceptions, been limited to univariate and bivariate analyses, occasionally supplemented with the introduction of a few controlling variables to partial out the influence of national or community resources. In Chapter 6, however, a more elaborate multivariate analysis was presented, including a path model on the impact of teaching conditions and instructional practices.

In the present chapter, some further steps in multivariate analyses of the data will be taken. The general approach of the whole IEA study was to measure the important explanatory variables of reading achievement, and the tests and questionnaires were therefore designed to be analyzed with modern techniques for multivariate analyses. The data were thought to be rich in potential for answering questions about which factors are important for student performance. The purpose of the analyses presented in this chapter is to make this kind of information visible using multivariate modeling on the whole data set for Population A, involving 4353 schools and 93,000 students. In an international study, including many countries with many different teaching conditions and instructional practices and with a wider spectrum of critical factors in the total set of countries than within any single educational system, the chances might be greater of detecting signals which are undetectable within a country where the variance of critical factors might be very low or even absent. The approach taken makes it possible to capture and explore the full international variation in the multivariate analyses. When the units of analysis are classrooms, there is normally not a sufficient number of them in each separate country to permit more elaborate analyses. This is an additional but more technical argument for utilizing a full international data set.

Selection of Variables for Multivariate Analysis

The questionnaires to teachers, school principals, and students in Population A included several hundred variables. Thus, a rather drastic reduction of the number of variables to be included in the multivariate analyses was necessary. The selection procedure followed a sequence of two steps:

1.   Bivariate correlations between each of the questionnaire variables and the outcome variables (Document reading, Expository reading, Narrative reading, and Voluntary reading) were computed for each country. The school and teacher questionnaires were normally answered by fewer than 200 teachers or school principals in each country. Thus, only variables which showed correlations with outcomes greater than .20 (or less than -.20) were considered significant. If correlations of that size or more were found in at least five countries, these variables could proceed to the next step in the selection procedure. As for student data, the criterion correlation for inclusion was .06, since the number of students in each country was normally close to 2000.

When this procedure was applied, the final number of explanatory variables selected for further between-class analyses was 48, most of them being teacher or school variables (see variable list in Appendix J).

2.   The set of 48 variables was entered in a multiple regression analysis with reading achievement (three domains) and voluntary reading as dependent variables. The proportion of explained variance of the outcome variables with this set of variables was between .57 and .59. However, several single variables did not contribute significantly to this explanation. Those variables without any significant *t*-value for the direct relation to any of the outcome variables were excluded from the further path models to be explored. The final set of explanatory variables which qualified for entering a between-class model on teaching was only 18 variables. Before this model is presented, the analysis of the international data set involved a few more steps still to be described.

Multiple Regression Analysis With Countries as Dummy Variables

The regression model is a tool for modeling means, and the statistical trick for describing the country means with such a model is to introduce a so-called dummy variable for each country. The new variable takes on the value 1 for all classes belonging to the country and the value of zero for all other classes. One country is chosen as a reference country (in this study, Spain). The multiple regression analysis of the three domains of reading includes data from all participating countries for Population A, which makes 27 school systems, but only 26 explanatory variables (the one for Spain is excluded) in the regression model. The unstandardized regression coefficients express the differences in means between these countries and Spain. The estimate of a country mean is obtained by adding (or subtracting if negative) the coefficient, which is expressed in Rasch scores, to the mean score of Spain.

No. of classes

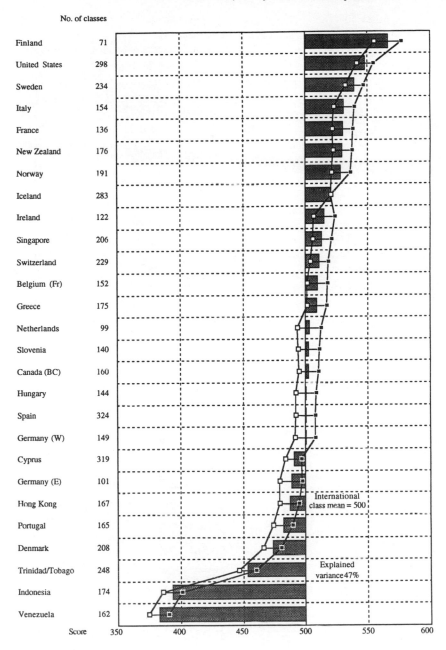

Figure 7.1: System Regression on Narrative Test Outcome: Between Class
Analyses on Pooled Population A Data (Rank Order According to Outcome)

No. of classes

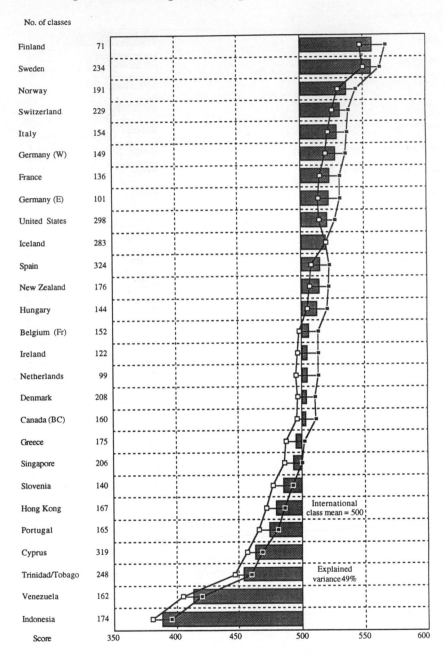

Figure 7.2: System Regression on Expository Test Outcome: Between Class
Analyses on Pooled Population A Data (Rank Order According to Outcome)

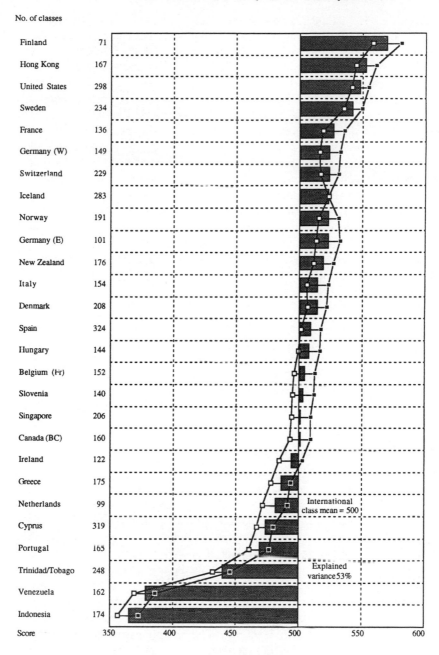

No. of classes

Finland	71
Hong Kong	167
United States	298
Sweden	234
France	136
Germany (W)	149
Switzerland	229
Iceland	283
Norway	191
Germany (E)	101
New Zealand	176
Italy	154
Denmark	208
Spain	324
Hungary	144
Belgium (Fr)	152
Slovenia	140
Singapore	206
Canada (BC)	160
Ireland	122
Greece	175
Netherlands	99
Cyprus	319
Portugal	165
Trinidad/Tobago	248
Venezuela	162
Indonesia	174

International class mean = 500

Explained variance 53%

Score   350   400   450   500   550   600

Figure 7.3: System Regression on Document Test Outcome: Between Class
Analyses on Pooled Population A Data (Rank Order According to Outcome)

Figures 7.1, 7.2, and 7.3 present the results of this first analysis step. The country-specific contribution to explaining the variance in the three achievement dimensions is expressed by the length of the bar for each country. These bars are subject to sampling fluctuations in the same way that the mean scores for each country are also only estimates of the true achievement levels. To indicate this uncertainty the figures show confidence intervals, except for Iceland where all students were tested. A lack of overlap in such confidence intervals leads to a conclusion that the corresponding country means differ significantly. The countries are ranked according to the size of their contributions, which are expressed in the same score scale as the individually based country means presented in Chapter 2. (The present score is based on class means, which are weighted with student weights within each country and pooled together, giving each country equal weight.) The total variance in achievement explained by country or system variation is .47 for the Narrative test, .49 for the Expository test, and .53 for the Documents test. Thus, just knowing what country a given class belongs to provides a substantial basis for prediction.

Adding the Full Set of Questionnaire Data

In the next step all 48 questionnaire variables obtained from step (2) in the procedure for variable selection were added to the country variables, and a new multiple regression analysis was run. At this stage, the total proportion of variance explained increased to between .62 and .65. Considering some unreliability in the outcome measures, there is certainly not much variance left to be explained. Thus, one could be very confident that the present data involve sufficiently strong signals to justify further, more detailed analyses.

Control of Community and Home Factors

A natural focus of the present study is the impact of the education system, the school, and teaching conditions on the level of reading literacy. It is well known that reading skills, to a large extent, are developed as an informal socialization process outside school, where the cultural capital of the families and the richness of stimulation in communities play a definitive role. If a more purified estimate of the impact of school conditions is attempted, a natural step is to control for the influence of home and community factors and examine what is left for remaining factors to explain. This step was taken by adding to the country dummies four variables related to home and community: (1) number of books at home, (2) degree of parental cooperation, (3) type of community, and (4) community resources. The latter construct included access to a bookstore, a public library, and secondary and higher education.

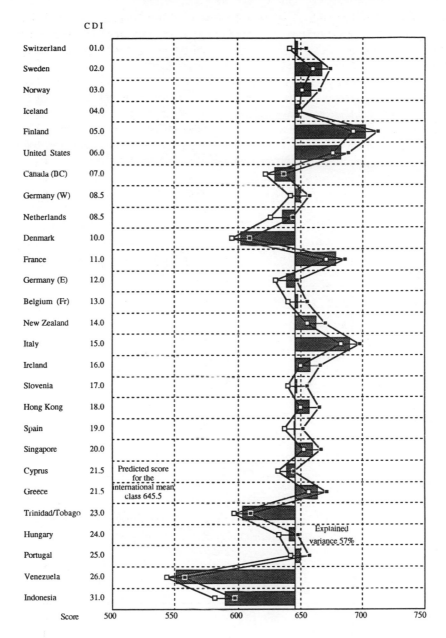

Figure 7.4: Deviation in Rasch Score from International Level of Narrative Test Outcome: Between-Class Regression on Pooled Population A Data Controlling for Community and Home Factors (Rank Order According to Composite Development Index (CDI))

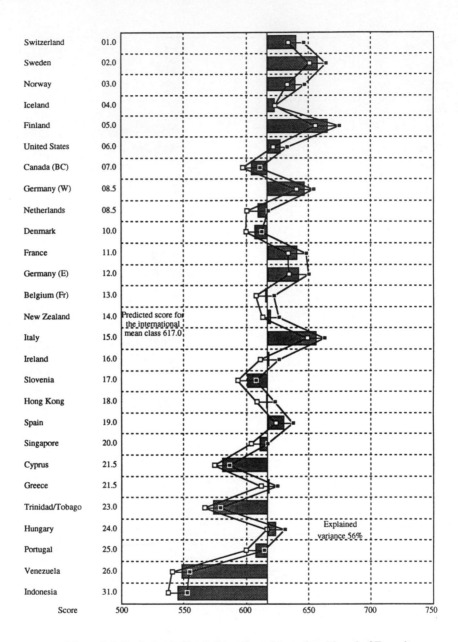

Figure 7.5: Deviation in Rasch Score from International Level of Expository
Test Outcome: Between-Class Regression on Pooled Population A Data
Controlling for Community and Home Factors (Rank Order According to
Composite Development Index (CDI))

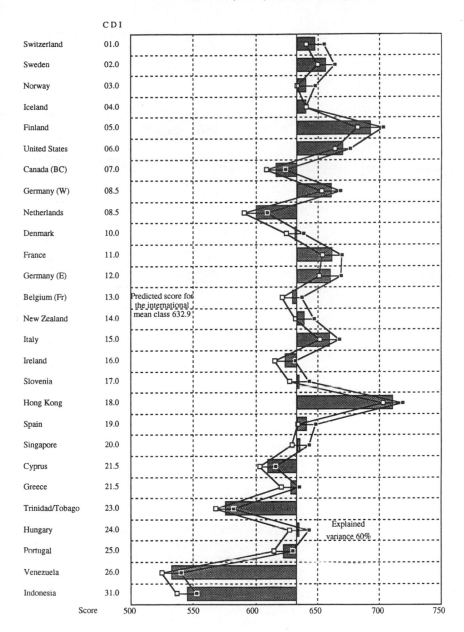

Figure 7.6: Deviation in Rasch Score from International Level of Document
Test Outcome: Between-Class Regression on Pooled Population A Data
Controlling for Community and Home Factors (Rank Order According to
Composite Development Index (CDI))

The results are presented in Figures 7.4, 7.5, and 7.6, where the countries are ranked according to the Composite Developmental Index, CDI (see Chapter 2). Countries with positions close to each other on this scale could now be compared under conditions for which most of the socioeconomic differences are controlled. The remaining differences between the country achievement levels reflect to a large extent differences in the effectiveness of the educational systems down to the classroom level. Figures 2.5 and 2.10 in Chapter 2 show very similar trends.

The results in Figures 7.4–7.6 are centered around the predicted score for the "International Class" (defined as taking on the grand mean value for all variables in the regression model).[1] One interpretation of the country bars in the Figures 7.4–7.6 is that they provide predicted outcome levels under equal community and home conditions.

In Figure 7.4 the narrative test outcome is taken as the measure of productivity of school systems, and those countries with means higher than the international mean level are listed downwards along the central line with a bar to the right. On the other hand, those countries with means lower than the international mean level show bars to the left. Switzerland, being ranked highest in CDI, was found at the international standard level only but was expected to perform well above this level. Sweden, Norway, Iceland, Finland, and the United States all achieved, as expected, above the international standard. Thus, the mean of the Narrative scores for each classroom in a country has been adjusted for country CDI, community resources, and home resources. What remains after this adjustment to a large extent reflects the impact of the school system on the average achievement of the classes in a country. For countries with a position in the mid-interval of the CDI (11–20) there were several countries performing above international standard. These were France, New Zealand, Italy, Ireland, Hong Kong, and Singapore. Other countries which were regarded as over-achieving in the Narrative domain were Greece, Hungary, and Portugal which had a low ranking in CDI but which nevertheless reached the international standard. There were other countries higher up on the CDI ranking which were clearly under-achieving, notably Denmark, Canada (BC), and the Netherlands. However, as has already been pointed out, Canada (BC) and the Netherlands tested younger children than most of the other countries and this could very well explain why they fell behind in this analysis.

The picture of over- and under-achieving in the two other domains, Expository and Documents, was quite similar with a few additional notable

---

[1] Technically this is calculated as the reference group mean (the mean of Spain) plus the sum of the product between the regression coefficients with their respective means for the community and home variables, and plus the mean of the 27 country contributions, the regression coefficients for the country dummy variables including zero for Spain.

observations to be made. Germany (East), with CDI in the mid-field, was over-achieving in both of these domains with an outcome level significantly above the international standard. Hong Kong could be taken as another example. The document score for Hong Kong, ranked second in the system regression in Figure 7.3, increased drastically when the community and home factors were taken into account. The top position of Hong Kong could well reflect specific influences, both out-of-school and within school, which promote skill in document reading. Is Hong Kong a pragmatic society where skill in reading signs, advertisements, instructions, or manuals has a clear "survival" value for young children?

Before turning to a summary of the country deviations from the international class mean in Figures 7.1–7.6, a word of caution is needed on interpreting the results from multivariate analysis. A crucial question to ask is, which factors of importance are left out of the analysis (the so-called omitted variables)? If there are such variables, which are very important for the outcome, and if the relative frequency distribution of these variables in the samples varies considerably from country to country, then the estimated regression coefficients will be biased. In this study, age is an example of this kind of disturbing variable. Unfortunately, the IEA Reading Literacy Study was designed to cover only one grade in each country, and the common ground for comparisons was defined to be the grade in which the largest percentage of 9-year-olds were found. Depending on the age of school start, repetition policies, etc., the obtained age distributions came out differently in different samples of the study. The reason why the multivariate study could not control for these differences is that the relationship between age and performance is not linear. Very young students for their grade often perform better than their classmates and very old students typically perform worse. As a consequence the age variable does not fulfill the basic assumption for simple regression of being linearly related to the outcome. Grade is another difficult variable to use in this context as it is a very vague indicator of length of schooling, not comparable between countries.

As a result, the statistical multivariate analysis creates a picture which controls for certain measurable and internationally comparable variables that fulfill certain assumptions about type of scale and linearity. The remaining missing factors have to be considered in the interpretation of the results. The Figures 7.4–7.6 may help the reader to do so when it comes to the developmental level of the country. Many other factors can be thought of as alternative candidates. One factor of specific relevance would be the percentage of the population under the age of 16. This indicator reflects, among other things, the degree of pressure on the educational system. The presentation offered here can only illustrate a very limited basis for explanations. It demonstrates the potential of multivariate analysis rather than gives any final answers.

Another way to improve the fairness of the comparisons of effectiveness of different educational systems is, of course, to group the countries according to very basic conditions of relevance for reading, such as type of language, historic traditions, and cultural patterns. The multivariate analysis is then performed within each group of comparison, and it is possible to discover to what extent different factors are important for performance in different settings. Again this more refined and detailed kind of analysis has not been included in the present report. A top-down approach has instead been taken, starting by giving a bird's-eye view of the global variation among those IEA variables which lend themselves to linear regression modeling.

Country Deviations from the International Class Mean in Rasch Scores

In order to summarize the results of the regression analysis from a country perspective, Rasch score deviations from the international class mean are reported for each country in Figure 7.7. As the general patterns reported in Figure 7.1–7.6 were very similar for the different domains, the results presented here are mean scores over the three domains. (In Table J.2 in Appendix J all score values are reported in detail for the domains and the means separately.)

For each country the outcome on reading is presented with three estimates of the unique contribution (*m1*, *m2*, and *m3*) corresponding to the results from the following three regression models:
1.   system regression with country variables only (*m1*)
2.   community and home factors plus country variables (*m2*)
3.   full set of questionnaire variables and country variables (*m3*).

The values for *m1*, *m2*, and *m3* are Rasch scores expressed as deviations from the "International Class Mean" level, here standardized to 0. The first bar, *m1*, provides a country's level in reading in relation to the other countries in the study (summary of Figures 7.1–7.3). The next bar, *m2*, has adjusted the level for differences between countries in community and home conditions (summary of Figures 7.4–7.6) and finally bar *m3* has adjusted the level for differences in the full set of questionnaire variables.

A drop in the reading level when controlling for community and home factors (*m1*–*m2* positive) means that the level of performance could partly be explained by these factors. Twelve countries showed this pattern clearly including all the Nordic countries, Canada (BC), the United States, the Netherlands, Switzerland, and New Zealand. Belgium (French) and Hungary also tended to drop in the adjusted level controlling for community and home factors, which actually placed them very near the international mean level. However, these two countries both improved their position when all school and teacher variables were considered, which is represented in the third bar. This points toward a positive predicted improvement in class achievement if they invest in schooling like that which is represented by the "International Class."

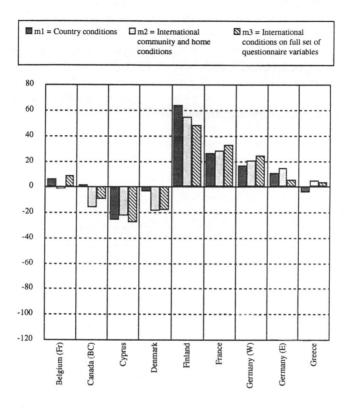

Figure 7.7A

Figure 7.7A–C: Country Outcome on Reading Adjusted to International Class
Conditions

If a country shows an increase between *m1* and *m2*, the interpretation may be that this country has a handicap in terms of community and home resources, and the adjusted level of performance, *m2*, takes this fact into account. The developing countries Indonesia, Trinidad and Tobago, and Venezuela showed, as expected, higher adjusted performance than their original outcome level. Hong Kong also improved its position considerably when taking the out-of-school factors into account. Among the European countries, France, Italy, Portugal, Germany (West), and Germany (East) all seemed somewhat handicapped by their level of community and home resources. More can be done in the community and home to stimulate reading and the tentative prediction from this study is that such investments would raise the level of reading in the future.

One focus in the multivariate analysis has been to make comparisons between the countries concerning the reading outcome as fair as possible. The third bar, $m3$, makes a comparison between countries possible by adjusting for the most important background variables in community, home, and school. It represents a unique contribution which has not been possible to explain even though nearly all relevant factors simultaneously have been included in the analysis. In the case of Finland, ranked top in the univariate analysis, the deviation in Rasch Score from the "International Class Mean" level dropped from $m1 = 64$ to $m2 = 55$ and down to $m3 = 48$. Among the fully adjusted $m3$-values it is still the greatest, indicating that specific explanations must be looked for connected with the Finnish school system and its cultural background.

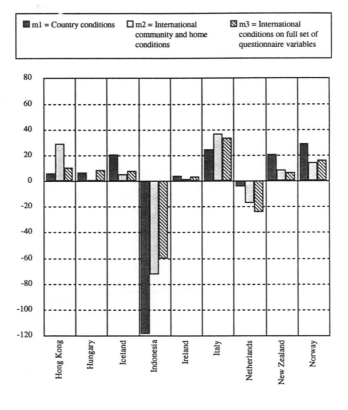

Figure 7.7B

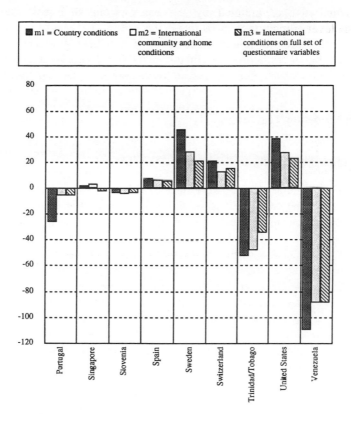

Figure 7.7C

Looking at the countries for which the relative level of performance increased when adjusting for community and home, France and Germany (West) demonstrated an upward trend from *m1* to *m2* and also from *m2* to *m3*. Some of the resource variables represented in the analysis are probably kept at a lower level of investment than the international class conditions in this study. The regression analysis points toward a positive predicted improvement in class achievement if these countries could invest more in these aspects of their system.

Five countries show a very stable position near to the international standard in all three analyses. These are Greece, Ireland, Singapore, Slovenia, and Spain. With the investment in resources captured in this study, the students in these countries perform at the expected level considering the information we have about efficiency in all 27 participating countries. For these countries the unique contribution of explained variance between classes in reading was not affected by the assumptions of equal conditions in community and home factors or in all the school and teacher variables. The IEA variables strongly related with outcome then give guidance for resource allocation, but there is nothing in the results that points at special, unique factors of importance for reading achievement that are operating in these countries.

A Path Model on Teaching

In Chapter 6, a between-class model with the focus on teaching conditions and teaching strategies was presented (see Figure 6.5). This model will now be used as a reference model to illustrate how the international potential of this study can be more fully exploited. Other models with different foci than teaching could, of course, have been selected as examples. However, for illustrative purposes, the present model was judged to be sufficiently clear and useful.

The first analysis of the model was a path analysis based on the pooled international data set with 4800 classes, excluding Venezuela because of some omissions in the data set. The next step involved multigroup comparisons, which means that the data from each of the countries were, one at a time, confronted with the international results (Munck, 1979, 1991) Those parts of the model were located where a given country deviated significantly from the international model, as indicated by the modification indices. By examining each single path of the model in this way, country by country, it was possible to identify those parts of the model where a high level of international invariance was obtained, i.e., where only few countries showed significant deviations. Valid generalizations, in this case over and above specific country contexts, are, of course, a desired goal in all scientific endeavors.

An important prerequisite for the outlined approach with multigroup comparisons is a fully specified path model where each variable at one stage is related to all variables at succeeding stages in the causal relationships. Otherwise, it would not be possible to identify all possible loci of deviations. Thus, no degrees of freedom are available and the path model is a fully identified model with perfect fit to any data. The estimation of the country-specific deviations from the international structure is using the pooled international data set with close to 5000 units of observation as well as a country-specific data set with number of observations (classes) ranging from 71 to 324. As there are hundreds of parameters to be estimated, there is no way of doing it at the country level, where normally less than two hundred classes are available.

The teaching model under consideration now involves four stages (see Figure 7.8). The first stage includes four controlling variables, two related to community ("Type of Community" and "Community Resources") and two to home factors ("Parental Cooperation" and "Number of Books at Home"). It is assumed that teaching conditions and teaching patterns are dependent to some extent on wealth and resources of the environment. When the main issue concerns the importance of teaching factors per se in explaining the student achievement variance, it is obviously relevant to control for environmental resources. One strong candidate as a variable for home control is the number of home possessions and the students' own possessions. Within many countries this variable had a substantial impact on student achievement. At the international level, however, this variable was less suitable, since the item list of possessions was adapted to the specific conditions in each country. If this adaptation had been equally successful in each country, the between-country variance would have been minimized. However, the degree of success of the adaptation in each country varied too much to allow this variable to qualify for the international model.

The second stage includes four variables related to school conditions ("Type of School," "Pupil/Teacher Ratio," "Size of School," and "Size of School Library"). The school environment obviously sets critical constraints on the teaching conditions as well as the instructional practices.

The second stage of the model also includes a group of five variables labeled proximal teaching conditions, i.e., classroom characteristics such as "Class Size," "Instructional Time," "Proportion Students with Other Language," "Proportion Students Needing Help," and "Time (with) Same Teacher." Here the teaching environmental net has been brought to its tightest level. In addition, a number of teacher characteristics ("Teacher Education," "Teacher Experience," "Teacher Sex," and "High Demand Views") have been included at this stage (see Chapter 6). The type of teacher who is responsible for the reading instruction determines the way teaching is done within the constraints set up by the external conditions.

The third stage is the very focus of the model. It concerns the teacher's instructional behavior and practices. Five of the nine teaching factors or constructs described in Chapter 6 are included here, namely, "Comprehension Instruction," "Phonics Teaching," "Assessment Emphasis," "Assessment of Low-Order Skills," and "Student-Oriented Reading." They were selected because they had the highest number of significant bivariate correlations with the outcome variables when within-country data were examined. They also tended to stand out in the multiple regression test referred to above. From a construct perspective, they are also some of the clearest and most interpretable constructs on teaching available.

The final stage represents the outcome which here includes student achievement on the three reading domains: Document Reading, Expository Reading, and Narrative Reading. Voluntary Reading could also be regarded as an outcome variable. However, it was decided not to include it among the outcomes in this model, partly because of its unclear status and partly because of a desire to keep the model simple.

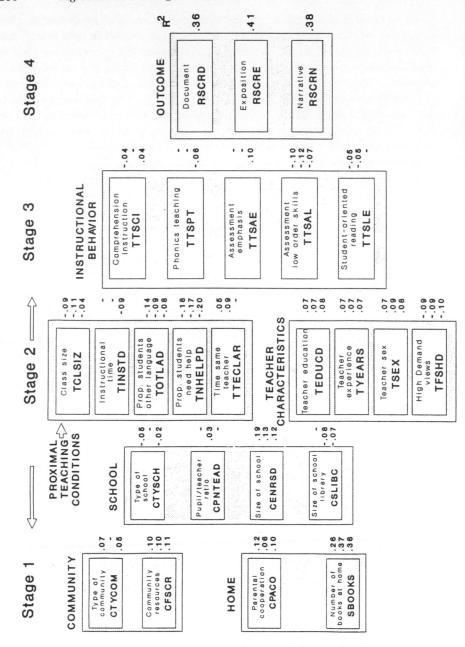

Figure 7.8: Path Model on Teaching: Direct Effects on Outcome; Significant
Effects Only

Table 7.1

Estimated Path Coefficients for the Teaching Model Based on
Between-Class Analysis on Pooled Population A Data

Path to:	ACTYCOMD	ACFSCR	ASBOOKS	ACPACO	ACTYSCH	ACPNTEAD	ACENRSD	ACSLIBC	ATCLSIZ	ATINSTD	ATOTLAD
ACTYSCH	0.03*	-0.00	0.11*	0.07*	—	—	—	—	—	—	—
ACPNTEAD	-0.09*	0.04*	0.10*	-0.06*	—	—	—	—	—	—	—
ACENRSD	0.36*	0.01	-0.07*	0.06*	—	—	—	—	—	—	—
ACSLIBC	0.15*	0.04*	0.19*	0.04*	—	—	—	—	—	—	—
ATCLSIZ	0.08*	0.01	-0.16*	0.14*	0.10*	-0.14*	0.41*	-0.09*	—	—	—
ATINSTD	-0.03*	-0.00	-0.16*	0.03*	0.15*	-0.07*	0.08*	-0.07*	—	—	—
ATOTLAD	0.06*	-0.11*	-0.20*	-0.11*	0.00	0.04*	0.25*	0.12*	—	—	—
ATNHELPD	0.00	-0.05*	-0.12*	-0.15*	-0.05*	-0.02	-0.02	0.08*	—	—	—
ATTECLAR	-0.01	-0.02	0.08*	-0.11*	-0.02	0.11*	-0.10*	-0.00	—	—	—
ATEDUCD	0.11*	0.11*	0.06*	0.06*	-0.05*	-0.03*	-0.16*	0.11*	—	—	—
ATYEARS	-0.01	-0.01	0.03*	-0.01	-0.03*	0.03*	0.03	-0.03	—	—	—
ATSEX	0.06*	0.04*	0.05*	-0.04*	-0.07*	0.07*	0.08*	0.07*	—	—	—
ATFSHD	-0.02	-0.07*	-0.36*	0.04*	0.09*	-0.01	0.14*	-0.17*	—	—	—
ATFSCI	-0.05*	0.07*	-0.11*	0.08*	-0.06*	-0.02	0.00	0.08*	-0.05*	0.04*	-0.07*
ATFSPT	-0.04*	-0.06*	-0.13*	-0.01	0.05*	-0.01	0.10*	0.10*	0.07*	0.06*	-0.05*
ATFSAE	-0.04*	-0.03	-0.08*	-0.02	0.02	-0.01	0.12*	-0.04*	-0.01	0.03	-0.03*
ATFSAL	-0.00	-0.03*	-0.16*	0.02	-0.04*	-0.04*	0.05*	0.09*	-0.05*	0.04*	-0.09*
ATFSLE	0.00	-0.03	0.05*	0.01	-0.03*	-0.06*	-0.16*	0.15*	0.16*	0.15*	0.08*
RSCRD	0.07*	0.10*	0.26*	0.12*	-0.05*	0.02	0.19*	-0.03	-0.09*	0.02	-0.14*
RSCRE	0.03	0.10*	0.37*	0.06*	-0.01	0.03*	0.13*	-0.08*	-0.11*	0.02*	-0.09*
RSCRN	0.05*	0.11*	0.36*	0.10*	-0.02*	0.01	0.12*	-0.07*	-0.04*	0.09*	-0.08*

Path from: †

Path to:	ATNHELPD	ATTECLAR	ATEDUCD	ATYEARS	ATSEX	ATFSHD	ATFSCI	ATFSPT	ATFSAE	ATFSAL	ATFSLE
ATFSCI	-0.02	-0.09*	0.07*	0.05*	0.13*	0.27*	—	—	—	—	—
ATFSPT	0.11*	-0.06*	0.07*	0.09*	0.08*	0.19*	—	—	—	—	—
ATFSAE	0.05*	0.03*	0.06*	0.10*	0.03*	0.38*	—	—	—	—	—
ATFSAL	0.07*	-0.07*	0.12*	0.05*	0.05*	0.32*	—	—	—	—	—
ATFSLE	0.00	-0.08*	0.05*	-0.02	0.10*	0.02	—	—	—	—	—
RSCRD	-0.18*	0.05*	0.07*	0.07*	0.07*	-0.09*	-0.04*	0.02	0.02	-0.10*	-0.05*
RSCRE	-0.17*	0.09*	0.07*	0.07*	0.09*	-0.09*	0.02	-0.01	0.01	-0.12*	-0.05*
RSCRN	-0.20*	0.02	0.08*	0.07*	0.08*	-0.10*	0.04*	-0.06*	0.10*	-0.07*	-0.01

* Significant at the 5% level

† For key to labels, see Appendix J

A majority of the explanatory variables in this model are based on information obtained from the teacher and school questionnaires, i.e., they are clearly between-class variables. The only exception is the home variable "Number of Books at Home," which is drawn from the student questionnaire. In such cases, there is a high risk of introducing a bias in the estimation of the relationships. When data from a lower level is aggregated up to a higher level, one should be careful (see, e.g., Keeves, 1992). However, when the aggregated variable only serves as a basic controlling factor, the aggregation bias may be less critical. In fact, the control here implies only that the impact on outcomes of teaching factors at later stages in the model is conditioned by the average number of books at home.

To sum up, the model is basically a between-class model dealing with the impact of teaching factors on student achievement with controls for community and home factors. The path coefficients are estimated from the international data set, describing the international structure of the relationships. The estimated path coefficients are presented in full in Table 7.1 and the direct effects on the three outcome variables are inserted in Figure 7.8.

Table 7.2

Path Model on Teaching. Direct and Total Effects of Community and Home Factors on Reading Outcome: Between-Class Analyses on Pooled Population A Data (Standardized Coefficients with Standard Error Approximately Equal to .01)

| Explanatory Variable | Outcome | | | | | |
| | Narrative | | Expository | | Documents | |
	Direct Effect	Total Effect	Direct Effect	Total Effect	Direct Effect	Total Effect
Type of Community	.05*	.06	.03	.02	.07*	.09
Community Resources	.11*	.14	.10*	.14	.10*	.14
Parental Cooperation	.10*	.13	.06*	.05	.12*	.13
Number of Books at Home	.36*	.42	.37*	.48	.26*	.37

* = direct paths with t-value ≥ 1.96.

In order to summarize the influence on reading exerted by each explanatory variable the total effects are also reported. Table 7.2 presents the direct and the total effects of the four controlling variables at the first stage, community and home factors, on all subsequent variables in the model. The results will be successively presented in the same way, where direct and total effects for each successive level in the model are given one stage at a time.

Table 7.3

Path Model on Teaching. Direct and Total Effects of School Factors, Proximal Teaching Conditions and Teacher Characteristics on Reading Outcome: Between-Class Analyses on Pooled Population A Data (Standardized Coefficients with Standard Error Approximately Equal to .01)

Explanatory Variable	Outcome					
	Narrative		Expository		Documents	
	Direct Effect	Total Effect	Direct Effect	Total Effect	Direct Effect	Total Effect
Type of School	-.02*	-.03	-.01	-.03	-.05*	-.06
Pupil/Teacher Ratio	.00	.02	.03	.07	.02	.05
Size of School	.12*	.08	.13*	.05	.19*	.11
Size of School Library	-.07*	-.08	-.08*	-.09	-.03	-.04
Class Size	-.04*	-.05	-.11*	-.11	-.09*	-.09
Instructional Time	.09*	.08	.02	.01	.02	.01
Prop. Students Other Language	-.08*	-.07	-.09*	-.08	-.14*	-.14
Prop. Students Need Help	-.20*	-.21	-.17*	-.18	-.18*	-.18
Time Same Teacher	.02	.03	.09*	.10	.05*	.06
Teacher Education	.08*	.08	.07*	.05	.07*	.06
Teacher Experience	.07*	.07	.07*	.07	.07*	.07
Teacher Sex	.08*	.08	.09*	.08	.07*	.06
High Demand Views	-.10*	-.09	-.09*	-.12	-.09*	-.12

"Type of Community," expressed as urban or rural, was the weakest of the first stage variables, significantly influencing narrative and document outcome but not expository (*t*-value = 1.92). "Community Resources," a composite of questions about public library, bookstore, secondary level schools, and higher education institutions, were of importance for the students' reading level and the total effects all reached .14. The effects of "Number of Books at Home" were high, with total effects around .40. The degree of parental cooperation significantly influenced reading results and the effect is mainly direct, around .10.

Among the school input factors it was the "Size of School" variable that showed the highest path and overall significance for the three domains. For the proximal teaching conditions it turned out to be the characteristics of the students (needing help or having another mother tongue) that were the most highly significant explanatory variables after controlling for the community, home and school factors. Finally, it can be seen from Table 7.3 that the teacher characteristics included in the model had significant influences on the outcome with direct effects around .08.

Table 7.4

Path Model on Teaching. Direct and Total Effects of Instructional Behavior on Reading Outcome: Between-Class Analyses on Pooled Population A Data (Standardized Coefficients with Standard Error Approximately Equal to .01)

	Outcome					
	Narrative		Expository		Documents	
Explanatory Variable	Direct Effect	Total Effect	Direct Effect	Total Effect	Direct Effect	Total Effect
Comprehension Instruction	.04*	.04*	.02	.02	-.04*	-.04*
Phonics Teaching	-.06*	-.06*	.00	.00	.02	.02
Assessment Emphasis	.10*	.10*	.01	.01	.02	.02
Assessment Low Order Skills	-.07*	-.07*	-.12*	-.12*	-.10*	-.10*
Student-oriented Reading	-.01	-.01	-.05*	-.05*	-.05*	-.05*

Turning to the instructional behavior factors in Table 7.4, its effects were fairly weak. The only factor that was significant overall for the three domains was "Assessment of Low-Order Skills." For further discussion of the results of the path analysis, see Chapter 6.

Cross-Country Deviations from the International Structure

Each of the 26 countries was compared with the international path model in a two-group analysis with LISREL constraining all the path coefficient parameters to be equal between the two groups. In order to take the different variances in the country-specific data and in the pooled data into account, covariance matrices were analyzed. In some countries, certain variables in the model did not vary at all and as a consequence the model had to be reduced for these analyses with the zero-variance variable(s). The most problematic variable was "Type of School" (state school or private school). Several countries reported no private schools, and this variable was therefore excluded from the international teaching model. The estimated teaching model was further simplified through not including the paths between school factors and proximal teaching conditions plus teacher characteristics at the second stage, but instead letting the residuals of these variables correlate to keep the model fully identified.

The goodness-of-fit results from the simultaneous test for invariance in all paths of the reduced teaching model are presented in Table 7.5. The degrees of freedom are 218 in general but less when one or several variables were excluded because of the zero-variance problem. The chi-square values were all significant, indicating that there was no single country that came really close in all paths to the international structure. But there are big differences between countries. Belgium (French), Canada (BC), Denmark, Germany (West), Ireland, the Netherlands, New Zealand, Norway, and Slovenia came relatively close to the overall structure, whereas Cyprus, Hong Kong, Indonesia, and Trinidad and Tobago deviated considerably from a common pattern.

The chi-square measure was used for the overall test of the invariance hypothesis (all paths equal to the international structure). The modification indices could then be used to locate the paths which contribute most to a high value on the overall test. They provided a local test for each path parameter, also a chi-square statistic, but with only one degree of freedom. If the outcome was significant (chi-square value above approximately 8 for $p < .05$) for a specific country and parameter, then a deviation from the international structure was traced.

Table 7.5

Goodness-of-Fit Results for Teaching Model: Simultaneous Test
for Invariance in All Paths Between International Pooled Data and
Each Country's Data: Population A

Country	Number of Classes	Chi-Square	Degrees of Freedom
Belgium/Fr	152	478.45	218
Canada/BC	154	544.31	218
Cyprus	319	1308.96	203
Denmark	209	568.13	218
Finland	71	641.57	218
France	136	641.62	218
Germany/W	149	549.17	218
Germany/E	101	776.45	218
Greece	175	843.15	218
Hong Kong	167	1192.62	218
Hungary	144	745.75	218
Iceland	282	710.98	218
Indonesia	174	1201.61	218
Ireland	122	564.98	218
Italy	154	747.57	203
Netherlands	99	597.43	198
New Zealand	176	532.37	218
Norway	191	594.72	218
Portugal	165	884.19	218
Singapore	206	995.89	178
Slovenia	140	522.35	203
Spain	324	794.50	218
Sweden	234	698.48	203
Switzerland	229	687.51	198
Trinidad/Tobago	248	1409.34	203
United States	294	735.85	178

The chi-square value mentioned above can be looked upon as a distance measure. These values can be directly compared between different paths within a two-group analysis and ranked. Low values indicate a high degree of invariance and high values the opposite. When corresponding modification indices are compared across countries, the number of classes has to be taken into account. Finland, with only 71 classes, is therefore expected to produce a lower chi-square than, for example, Spain with 324 classes, assuming the two countries lie at the same distance from the international estimate. This complication in the interpretation of chi-square values has to be kept in mind in the following presentation of the results from the modification indices.

The output from the 26 two-group analyses is indeed very comprehensive and contains 191 modification indices each corresponding to a country-specific path estimate.[2] Two summary tables present the main trends. Table 7.6 provides the maximum deviations found for each path in the model and for which country, and Table 7.7 presents the sums of the corresponding modification indices as a measure of degree of invariance. As these were all chi-square measures with one degree of freedom and the countries constitute independent samples, which make these estimates independent, the sum is also chi-square distributed with 26 degrees of freedom. In order to guide the reader about the importance of the path, it is marked out in both summary tables if the corresponding path provided a significant path estimate at the 5% level on the international pooled data, according to Table 7.1.

In Table 7.6 highly significant modification indices are reported for paths from community and home factors to school conditions, to proximal teaching conditions and to teacher characteristics. These are the reflection of differences between countries in the basic schooling conditions and how these are related within each country. When community and home factors were controlled for, the paths from the second stage variables to the reading outcome showed relatively low deviations from the international model. Seventy-five percent of the 36 paths were not significant. This can be seen in Table 7.7, where especially the relationships between teacher characteristics and reading outcome were practically all invariant at the 1% significance level. For the interpretation of the results of the international path analysis this means that paths from School, Proximal Teaching Conditions, and Teacher Characteristics to Outcome variables reported in Figure 7.8 are reasonably adequate and generally valid. The significant effects found in the international parameter estimation of these relationships are supported in almost all participating countries and show a similar strength. When it comes to the relationships between the Instructional Behavior and the Outcome, the degree of invariance is low; only 25% of the 15 paths were not significant. In order to understand the effects of different teaching strategies, one has to explore the results from each individual country, whereas the influence of school resources seems to be of similar importance globally for reading performance.

---

[2] Appendix 7.3 is available on request from Ingrid Munck, Institute of International Education, University of Stockholm, S-106 91 Stockholm, Sweden.

Table 7.6

Maximum Modification Index for Path Model on Teaching by Country. Results from LISREL Two-Group Analysis on Covariance Matrices for International Pooled Data and Each Country's Data: Population A

Path from: Path to:	Stage 1 variables				Stage 2 variables						
	Type of community	Community resources	Number of books at home	Parental cooperation	Pupil/teacher ratio	Size of school	Size of school library	Class size	Instructional time	% students other tongue	% students need help
Stage 2											
Pupil/Tch. ratio	FIN 16.3*	CAC 14.8*	SIN 33.6*	FIN 15.9*	...	...	...	...	...	...	...
Size of school	CYP 73.3*	CYP 5.6	POR 32.6*	SIN 7.2*	...	...	...	...	...	...	...
Size of library	GRC 62.4*	GRC 38.1*	SWE 109.2*	GE2 18.8*	...	...	...	...	...	...	...
Class size	NOR 23.7*	ICE 18.9	ITA 30.2*	POR 9.7*	...	...	...	...	...	...	...
Instruct. time	CYP 60.7*	CYP 43.1	SIN 70.1*	BEF 10.4*	...	...	...	...	...	...	...
% Std. other lang.	HKO 20.9*	CYP 55.5*	TRI 120.8*	ITA 21.6*	...	...	...	...	...	...	...
% Std. need help	SWI 16.2	ICE 5.9*	USA 24.7*	INS 4.3*	...	...	...	...	...	...	...
Time same tchr.	NOR 9.5	DEN 4.8	USA 22.9*	HKO 13.8*	...	...	...	...	...	...	...
Teacher educ.	USA 16.7*	GRC 13.1*	IRE 6.7*	GRC 8.7*	...	...	...	...	...	...	...
Teacher exp.	DEN 5.8	POR 6.1	NET 8.4*	NET 7.0	...	...	...	...	...	...	...
Teacher sex	HKO 13.7*	INS 8.1*	NET 12.7*	SWE 45.0*	...	...	...	...	...	...	...
High dem. views	POR 12.8	POR 5.3*	CYP 64.5*	INS 7.5*	...	...	...	...	...	...	...
Stage 3											
Comprh. inst.	SPA 11.5*	INS 10.2*	SIN 7.5*	SIN 10.3*	SPA 13.6	GRC 4.4	SPA 5.8*	GRC 9.8*	CYP 8.6*	NET 7.7*	TRI 8.2
Phonics teaching	ICE 18.3*	INS 5.6*	INS 10.0*	FRA 5.3	ICE 10.9	ICE 38.9*	ICE 16.2*	ICE 44.0*	CYP 12.3*	GEI 3.0*	INS 4.7*
Assessm. emph.	GE2 13.3*	GE2 15.5	INS 10.9*	TRI 5.2	CAC 12.1	HUN 5.0*	USA 6.9*	ITA 27	ITA 7.4	SWE 6.3*	GRC 8.7*
A. low order skills	POR 5.1	POR 9.8*	TRI 12.8*	POR 5.0	BEF 9.1*	ICE 2.6*	BEF 2.0*	ICE 10.3*	SWI 7.3*	SWE 3.2*	POR 7.6*
Std-oriented rdg.	FRA 5.7	SWE 12.0	NEZ 8.6*	SWE 6.6	NEZ 5.7*	IRE 8.5*	SLO 12.5*	NEZ 12.9*	TRI 28.0*	SWE 6.6*	NET 27
Outcome											
Document	USA 20.1*	TRI 16.2*	SPA 24.9*	SIN 25.1*	SIN 13.3	GRC 36.6*	SIN 10.1	SIN 16.5*	ICE 11.6	GRC 27.4*	SIN 15.9*
Exposition	INS 11.3	NOR 9.3*	NOR 13.3*	SPA 10.6*	CYP 5.8*	INS 7.0*	SIN 8.9*	INS 173*	SPA 12.9*	SWE 5.5*	ICE 2.8*
Narrative	CAC 8.9*	TRI 4.7*	USA 14.5*	HUN 5.8*	SIN 5.5	SWI 5.0*	SWE 5.7*	CYP 6.4*	TRI 15.8*	SIN 19.0*	INS 8.7*

Path from:	Stage 2 variables (Cont.)					Stage 3 variables				
Path to:	Time same teacher	Teacher education	Teacher experience	Teacher Gender	High Demand views	Comprehen- sion instruct.	Phonics teaching	Assessment emphasis	Assessm. low order skills	Stdn- oriented reading
Stage 3										
Comprh. inst.	GE2 5.3*	USA 3.2*	HKO 11.8*	SWI 9.0*	USA 15.8*	--	--	--	--	--
Phonics teaching	SPA 4.6*	CAC 10.0*	NOR 3.3*	CYP 5.3*	USA 11.4*	--	--	--	--	--
Assessm. emph.	CYP 9.1*	SIN 4.4*	SWI 19.7*	SWI 7.1*	SIN 19.0*	--	--	--	--	--
A. low order skills	INS 12.6*	INS 8.9*	HKO 8.0*	NEZ 5.9*	USA 13.0*	--	--	--	--	--
Std-oriented rdg.	ITA 9.3*	GRC 5.2*	CYP 15.1	ITA 4.0*	CYP 10.0	--	--	--	--	--
Outcome										
Document	GRC 12.1*	FIN 6.2*	SPA 8.4*	FRA 8.1*	SPA 4.5*	IRE 13.0*	SPA 73	CAC 62	SIN 6.1*	SPA 11.5*
Exposition	POR 17.3*	POR 4.5*	POR 6.8*	FRA 5.2*	GE1 3.6*	GRC 11.9	POR 59	SPA 9.2	SPA 18.2*	HKO 8.0*
Narrative	BEF 73	CAC 9.4*	POR 7.0*	FRA 11.9*	NOR 2.9*	SIN 8.9*	NET 8.6*	GE2 14.7*	IRE 7.8*	SIN 11.1

* Significant path estimate at the 5% level (according to Table 7.1)

Table 7.7

Degree of Invariance over Countries in Path Model on Teaching.
Sums of Corresponding Modification Indices Over All Countries:
Population A. Degrees of Freedom = 26

Path from:	Stage 1 variables				Stage 2 variables						
Path to:	Type of community	Community resources	Number of books at home	Parental cooperation	Pupil/teacher ratio	Size of school	Size of school library	Class size	Instructional time	% students other tongue	% students need help
Stage 2											
Pupil/Tch. ratio	95.8α*	46.0α*	185.4α*	74.8α*	---	---	---	---	---	---	---
Size of school	395.4α*	47.7α	206.4α*	54.3α*	---	---	---	---	---	---	---
Size of library	252.9α*	164.2α*	668.9α*	87.8α*	---	---	---	---	---	---	---
Class size	120.5α*	91.4α	193.4α*	48.2α*	---	---	---	---	---	---	---
Instruct. time	128.2α*	63.6α	265.2α*	50.9α*	---	---	---	---	---	---	---
% Std. other lang.	132.5α*	231.8α*	457.5α*	186.6α*	---	---	---	---	---	---	---
% Std. need help	49.2α	38.4*	61.4α*	29.3*	---	---	---	---	---	---	---
Time same tchr.	44.1	31.5	50.2α*	92.5α*	---	---	---	---	---	---	---
Teacher educ.	96.7α*	88.6α*	56.1α*	68.0α*	---	---	---	---	---	---	---
Teacher exp.	30.9	26.8	41.5*	32.5	---	---	---	---	---	---	---
Teacher sex	56.7α*	35.8*	45.8α*	68.6α*	---	---	---	---	---	---	---
High dem. views	44.0	37.1*	345.3α*	41.1*	---	---	---	---	---	---	---
Stage 3											
Comprh. inst.	44.4α*	67.0α*	49.7α*	39.1*	39.1	35.6	24.0*	75.9α*	34.4*	25.8*	36.1
Phonics teaching	58.1α*	31.0*	54.2α*	26.0	49.2α	93.3α*	64.8α*	96.3α*	37.4*	13.8*	17.2*
Assessm. emph.	37.3*	40.6α	51.4α*	33.0	23.0	25.8*	21.3*	19.8	26.6	15.1*	22.2*
A. low order skills	32.3	38.4*	101.4α*	28.0	50.9α*	21.6*	12.1*	49.4α*	26.7*	14.7*	36.3*
Std-oriented rdg.	34.5	34.8	43.2*	43.8	34.8*	55.5α*	50.1α*	90.4α*	74.0α*	44.7*	19.1
Outcome											
Document	110.7α*	50.8α*	132.0α*	66.2α*	40.1	152.1α*	61.4α	55.4α*	38.8	120.1α*	56.9α*
Exposition	35.8	36.0*	82.3α*	75.5α*	28.9*	45.1*	40.1*	68.2α*	42.9*	30.6*	21.6*
Narrative	31.1*	21.4*	80.8α*	28.9*	29.6	31.5*	20.6*	38.6*	70.5α*	36.4*	48.6α*

Path from:	Stage 2 variables (Cont.)					Stage 3 variables				
Path to:	Time same teacher	Teacher education	Teacher experience	Teacher Gender	High Demand views	Comprehension instruct.	Phonics teaching	Assessment emphasis	Assessm. low order skills	Stdn-oriented reading
Stage 3										
Comprh. inst.	35.8*	22.9*	44.0*	42.8*	81.3¤*	--	--	--	--	--
Phonics teaching	29.3*	24.4*	25.2*	28.1*	48.5¤*	--	--	--	--	--
Assessm. emph.	45.8¤*	25.7*	69.0¤*	40.7*	108.2¤*	--	--	--	--	--
A. low order skills	47.5¤*	43.7*	47.4¤*	34.1*	87.6¤*	--	--	--	--	--
Std-oriented rdg.	52.7¤*	22.6*	76.5¤	15.7*	73.7¤	--	--	--	--	--
Outcome										
Document	39.3*	29.9*	44.0*	22.2*	26.9*	72.8¤*	38.3	55.7¤	28.4*	68.4¤*
Exposition	75.2¤*	27.2*	34.3*	32.9*	25.1*	40.5	23.4	61.0¤	72.5¤*	49.0¤*
Narrative	45.0	30.2*	35.7*	34.9*	18.6*	55.2¤*	46.2¤*	102.2¤*	53.1¤*	74.8¤

¤   The test for invariance is significant at the 1% level.

*   Significant path estimate at the 5% level (according to Table 7:1).

Discussion

To conclude, one might ask if the modeling approach presented above is sufficient in terms of capturing the main trends about the relationships in the reading literacy data. Certainly not, is the answer, and the analyses are also presented as a first step towards seeing the results with a bird's-eye view, in a broad perspective. One line of refinement is to reduce some of the assumptions made for the statistical analysis. The path analyses can be improved by introducing latent variables and reducing measurement error, which is especially important for the explanatory variables which may also vary in precision across countries (Munck, 1991). Another way of approaching the multivariate analysis is to take into account the hierarchical structure of the data and the dependencies imposed on the data by the sampling. It has become more and more evident that a multilevel analysis strategy is required in order to explore IEA data more adequately (Keeves, 1992). This can be done with so-called Hierarchical Linear Models within the framework of traditional regression models without latent variables (Bryk & Raudenbush, 1992). In recent years there has also been a dynamic development of applications of Multilevel Covariance Structure Analysis using the multiple-group structural equation software such as LISREL, LISCOMP, and EQS (Muthén, 1989, 1992; Härnqvist, Gustafsson, Muthén & Nelson 1993). According to Muthén (1992), the initial analyses of multilevel covariance structures consist of four steps: (1) conventional factor analysis based on the covariance matrix for the students, (2) estimation of the variance components and intraclass correlations of the different levels, (3) estimation of within-level covariance structures, and finally (4) estimation of between-level covariance structures. From these four steps, one proceeds to formulate a MFA (Multilevel Factor Analysis) model.

The large between-class model estimated and tested in this study can be looked upon as a contribution to the estimation of the between-class structure. It resulted in a model explaining about 40% of the variance in reading achievement on the class level and identified a number of invariant influences from school resources and teacher characteristics on the outcome performance of the class. As a next step these results have to be combined with student level influences into more complete models, including information from all questionnaires. During the period 1993–95, the Swedish research project Mutivariate Analyses of Literacy, MALI, will apply the methods of MFA to the IEA Reading Literacy data and explore the factor structures at the within- and between-country levels simultaneously. The work will begin with the test items, but will also consider the structure of the background variables. The plan for these analyses also covers the estimation of some hierarchical modeling, including latent variables and variables measured at different levels. Such modeling, with the available software and computer capacity, is very complex, and certainly the results will only scratch the surface of a more complete multivariate analysis of the rich IEA Reading Literacy data set.

8

Conclusions

WARWICK B. ELLEY

The IEA study of Reading Literacy was designed to assess the levels of student reading achievement in 32 education systems, and to investigate some of the hypothesized reasons for the observed differences in these levels, within and between countries. A major rationale for conducting such studies internationally is that the influence of a greater range of variables can be studied, variables which differ substantially between countries, but very little within countries. This chapter outlines the major findings of the project, the kinds of policy implications emanating from these findings, and some suggestions for further research on the data collected.

Findings on Relative Achievement Levels

To interpret the differences in achievement levels observed, readers need to accept the two assumptions that the national samples of students selected for study were comparable, and that the tests used were equally fair across school systems. The evidence presented in this report about the validity of these two assumptions is heartening. It is true that there were minor differences in age and grade between student samples in the 32 systems (see Figure 2.2), but the slight relationships found between these variables and achievement levels suggests that their influence on relative means and on correlations was negligible in all but a few cases (see Appendix G). As for the comparability of the tests, the statistical checks showed a very good fit for all test items after a screening process had been applied to remove the few exceptions. There are continuing concerns about possible cross-cultural differences in test-taking strategies, particularly at the younger age levels, in a few countries where children are not accustomed to formal testing (e.g., Denmark and West Germany). These caveats aside, the following findings can be stated with some confidence.

1.   National levels of reading literacy at school are highly correlated with the levels of economic and social development of the participating countries. In those countries where the indicators reveal strong economies, and high levels of health and adult literacy, most students become competent readers, regardless of such factors as the age of beginning instruction or the number of days in a school year. In this sense, schools appear to reflect the conditions

existing in their respective societies. Schools in poor communities rarely rise
above their prevailing circumstances in literacy development.
2.   A few school systems achieved above what would have been expected
according to their indices of national development. Students in Finland,
Hungary, Singapore, Hong Kong, and New Zealand achieved well above
expectation at both grade levels tested. The particular educational and cultural
factors responsible for these deviations deserve more investigation than they
have received.
3.   In absolute terms, the students of Finland showed the highest
achievement in reading in both populations despite the fact that they have had
fewer years in school than their counterparts in most countries. Among the
more plausible interpretations of their students' marked superiority are a long
literacy tradition in Finland, a high GDP per capita, the elevated status of
teachers, and a relatively homogeneous society, culturally and linguistically.
The small number of non-readers in Finland could also be related to the
phonetically regular orthography of their language. When there is (typically)
only one symbol for every sound, the acquisition of decoding skill is believed
to be simpler. After controlling for home and community resources and for
instructional factors, Finland remained the leading country. No doubt there are
further critical variables in the quality of the Finnish teaching programs, not
detected by the methodology of this IEA study.
4.   Other countries with consistently high performance levels, across all
domains and both populations, were Sweden, France, and New Zealand, while
the United States and Italy produced strong results at the Population A level.
Among the educational factors which differentiated such countries from the
low scoring countries, over and above economic and social development, were
the ready availability of books in school and a teaching force with more
education. Several variables predicted to be crucial, such as typical class size,
length of school year, age of beginning instruction, frequency of tests, and
level of preschool enrollment were not consistent or powerful in the extent to
which they differentiated between high and low scoring countries.
5.   Another measure of literacy expectation at the Population B level was
provided by national panels of judges in 12 countries. They studied the tests
and made estimates of the levels of achievement required for specified literacy
standards in their respective societies. Judged against those expected
standards, students of some low scoring countries performed almost as well as
those of high scoring countries. With minor exceptions, national achievement
levels appear to reflect local community expectations.

Findings on Voluntary Reading Activities

A prominent goal in most countries is to develop in students a lasting
interest in reading. Despite a disconcerting tendency toward "compliance

effects" (a tendency to respond favorably) in responding to the questionnaires in a few countries, the following major findings are well warranted.
1.   Gender differences generally supersede national differences in most aspects of voluntary reading. Thus girls in Population A reported more book reading than boys in nearly every country, but the pattern was reversed for the reading of comics and of directions. By age 14, however, boys reported more reading of books, and of magazines than girls did in most countries, while girls reported more interest in document reading than boys did.
2.   There were some differences in frequency of reading by country, however. Nordic countries reported heavy reading of newspapers, third world students claimed to devote more attention to books, while several European countries reported greater frequency of magazine reading.
3.   Popular themes in reading for Population B students are remarkably consistent across countries. Thus, humor, sports, music, and adventure are preferred book themes in nearly all countries; poetry, biography, and classics are popular in none. In magazines, 14-year-olds everywhere select the entertainment, sports, and music sections first, while in newspapers they devote prior attention to information about entertainment and to the comic strips and sports sections. Trends such as these have shown little change since an earlier IEA survey in 1971, although music and sports themes appear to have gained ground.
4.   In most countries frequent readers are better readers. In 15 of the 27 countries at Population A level, there was a positive linear relationship between frequency of reading and achievement; at Population B the same trend was observed in several Nordic and third world countries, but more often at this age the best readers reported no higher frequency levels than average readers. Apparently, frequency of voluntary reading is more important in the early stages of reading acquisition.

Home Background Influences on Reading

As in most surveys of this kind, home background and student level factors showed consistent relationships with achievement. In-depth analyses of these influences were precluded by the limitations of the data-gathering techniques and the restrictions placed on information collection in some countries, but the trends were clear, nevertheless.
1.   Socioeconomic status, as measured by material possessions at home, showed positive correlations with achievement between countries, to a marked degree, and within countries to a lesser degree. The trends were clearest in developing countries and least obvious in the wealthiest countries and in Hong Kong.
2.   Homes with a plentiful source of books and newspapers apparently provide more advantages for children's literacy development in all countries,

with similar effects in all domains. Correlations across countries were close to .40; those within countries between .15 and .30.

3.   Students with a home language different from that of the school scored considerably lower in the literacy tests used in this survey, especially in New Zealand, Germany (West), and Sweden. However, Singapore students, who acquire literacy in a non-native tongue from the beginning of their schooling, achieved at unexpectedly high levels.

4.   As in earlier surveys, heavy TV viewers were found to have lower reading scores in most countries. Nevertheless, in one group of European countries, higher achievement was shown by those who viewed TV for as many as 3–4 hr per day. A common factor there was regular exposure to foreign films with sub-titles in the local language. Frequent experience of captioned television may well be a highly motivating and effective context for improving reading ability.

5.   Gender differences were pervasive in achievement as well as in voluntary reading. In Population A, girls achieved at higher levels in all countries, especially in the Narrative domain. By age 14, however, the boys had halved the gender gap. They showed slightly better performance overall than girls in the Documents domain, but were still lagging in Narrative. There was some support for the hypothesis that a preponderance of women teachers increases the size of the gender difference. In addition, it was found that in countries where formal instruction begins at age five, the boys fell further behind the girls in both comprehension and in word recognition. An early start to formal instruction may not be beneficial for many later maturing boys.

6.   Students living in urban areas tend to show higher achievement than those from rural or small town environments, but this pattern is not universal. In a few countries the provision of rural facilities is such that no apparent disadvantage is observed, and in others a pattern of depressed living conditions in urban areas has reduced the size of the gap. Rural location need not be a handicap in literacy acquisition.

7.   Within most countries, the majority of students showed moderate skill in assessing their own reading ability. Only in a few developing countries did the correlations fall below .20. In most cases, students tended to overestimate their achievement level, except in the case of Finland, Hungary, Hong Kong, and Singapore. Girls rated themselves more highly than boys, usually with justification. There are clearly cultural explanations for the fact that some countries show greater modesty than others in rating their ability on an international scale.

8.   Student beliefs about how one becomes a good reader were found to vary somewhat cross-nationally. While most supported the view that one needs to like reading, and be able to concentrate well, there were systematic differences, internationally, in the priorities of the best readers. In high scoring countries they valued the presence of many good books, a lively imagination,

and the importance of vocabulary building; in low scoring countries they stressed the importance of learning to sound out words and having lots of drill at the hard things. These differences in student metacognitive beliefs may well reflect differences in the value systems of their teachers. Where many students are weak readers the teachers emphasize the value of disciplined effort; where standards are higher, teachers and students see more benefit in reading for enjoyment. The causal links in these contrasts deserve further study.

Findings on School Resources

Schools need resources to provide quality instruction. Without ready access to good books, well qualified teachers, cooperative parents, and satisfactory physical circumstances, teachers' efforts are believed to count for little. Just how important are these factors in literacy education?

1.   Access to books in the school's local community is one clear indicator of literacy standards between countries. The correlations between achievement and access to public libraries and bookstores were .72 and .57 between countries for Population A, and .86 and .82 for Population B. However, the within-country correlations dropped in most cases to less than .10, largely due to lack of variation within countries. Where provision within countries is homogeneous, clear relationships cannot be established.

2.   Certain teacher characteristics, such as native language and years of post-secondary education, also differentiated clearly between high scoring and low scoring countries.

3.   Countries with generally smaller classes and smaller schools produced better scores, on average. Within countries, however, schools which had larger school rolls and classes tended to produce better results, partly because they were located in more favored communities. Small rural schools are frequently disadvantaged in these respects, and the tendency for schools to place weaker pupils in smaller classes, so that they might attract greater individual attention from teachers, complicates this relationship within countries.

4.   Book resources in the school constituted a major variable in differentiating between countries. Those education systems which had built up large school libraries, classroom libraries, and teacher libraries produced better achievement levels in both populations, before and after adjustment for differences in economic and social development. However, when home and other community resources were partialled out, the correlation for size of school library at the elementary school level dropped to zero.

Findings on Teaching

1.   In Population A, the students of female teachers outperformed those of male teachers in most countries, and significantly so in ten; in Population B, the students of female teachers showed significantly better results in six countries, those of males in only two countries. Probable explanations are

found in differences in recruitment patterns due to the sex role expectations of academically successful young people.

2.   When teachers ranked their aims in teaching reading, greatest priority was given in most countries to improving reading comprehension and to developing a lasting interest in reading. High scoring countries however, gave greater weight to encouragement–interest aims, low scoring countries to skill emphasis.

3.   In most countries teachers reported devoting more instructional time to narrative reading, and least to documents, at both age levels.

4.   Nearly all teachers use some form of grouping for reading instruction, usually arranged by ability. Only in Finland and Italy was grouping by interest level more common. Grouping was used more extensively in large classes. There was no substantial correlation between grouping practice and achievement levels.

5.   A LISREL analysis of a pooled international data set representing 4800 classrooms in Population A showed that most variance in reading achievement was attributed to the literacy level of the home. After adjustment for differences in home and community resources, few international variables showed consistent influence across the whole data set. Most notable were the positive effects of smaller classes, more instructional time, and the proportion of female teachers. The number of students in a class needing remedial help was negatively associated with achievement, as one might expect. The potential value of other instructional factors was difficult to determine, partly because of pervasive compliance effects.

6.   Within countries, significant correlations between teaching constructs and achievement, after adjustment for home and community resources, were few and varied. Where the teacher reported a strong emphasis on student-oriented reading, achievement was significantly higher in six countries; where they stressed the assessment of low-order skills it was lower in six countries. A comprehension instruction emphasis correlated positively with achievement in only three countries and a phonics emphasis negatively in two.

7.   When the 20 classrooms within each country that achieved most above expectation (relative to their level of home resources), were compared with the 20 classrooms that achieved furthest below expectation, a variety of different factors emerged as significant. In 17 countries, the extent to which teachers read in their leisure time discriminated between high and low classrooms. Other strong factors were teacher gender (favoring females) and length of teaching experience (favoring the more experienced). Effective teachers more often valued accuracy and order in eight countries; they emphasized assessment, comprehension instruction, and student-centered reading in nine or more countries; they often encouraged students to read and took their interests into account in five or more countries.

Implications for Policy-Makers

Cross-sectional surveys rarely produce findings with definitive recommendations for educators. Rather they have the potential to build up the knowledge base of policy-makers, and to confirm or reject common beliefs about what is effective and what is irrelevant to raising educational achievement levels.

It was perhaps not surprising that relatively few relationships were found to be stable and consistent across all countries. Certain findings, like the gender differences in achievement, are clear-cut, but these are not readily changed. Others, like the link between provision of books and achievement, are strong and are more often under the control of the educator. The following section lists those findings which have emerged internationally, and which educators would be wise to take account of, if they are to make more informed decisions in raising literacy levels.

Many other implications, which apply in specific cases, will no doubt be detected at national and local levels.

1.   Countries which allocate more funds into education do produce better achievement results. No country with low GNP per capita was among the high scoring countries. National efforts and international aid should be devoted to equalizing funding efforts if greater equality of outcomes is to be achieved.

2.   Access to large stocks of books is a prerequisite of good reading comprehension. Schools and communities with a dearth of books need compensatory provision in schools if it is desired to avoid a group of low achievers in schools.

3.   A strong literacy tradition in the society is another prerequisite for high literacy levels in the school. Countries with higher newspaper circulation, and many books in homes (sure indicators of the priority accorded to reading), were mostly in the forefront in this survey. National campaigns to stress the importance of role models and reading in the community at large are indicated by these findings.

4.   A general policy of a late start to formal instruction in schools is not a serious handicap for most students in learning to read. By age 9, countries in which students began formal instruction in reading only at age 7 are frequently among the best readers. The same trend was found in the first IEA Reading Survey, at age 10 (Thorndike, 1973). However, there are probably other reasons for their advantage, and across all countries, an earlier start (6 years), other things being equal, was found to be linked with slightly higher levels of achievement at age 9 (Elley, 1992).

5.   The degree of parental cooperation for the school's goals in literacy was a regular concomitant of high achievement. Thus, efforts to improve this kind of cooperation appears to be indicated in most countries.

230   *Warwick B. Elley*

6.   A school's own initiatives to raise standards were regularly associated with higher literacy levels. Where schools devoted effort to school newspapers, drama clubs, teacher libraries, literature clubs, and the like, students appeared to benefit.
7.   The more reading students do in their leisure time, the higher their achievement levels. Thus, efforts should be made to promote the reading habit outside of school hours, and to ensure that time is set aside for independent reading at school.
8.   Countries which have worked to reduce class size and to improve teacher/pupil ratios have produced higher achievement levels. This link is less apparent within some countries, as many schools deliberately arrange for weaker students to be put in small classes. Thus, these classes tend to show lower literacy levels. But when averages are calculated between countries, the confusing effects of these within-country tendencies are reduced so that the expected pattern of advantage for smaller classes is revealed.
9.   The more years of education teachers have, the better their students' literacy levels, even after adjusting for differences in wealth. Thus, policies designed to raise teachers' educational levels are likely to be productive.
10.   Good readers' own perceptions of the best ways to become a good reader suggest that internationally high reading standards are more likely with a school policy which encourages students to enjoy reading rather than one which overemphasizes skill building at the expense of interest.

Further Tasks for Researchers

A project that collects hard data from 210,000 students and 10,000 teachers in 32 countries cannot yield all its secrets in the first analyses. There is information generated in the IEA Reading Literacy survey which should continue to occupy secondary analysts for years to come.

In this report, findings have focused on differences in national means and the correlates of those differences. Some multivariate analyses were conducted, and contrasts between more and less effective schools were examined. However, further analysis is clearly warranted, at the national and international level.

Some international studies that could well be profitable are listed below.
1.   A comparative study of minority language groups in each country may help identify policies which are productive for meeting the needs of such groups.
2.   A contrastive analysis of the best and worst readers in each country could reveal variables which are consistently linked with high levels of achievement in reading.
3.   A qualitative study of the most successful teachers and schools in each country could be productive in generating new hypotheses.

4.   Ethnographic studies of schools in disadvantaged contexts which produce high literacy levels may be helpful.

5.   An extension of the national panel ratings exercise to include all countries would help establish with greater confidence the relationships between expectations and achievement.

6.   A comparison of language groups might identify likely causes of semantic or orthographic difficulties in reading tests.

7.   Further validity studies of the IEA tests could help establish what other kinds of literacy tasks students at different score levels are capable of performing.

8.   A comparison of performance levels in adjacent grades on the Reading Literacy tests in order to confirm the accuracy of age adjustments in different countries and different language groups (see Appendix G).

9.   Administration of the Population B tests to grades in which most students are 15 and 16 years of age, in order to judge how much growth occurred beyond the Population B level.

10.   Further exploration of the compliance effect in responding to questionnaires, to determine the conditions under which it is most likely to occur. Such a study would be helpful for future IEA surveys.

11.   The voluntary reading patterns of Population B students should be analyzed by gender to determine the extent to which popular themes are universal in their gender-relatedness.

12.   Qualitative analyses could be conducted on the schools which produced the highest and lowest scores on book reading indices at both age levels in order to determine the kinds of policies which foster such habits.

13.   Hierarchical linear modeling (HLM) analyses, for both populations, may well throw more light on the relationships between achievement levels and different categories of home and school variables.

Further studies are already underway on gender and cultural influences on literacy achievement, and an analysis of the effects of school climate is also envisaged. Many other analyses are also planned at the national level for both populations, and some are envisaged across sets of related countries.

References

Akinnaso, F.N. (1991). Literacy and the individual consciousness. In E.M. Jennings & A.C. Purves (Eds.), *Literate systems and individual lives: perspectives on literacy and schooling* (pp. 73–94). Albany, NY: State University of New York Press.

Anderson, R.C., Wilson, P.T., & Fielding, L.G. (1988). Growth in reading and how children spend their time outside of school. *Reading Research Quarterly, 23,* 3, 285–303.

Angoff, W.H. (1971). Scales, norms and equivalent scores. In R.L. Thorndike (Ed.), *Educational measurement* (2nd Ed. pp. 508–600). Washington, DC: American Council on Education.

Archer, A.J., & Elley, W.B. (1993). Do print size and line length affect children's reading comprehension? *Research in Education, 49,* May, 75–76.

Barr, R., & Dreeben, R. (1991). Grouping students for reading instruction. In R. Barr, M.L. Kamil, P.B. Mosenthal, & P.D. Pearson (Eds.), *Handbook of reading research* (Vol. 2). New York: Longman.

Beaton, A. (1994). *IEA reading literacy study: A technical report.* The Hague: IEA.

Bryk, A.S., & Raudenbush, S.W. (1992). *Hierarchical linear models: Applications and data analysis methods.* Newbury Park: Sage Publications.

Calfee, R., & Drum, P. (1986). Research on teaching reading. In M.C. Wittrock (Ed.), *Handbook of research on teaching* (3rd Ed.). New York: Longman.

Carceles, G. (1990). World literacy prospects at the turn of the century. *Comparative Education Review, 34,* 1, 4–20.

Cheung, K.C., Keeves, J.P., Sellin, N., & Tsoi, S.C. (1990). Multilevel analysis in educational research. *International Journal of Educational Research, 14,* 3, 215–319.

Clifford, G.J. (1984). Buch und Lesen: Historical perspectives on literacy and schooling. *Review of Educational Research, 54*(4), 472–500.

Coleman, J.S. (1990). Social Capital. In T. Husén & T.N. Postlethwaite (Eds.), *International encyclopedia of education supplementary volume 2,* pp. 580–582.

Coleman, J.S., Campbell, E.R., Hobson, C.J., McPartland, J., Mead, A.M., Weinfeld, F.B., & York, R.L. (1966). *Equality of educational opportunity.* Washington, DC: U.S. Government Printing Office.

Connerton, P. (1989). *How societies remember.* Cambridge: Cambridge University Press.

Cunningham, A.E., Stanovich, K.E., & Wilson M.R. (1991). Cognitive variation in adult students differing in reading ability. In T. Carr & B. Levy (Eds.), *Reading and development: Component skills approaches.* New York: MacMillan.

Downing, J. (1973). *Comparative reading.* New York: MacMillan.

Elley, W.B. (1991). Acquiring literacy in a second language: The effect of book-based programs. *Language Learning, 41,* 3, 375–411.

Elley, W.B. (1992). *How in the world do students read?* Hamburg: IEA.

Elley, W.B., & Mangubhai, F. (1992). Multiple choice and open-ended items in reading tests. *Studies in Education Evaluation, 18*(2), 191–199.

Fishbein, M., & Ajzen, I. (1975). *Belief, attitude, intention, and behavior. An introduction to theory and research.* London: Addison-Wesley.

Foster, P.J., & Purves, A.C. (1990). Literacy and society, with particular reference to the non-Western world. In R. Barr, M.L. Kamil, P.B. Mosenthal and P.D. Pearson (Eds.), *Handbook of reading research* (Vol. 2). White Plains, NY: Longman.

Fuller, B. (1987). What school factors raise achievement in the third world? *Review of Educational Research, 57,* 3, 255–292.

Gorman, T., Purves, A.C., & Degenhart, R.E. (1988). The IEA study of written composition In *The international writing tasks and scoring scales.* Oxford: Pergamon Press.

Graff, H. (Ed.). (1981). *Literacy and social development in the west: A reader.* Cambridge: Cambridge University Press.

Greaney, V., & Neuman, S.B. (1990). The functions of reading. *Reading Research Quarterly, 25,* 3, 172–195.

Guthrie, J.T. (1981). Reading in New Zealand: Achievement and volume. *Reading Research Quarterly, 17,* 1, 6–27.

Guthrie, J.T., & Greaney, V. (1991). Literacy Acts. In R. Barr, M.L. Kamil, P. Mosenthal, & P.D. Pearson (Eds.) *Handbook of reading research* (Vol. 2). New York: Longman.

Guthrie, J.T., & Seifert, M. (1984). *Measuring readership: Rationale and technique.* Paris: UNESCO.

Haddad, W., Carnoy, M., Rinaldi, R., & Regel, O. (1990) *Education and development.* Washington, DC: World Bank.

Härnqvist, K., Gustafsson, J.-E., Muthén, B.O., & Nelson, G. (1993). Hierarchical models of ability at individual and class levels. Manuscript submitted for publication.

Heynemann, S., & Loxley, W. (1983). The effects of primary school quality on academic achievement in twenty-nine high- and low-income countries. *American Journal of Sociology, 88,* 6, 1162–1194.

Hulin, C.L. (1987). A psychometric theory of evaluations of item and scale translations. *Journal of Cross-Cultural Psychology, 18,* 2, 115–142.

Human development report (1991). New York: UNDP.

Johnson, D.D. (1974). Sex differences in reading across cultures. *Reading Research Quarterly, 9,* 1, 67–86.

Jöreskog, K.G., & Sörbom Dag. (1989). *LISREL 7: A guide to the program and applications* (2nd Ed.). Chicago: SPSS Inc.

Keeves, J.P. (1992). *The IEA technical handbook.* The Hague: IEA.

Keeves, J.P., & Sellin, N. (1988). *Multilevel data. Educational research, methodology and measurement: An international handbook.* Oxford: Pergamon Press.

Kirsch, I.S., & Guthrie, J.T. (1984). The concept and measurement of functional literacy. *Reading Research Quarterly, 13,* 4, 485–507.

Kyostio, O.K. (1980). Is learning to read easy in a language in which the grapheme–phoneme correspondences are regular? In J.F. Kavanagh & R.L. Venezky (Eds.), *Orthography, Reading, and Dyslexia.* Baltimore, MD: University Press.

Langer, J. A., & Allington, R. L. (1992). Curriculum research in reading and writing. In P. W. Jackson (Ed.), *Handbook of research on curriculum* (pp. 687–725). New York: Macmillan.

Levine, K. (1986). *The social context of literacy.* London: Routledge & Kegan.

Lohnes, P.R., & Gray, M.M. (1972). Intellectual development and the cooperative reading studies. *Reading Research Quarterly, 8,* 52–61.

Lundberg, I., & Linnakylä, P. (1993). *Teaching reading around the world.* Hamburg: IEA.

Munck, I.M.E. (1979). Model building in comparative education: Applications of the LISREL method to cross-national survey data. *IEA monograph studies, No. 10.* Stockholm: Almqvist & Wiksell International.

Munck, I.M.E. (1991). A path analysis of cross-national data taking measurement errors into account. In P.P. Biemer et al (Eds.), *Measurement errors in surveys.* New York: John Wiley & Sons, Inc.

Muthén, B.O. (1989). Latent variable modeling in heterogeneous populations. *Psychometrika, 54,* 557–585.

Muthén, B. (1990). Mean and covariance structure analysis of hierarchical data (unpublished). UCLA Statistics Series, 62.

Muthén, B. (1991). Multilevel factor analysis of class and student achievement components. *Journal of Educational Measurement, 28.*

Muthén, B. (1992). Multilevel covariance structure analysis. Version 2. *Sociological Methods & Research.*

Muthén, B. (1994). Multilevel covariance structural analysis. *Sociological Methods & Research.*

NAEP (1985). *The reading report card.* Princeton, NJ: Educational Testing Service.

Neuman, S.B., & Kostinen, P. (1992). Captioned television as comprehensible input: Effects of incidental word learning from context for language minority students. *Reading Research Quarterly, 27,* 1, 94–106.

Osgood, C.E., May, W.H., & Miron, M.S. (1975). *Cross-cultural universals of affective measuring.* Urbana, IL: University of Illinois Press.

Palincsar, A.A., & Brown, A.L. (1984). Reciprocal teaching of comprehension-fostering and comprehension-monitoring activities. *Cognition and Instruction, 1,* 117–175.

Peaker, G. (1967). The regression analyses of the national survey. In United Kingdom, Dept. of Education and Science, *Children and their primary school* (Vol. 2, Appendix 4). London: HMSO.

Peaker, G. (1971). *The Plowden children four years later.* London: NFER.

Pearson, P.D., & Dole, J.A. (1987). Explicit comprehension instruction: A review of research and a new conceptualization of instruction. *Elementary School Journal, 88*(2), 151–165.

Pearson, P.D., & Fielding, L. (1991). Comprehension instruction. In R. Barr, M.L. Kamil, P.B. Mosenthal, & P.D. Pearson (Eds.), *Handbook of reading research* (Vol. 2). New York: Longman

Postlethwaite, T.N., & Ross, K. (1992). *Effective schools in reading: Implications for educational planners.* Hamburg: IEA

Preston, R.C. (1962). Reading achievement of German and American children. *School and Society, 90,* 350-354.

Purves, A.C. (1973). *Literature education in ten countries.* Stockholm: Almquist and Wiksell.

Purves, A.C. (1992). *The IEA study of written composition II: Education and performance in 14 countries.* Oxford: Pergamon Press.

Rosenshine, B., & Stevens, R. (1984). Classroom instruction in reading. In P.D. Pearson, R. Barr, M.L. Kamil, & P. Mosenthal (Eds.), *Handbook of reading research* (Vol. 1). New York: Longman.

Ross, K.N., & Mählck, L. (1990). *Planning the quality of education: The collection and use of data for informed decision-making.* Oxford: Pergamon.

Ross, K.N., & Postlethwaite, T.N. (1989). *Indonesia: Quality of basic education* (Vol. 1). Jakarta, Indonesia: Ministry of Education and Culture.

Ross, K.N., & Postlethwaite, T.N. (1992). *Indicators of the quality of education: A summary of a national study of primary schools in Zimbabwe, IIEP Report No. 96.* Paris: IIEP.

Schiefelbein, E., & Simmons, J. (1981). *Determinants of school achievement: A review of research for developing countries.* Ottawa, Canada: International Development Research Center.

Stahl, S.A. (1992). Reading Instruction: The State of the Art. Commissioned by the International Institute for Educational Planning, Paris (unpublished).

Stahl, S.A., & Miller, P.D. (1989). Whole language and language experience approaches for beginning reading: A quantitative research synthesis. *Review of Educational Research, 59,* 87–116.

Stanovich, K. (1986). Matthew effects in reading: Some consequences of individual differences. *Reading Research Quarterly, 21,* 360–407.

Stanovich, K.E. (1991). Word recognition: Changing perspectives. In R. Barr, M.L. Kamil, P. Mosenthal, & P.D. Pearson (Eds.), *Handbook of reading research* (Vol. 2). London: Longman.

Stevenson, H.W., & Stiegler, J.W. (1992). *The learning gap.* New York: Summit Books.

Teale, W., & Sulzby, E. (1986). *Emergent literacy: Writing and reading.* Norwood, NJ: Ablex.

Thorndike, R.L. (1973). *Reading comprehension education in fifteen countries. International studies in evaluation III.* Stockholm: Almqvist and Wiksell.

UNESCO (1991). *World Education Report.* Paris: UNESCO.

Wagner, D.A. (1990). Literacy assessment in the third world: A preview and proposed schema for survey use. *Comparative Education Review, 34,* 1, 112–138.

Wagner, D.A. (1991). Literacy in a global perspective. In I. Lundberg & T. Husén (Eds.), *Literacy in a world of change: Perspectives on reading and reading disability.* Stavanger: Stavanger Center for Reading Research.

Wagner, D. (1993). *Literacy in Morocco.* Cambridge: Cambridge University Press.

Wells, G. (1986). *The meaning makers. Children learning language and using language to learn.* Portsmouth, NH: Heinemann.

Williams, J., & Batten, M. (1981). The quality of school life. *Research Monograph, No. 12.* Melbourne, Australia: Australian Council for Educational Research.

Wolf, R.M. (1993) Data quality and norms in international studies. *Measurement and Evaluation in Counseling and Development,* April 1993.

World Declaration on Education for All (1990). *Meeting basic needs: A vision for the 1990s.* New York: Inter-Agency Commission for World Conference on Education for All.

Appendix A

Personnel of the IEA Reading Literacy Study

International Coordinating Center Staff (University of Hamburg, Germany)

Professional Staff

T. Neville Postlethwaite, International Coordinator (1989–1991)
Andreas Schleicher, International Data Manager (1989–1992); International Coordinator (1992)
Dieter Kotte, Assistant International Coordinator (1989–1990)
R. Elaine Degenhart, Assistant International Coordinator (1990–1992)
Stefan Seyfert, Assistant International Data Manager

Data Processing Team

Michael Bruneforth
Dirk Hastedt
Heiko Jungclaus
Knut Schwippert

Administrative and Publications Staff

Julianne Friedrich
Jedidiah M. Harris
Britta Niemann
Bettina Westphalen
Ellen Ziesmann

International Steering Committee

Albert E. Beaton, Educational Testing Service, Princeton, NJ, United States
Warwick B. Elley, University of Canterbury, New Zealand (Chair)
John Guthrie, University of Maryland, United States (1989–91)
Ingvar Lundberg, University of Umeå, Sweden
Francis Mangubhai, University of Southern Queensland, Australia

Alan C. Purves, State University of New York (Albany), United States (IEA Standing Committee Representative)
Kenneth N. Ross, Deakin University, Australia (Sampling Referee)

National Research Coordinators

Dominique and Annette La Fontaine, University de Liège, Belgium
Serara Moahi, Ministry of Education, Gabarone, Botswana
Victor Froese, University of British Columbia, Vancouver, BC, Canada
Constantinos Papanastasiou, Pedagogical Institute, Nicosia, Cyprus
Jan Mejding, Danish Institute for Educational Research, Copenhagen, Denmark
Pirjo Linnakylä, University of Jyväskylä, Finland
Emilie Barrier, Centre International d'Études Pédagogiques, Sèvres, France
Rainer Lehmann, University of Hamburg, Germany
Georgia Kontogiannopoulou-Polydorides, University of Patras, Greece
Cheung Yat-shing, Hong Kong Polytechnic, Hong Kong
Judit Kádár-Fülöp, National Institute of Public Education, Budapest, Hungary
Sigridur Valgeirsdottir, Institute of Educational Research, Reykjavik, Iceland
Jiyono, Balitbang Dikbud, Jakarta, Indonesia
Michael O. Martin, St. Patrick's College, Dublin 9, Ireland
Pietro Lucisano, Istituto di Filosofia (Pedagogia), Roma, Italy
Kees de Glopper and Martha Otter, S.C.O., Amsterdam, Netherlands
Hans Wagemaker, Ministry of Education, Wellington, New Zealand
Samuel O. Ayodele, University of Ibadan, Nigeria
Finn Egil Tønnessen, Senter for Leseforsking, Stavanger, Norway
Mona D. Valisno, National Educational Testing and Research Center, Manila, Philippines
Maria José Rau, Ministério de Educaçïo, Lisbon, Portugal
Beatrice Tay, Ministry of Education, Singapore
Marjan Setinc and Barbara Japelj, University of Ljubljana, Slovenia
Guillermo Gil, Ministerio de Educación y Ciencia, Madrid, Spain
Karin Taube, University of Stockholm, Sweden
François Stoll and Philip Notter, Psychologisches Institut, Zürich, Switzerland
Malee Nitsaisook, Suan Sunandha Teachers' College, Bangkok, Thailand
Hyacinth E. McDowall, Ministry of Education, Port-of-Spain, Trinidad and Tobago
Marilyn Binkley, U.S. Department of Education, Washington, DC, United States
Armando Morles, Universidad Pedagógica Experimental Libertador, Caracas, Venezuela
Rosemary Moyana, University of Zimbabwe, Harare, Zimbabwe

Appendix B

Target Populations and Samples

The two target populations were defined as follows:

Population A: All students attending mainstream schools on a full-time basis at the grade level in which most students were aged 9:00–9:11 years during the first week of the eighth month of the school year.

Population B: All students attending mainstream schools on a full-time basis at the grade level in which most students were aged 14:00–14:11 years during the first week of the eighth month of the school year.

From the above definitions it can be seen that students in separate special education schools were excluded from the defined populations.

Tables B.1 and B.2 present for Populations A and B the percentage of students omitted from the defined population, the percentage of students not given the tests in the classroom during the test administration, the number of schools or classes in the planned sample, and the number of schools or classes in the achieved sample (i.e., the number of schools or classes for which data are available in the data files handed in). Those not given the tests during the testing session were those deemed (1) unable to take any items on the test because of learning or physical disability (typically mainstreamed children), or (2) to have insufficient knowledge of the language of the test even to follow the general instructions (typically recent immigrants).

One prior requirement of the IEA Reading Literacy Study was that there should be a response rate of at least 80% of the schools or classes planned to be drawn. It will be noted that asterisks have been placed next to Nigeria, Thailand, and Zimbabwe, countries which participated in Population B only. The asterisks indicate that the response rates were lower than 80%. Care should be exercised with data from these three populations.

Information is given below on the nature of the students omitted from the defined population or on the definition of the population. For example, in the first row of Tables B.1 and B.2 it can be seen that 3.6 and 3.8% of Belgian students have been omitted from Populations A and B respectively. In the notes below, it will be seen that these are students from schools in the francophone administered part of Belgium who were instructed in Flemish or German.

Table B.1

Information on Omitted Population, Size of Sample and School Response Rates for Population A

	POPULATION A					
	Students			Schools		
Country	% Excluded from defined pop.	% Excluded during test	Number in final sample	Planned	Achieved	% Response
Belgium/Fr	3.6	0.32	2729	150	149	99.3
Canada/BC	1.2	2.33	2682	157	157	100.0
Cyprus	0.0	0.44	1515	182	181	99.5
Denmark†	0.0	3.27	3368	212	209	99.0
Finland	9.2	0.00	1557	71	71	100.0
France (State only)	16.0	0.00	1887	140	136	97.1
Germany/E	0.0	0.13	1906	100	100	100.0
Germany/W	0.5	0.85	2953	150	150	100.0
Greece	0.0	2.98	3616	176	175	99.4
Hong Kong	2.6	0.00	3312	167	167	100.0
Hungary	2.4	0.00	3174	144	144	100.0
Iceland (all schools)	0.5	1.43	4129	180	180	100.0
Indonesia (7 provinces only)	0.0	0.00	3393	176	174	98.9
Ireland	4.2	0.14	2783	134	122	91.0
Italy (state only)	8.6	1.10	2281	177	154	87.0
Netherlands	0.0	0.18	1737	91	91	100.0
New Zealand	0.0	0.32	3058	177	176	99.4
Norway	0.3	1.43	2566	191	191	100.0
Portugal (mainland only)	0.0	0.11	2799	165	145	87.9
Singapore (all schools)	0.0	0.68	7488	206	206	100.0
Slovenia	0.0	0.10	3421	140	140	100.0
Spain	11.1	0.00	8674	324	324	100.0
Sweden	0.0	0.91	4358	124	123	99.0
Switzerland	0.0	0.80	3411	225	225	100.0
Trinidad/Tobago †	0.0	0.01	3687	184	182	98.9
United States	4.9	2.33	6848	200	165	82.5
Venezuela	0.2	0.22	4819	181	161	89.0

†These systems sampled classes and not schools.

Table B.2

Information on Omitted Population, Size of Sample and School
Response Rates for Population B

	POPULATION B					
	Students			Schools		
Country	% Excluded from defined pop.	% Excluded during test	Number in final sample	Planned	Achieved	% Response
Belgium.(Fr)	3.8	0.00	2796	153	144	91.7
Botswana	0.0	0.00	4768	137	137	100.0
Canada (BC)	1.1	0.38	4830	216	197	91.2
Cyprus (all schools)	0.0	0.07	1459	52	52	100.0
Denmark†	0.0	0.51	3832	207	209	100.0
Finland	12.4	0.00	1352	71	71	100.0
France (State only)	21.0	0.00	2582	140	136	97.1
Germany (E)†	0.0	0.12	1885	100	100	100.0
Germany (W)†	0.5	0.36	4302	200	196	98.0
Greece	1.4	0.39	3968	148	147	99.3
Hong Kong	1.2	0.00	3160	158	158	100.0
Hungary	0.25	0.00	3455	144	144	100.0
Iceland (all schools)	2.6	0.10	4000	124	124	100.0
Ireland	0.0	0.11	3817	162	151	93.2
Italy (state only)	4.8	0.80	3180	175	173	98.9
Netherlands	0.0	0.00	3897	174	162	93.1
New Zealand	0.0	0.34	3174	125	124	99.2
Nigeria* (six states only)	0.0	0.00	2365	136	80	58.8
Norway	0.2	0.47	2446	142	138	97.2
Philippines	39.0	0.00	9713	245	244	99.6
Portugal (mainland only)	0.0	0.00	3529	136	130	95.6
Singapore (all schools)	0.0	0.00	4893	142	142	100.0
Slovenia	0.0	0.00	3328	139	139	100.0
Spain	6.5	0.00	8945	318	318	100.0
Sweden	0.0	0.52	3618	149	149	100.0
Switzerland	0.0	0.34	6488	362	322	89.0
Thailand*	0.8	0.00	2753	217	139	64.0
Trinidad/Tobago	0.0	0.00	3044	93	93	100.0
United States	4.9	0.58	3587	204	165	80.9
Venezuela	1.2	0.20	4434	178	162	91.0
Zimbabwe*	0.0	0.00	2749	192	143	74.5

*These systems had a response rate of less than 80 percent.
†These systems sampled classes and not schools.

Notes on Excluded Students From Defined Target Populations

Belgium/Fr.: All students in French-speaking Belgium instructed in Flemish or German were excluded.

Canada/BC: Students in Government Native Indian schools excluded.

Finland: Swedish-speaking and laboratory schools excluded.

France: Overseas territories and private schools in mainland France were excluded. Private schools = 16% of all students at Population A, 21% of all students at Population B.

Germany/W: Students in non-graded private schools were excluded (0.5%).

Greece: In Population B, 1.4% in evening schools excluded.

Hong Kong: International schools, ESF Foundation schools, schools not participating in Secondary School Places Allocation System (SSPA), and schools with class size of less than 20 were excluded.

Hungary: Very small schools in remote areas and ungraded schools were excluded.

Iceland: Schools where there were fewer than five students in target population were excluded.

Indonesia: Excluded schools outside of Java, Riau (Sumatra), and East Nusa Tenggara. The included population accounts for 70% of the population.

Ireland: Private schools and schools with fewer than five students in the target population were excluded.

Italy: Non-government schools excluded.

Nigeria: Excluded schools outside of Lagos, Ogun, Oyo, Ondo, Bendel, and Kwara.

Norway: Schools for Lapps excluded.

Philippines: Schools in earthquake and insurgency areas (about 39% of the population) excluded.

Spain: Students from schools with fewer than ten students in the defined grade and from schools where medium of instruction not Castillian Spanish were excluded.

Thailand: Laboratory schools and schools controlled by the Department of Fine Arts and Culture were excluded. However, only 33% of 14-year-olds were in school.

United States: Fifty states (Mainland, Alaska, and Hawaii) constituted the target population. Students in eligible schools not capable of taking test (about 4.9% of each population) were excluded.

Venezuela: Students attending private rural schools were excluded.

Appendix C

Passages and Test Items

Table C.1

Passages and Items in Final Test: Population A

Passage	Number of items	Topic
Narrative /		
Bird and Elephant A/BIRD	5	A mother bird chases away an elephant who was bothering her family.
Boy and Dog A/DOG	6	A boy who wants a dog, pretends he has one, in order to show he can look after it.
Lonely Shark AB/SHARK	5	A family of sardines befriends a lonely shark, but suffers a cruel fate.
Grandpa A/GRANDPA	6	A frail old man is harshly treated by his family, until they realize that they too will become helpless.
Expository		
Postcard A/POST-CARD	2	Two children report to their parents on their holiday.
Walrus A/WALRUS	6	Description of walrus and its lifestyle.
Quicksand A/QUICKSAND	3	Description of quicksand and how to behave when caught in it.
Marmots AB/MARMOTS	4	Description of the habitat of a family of marmots.
Trees A/TREES	6	Description of method used to assess the age of trees.
Documents		
Map of Island A/ISLAND	4	Students asked to locate points on a simple map of an island.
School Timetable A/SCHOOL TIMES	3	Students locate lessons on school timetable.
Bar Graph A/BAR GRAPH	4	Students interpret bar graph showing number of bottles collected by four classes.
Bus Timetable A/BUS	4	Students locate places and times on bus timetable.
Table of Contents A/CONTENTS	3	Students identify authors and page numbers in table of contents.
Temperature Chart AB/TEMPERATURE	5	Students locate times and trends on temperature chart over 4 days.

Table C.2

Passages and Items in Final Test: Population B

Passage	Number of items	Topic
Narrative		
Killing the Fox B/FOX	5	A man kills a fox he comes on unexpectedly and reflects on what he has done.
The Village Mute B/MUTE	5	A mute alerts the village to the arrival of builders who transform a school.
Lonely Shark AB/SHARK	5	A family of sardines befriends a lonely shark, but suffers a cruel fate.
Magician's Revenge B/REVENGE	7	A magician plays a trick on a spectator who undermined his show.
Antonia's Grandmother B/ANTONIA	7	A girl helps her grandmother to recover from an illness with an act of kindness.
Expository		
Marmots AB/MARMOTS	4	Description of the habitat of a family of marmots.
Laser B/LASER	6	Magazine article on the development and contributions of lasers.
Learning to Read B/LEARNING	4	A Tanzanian illiterate woman describes her reactions on learning to read.
Paracutin, the Volcano B/PARACUTIN	6	Description of an unexpected volcanic eruption in Mexico.
Smoking and Cancer B/SMOKE	6	Technical description of the effects of smoking on the body.
Documents passage		
Travel Card B/CARD	7	Students fill in a traveler's card for a young woman, using information provided.
Resource Map B/RESOURCES	3	Students use a key to locate resources in a detailed map.
Job Vacancies B/JOBS	3	Students use job vacancy advertisements to locate jobs with particular features.
Bar Graph B/BAR GRAPH	3	Students interpret bar graph showing population numbers of hares and lynxes over 10 years.
Bus Timetable B/BUS TIMES	3	Students locate times, places and routes on a complex bus timetable.
Follow Directions B/DIRECTIONS	3	Students insert geometric figures and numbers in a rectangle, as directed, and respond to questions about completed figure.
Weather Chart B/WEATHER	4	Students locate places with particular weather features on a list of 38 world cities.
Temperature Chart AB/TEMPERATURE	5	Students locate times and trends on temperature chart over 4 days.
Aspirol Directions B/ASPIROL	3	Students respond to questions about use, dosage, composition for Aspirol tablets.

Appendix D

Preparation of Questionnaires

At the plenary sessions at NRC meetings, discussions were held to refine the aims of the study. In turn these were embedded into an overall conceptual model (see Table 1.9 in Chapter 1). A questionnaire subcommittee of NRCs was established under the chairmanship of the New Zealand NRC, Dr Hans Wagemaker. All of the NRCs were invited to submit to the subcommittee questions which were embedded in the conceptual framework and which would be suitable for all countries. The procedure adopted was first to identify indicators implied by the initial conceptual model developed for the study. Secondly, for each indicator an initial decision had to be made on the most appropriate source of information: student, teacher, or school principal. Finally questions were formulated which were intended to accommodate differences between countries, while at the same time capturing commonality of semantic meaning. The subcommittee met at each meeting of the NRCs in order to formulate questions and to prepare forms for administration. Inevitably the list of both indicators and questions was expanded as work proceeded. It was generally felt by the subcommittee that it would have been desirable for much more time to be made available for meetings for this aspect of the work.

Student Questionnaires

These questionnaires consisted of two independent parts: the first contained questions about the students' home and school conditions; the second contained questions about the students' voluntary reading activities. In view of the relative youth and the limited literacy skills of many 9-year-olds, the questions had to be simple and direct. Test administrators read the questions to the 9-year-olds. If the NRCs had national concerns which could not be accommodated in the international questionnaire, they were encouraged to add "national options," which were responded to and processed only in their own country.

Home and School Circumstances

Identification

Questions were asked about students' age, sex, and home language (and in some countries about the students' ethnic identity).

Socioeconomic Status

Previous IEA studies had identified problems in the comparability of occupational scales across countries, so questions in this area were confined to parents' educational level (number of years), material possessions in the home, and the frequency of students' meals. After the pilot study, parental educational level was dropped from the Population A questions because of unreliable data, but it was retained in Population B. For the material possession questions, each country selected its own list of ten items (TV., washing machine, computer, etc.) which would best discriminate between high and low socioeconomic levels of students' homes, and eight further items representing students' personal possessions (own bicycle, camera, place to study etc.). This approach represented an innovation in most countries.

Home Literacy Resources

Students were asked about the number of books in their homes and about their access to a daily newspaper.

Home Literacy Interaction

Questions in this section focused on parental interest in students' reading, the extent to which they read to one another, and the frequency with which students received help with homework.

Further Questions

Students were also asked to estimate how often they watched TV, how often they borrowed from a school or public library, how much homework they received, and "how good" they were, in their own view, at reading (on a four-point scale: "very good" to "not very good"). Finally, a question was asked about the students' beliefs about the best way to become a good reader. Students selected three ways, from a given list of eleven (liking it, knowing how to sound out words, having lots of good books around, etc.) It was expected that students' modal perceptions would reflect teachers' various emphases in instruction.

Student Voluntary Reading Activities

The purpose of this section was to determine how often students read different kinds of reading materials. Thus, Population A students were asked to state whether they read a book for fun last week (Yes/No), and then how often they read books for fun (four-point scale: "almost never" to "almost every day"). Similar questions were designed for comics, magazines, newspapers, written instructions, and reading aloud at home. Another set of questions sought information from students on their frequency of reading in school, especially on textbooks, storybooks, workbooks, and reference books. Again, most questions in this section (for Population A) required students to respond on a four-point scale to indicate frequency of reading. Revisions were made to the format of the questions after the pilot tests.

At Population B level, a more elaborate set of questions was prepared about the frequency of student voluntary reading of various levels of books, magazines, etc. (mystery, romance, travel, sports, etc.). Six-point scales were found to be appropriate for 14-year-olds, ranging from "almost never" to "almost every day." During the pilot phase several NRCs conducted reliability checks on the quality of the data obtained from 9-year-olds. As there was clearly some cause for concern about the accuracy of information gained from many 9-year-olds, questions requiring students to make complex judgments were dropped, or adapted. Nevertheless, some problems remained in certain questions which were subject to social desirability pressures. There are cultural differences in students' desire to please, which make for differential responses to questions, for example, about voluntary reading and book borrowing.

School Climate

Finally, a set of 29 questions was adapted from Williams and Batten (1981) *The quality of school life*, for the Population B questionnaire to assess students' perception of their school climate. Students responded by agreeing or disagreeing with statements such as "School is a place where: teachers are fair and just; I feel important; I feel lonely" (etc.). This section was optional, but was included by 27 countries.

Teacher Questionnaires

The design of the survey allowed for sampling of intact classes so that teacher variables could be related to student outcomes, within and between countries, and relevant relationships investigated. The teachers of each class which was selected for inclusion in the survey, were therefore asked to respond to 46 questions about their identity, training, experience, instructional practices, classroom context, and beliefs related to the teaching of reading. This section describes the major categories of questions designed for this purpose. The challenge here was to prepare a set of questions which was capable of capturing the experience of teachers at both primary and secondary level. It had to recognize that in some developing countries teaching methods used at the secondary level were those which teachers in developed countries would use at the primary school level.

Identification

Questions were prepared on teacher sex, home language, and years of teaching experience.

Training

Teachers were asked to state how many years of schooling, pre-service training, in-service training, and post-secondary education they had. Variations in systems of training presented several challenges in this section.

Readership

In order to examine the levels of literacy and commitment of teachers, questions were asked about the frequency with which they read articles on reading, books of various sorts, poetry, plays, and children's literature.

Classroom Conditions

Information was sought on the following kinds of variables, likely to affect teaching quality: size of class, whether multi-grade, length of time teacher had taught the class, frequency of meeting with parents, frequency of staff meetings, number of students needing and receiving remedial assistance, time spent teaching language, number of textbooks available, size of classroom library, size of school library, borrowing rules, etc. Questions were also prepared on the time spent teaching reading, but were not very successful as many teachers integrated their reading instruction into general language lessons, or other parts of their instruction.

Instructional Practices

Under this heading, teachers were asked to indicate how frequently they conducted some 60 specific activities (e.g., teaching new vocabulary in lists, listening to students read to the class, dramatizing stories, reading aloud to children, grouping children for reading, using multiple-choice questions, etc.). The intention was to group these activities, for greater reliability, into more generic concepts, postulated beforehand, and to check by factor analysis how they cohered. These concepts were the same as those listed in Table 1.9 (e.g., comprehension instruction emphasis, assessment emphasis, skills instruction).

Teacher Beliefs

Teachers were asked to rank their priority aims in reading instruction (5 out of 12 provided), and to respond on a Likert scale concerning 26 issues in reading instruction ("children should not guess," "they should choose their own books," "mistakes should be corrected at once," etc.). Once again, these responses were to be grouped into instructional constructs, as postulated in Table 1.9.

Further questions were designed to investigate teachers' beliefs about how they encourage their students to read more, how often they teach narration, exposition and documents, how often they are evaluated, and what topics they discuss at staff meetings.

School Principal's Questionnaire

Twenty-four questions were designed for the school principal's questionnaire about the size and type of school the students in the sample attended, the resources available in the community and the school, the size of the school library, details about the staff, the number of days of instruction, extent of absenteeism, special programs for reading, and the way the principal perceived his or her role in the school. Once again, these questions were grouped to fit the conceptual model presented in Table 1.9.

National Case Study Questionnaire

In cross-national studies the ability to compare countries allows an examination of the impact and effect of policies which are consistent within nations but which may vary across nations. Policies such as age of entry, hours of instruction, teacher training, and methods of instruction which characterize national education systems and which vary across countries, when compared, have the potential to provide new perspectives and insights in coming to understand differences in educational outcomes.

The National Case Study Questionnaire (NCSQ) was designed to gather educational, economic, social, political, and cultural data which may help explain variances in school achievement across nations or regions. Questions were framed around seven major interest areas, which included: the structure of the school system, curriculum in reading, teachers, instructional time, socioeconomic conditions, national language and culture, and a final section which requested any information which in the opinion of the NRC would assist with the interpretation of the results. In addition to providing an opportunity to compare policies, programs, and economic conditions directly at the national and/or regional level, data gathered from the NCSQ was used to contribute to the construction of a Composite Index of Development (CDI) (see Chapter 2).

The final format was decided by the Questionnaire Subcommittee after trialling with NRCs and subsequent revisions. Much of the information requested was expected to be available from existing published sources in each country and it was expected that completion would require the input from several sources. The experience of the trial revealed a need to get an estimate of the reliability of the information that was being provided. NRCs were asked to estimate the reliability for each question and the source from which the information was obtained. The final version of the questionnaire followed the format described below.

Structure of the School System

At the national level countries operate different policies as they relate to age of entry to school and length of compulsory schooling, and they are also likely to differ in terms of the provision and nature of pre-compulsory schooling. How do countries make provision for the more academically able students and what are the polices and practices with respect to vocational training and education? What impact do these differences have on performance in reading literacy? Does age of entry, for example, make a difference to how proficient children are in terms of their reading skills at age 9 or 14? Under this section NRCs were asked to provide information on their national policies in relation to compulsory schooling and the extent and nature of pre-school experience.

To provide a context in which to interpret a country's results, variations in official educational policies as they relate to enrollment are also important. For example, to what extent are students retained in the system during the compulsory and post-compulsory years and what proportion of a cohort receives pre-school care and education?

Curriculum in Reading

In many countries the curriculum as it relates to reading is centrally prescribed and this may be done at a national or regional level. Under this section of the questionnaire NRCs were asked to provide information on policies and practices as they related to the reading curriculum. Questions related to the degree of discretion teachers had in implementing the intended curriculum, the age at which children begin and cease formal reading instruction, and practices in relation to the first year of reading instruction. In those countries where a curriculum was centrally prescribed, NRCs were requested to provide the International Coordinating Center with a copy.

The Teachers

Teacher quality in terms of the levels of education and training they have received has long been thought to be positively associated with student outcomes. In addition to providing information on levels of education and training for both primary and secondary teachers, NRCs were asked to provide information on the percentage of teachers who were female, to describe briefly any current developments in teacher training, to describe how many teachers a typical child would have had in the first four years of school, and information on the status (remuneration) of the teaching profession in relation to other occupations.

Instructional time

Opportunity to learn is directly related to learning outcomes. At the national level policies with respect to the number of instructional days in the year, the length of the school day, and the proportion of instructional time devoted to instruction in reading and instruction in the language of the test were all thought to be related to achievement in reading literacy. This information was gathered for grades K to 9 in each country to supplement that provided by teachers.

Social and Economic Conditions

Under this section NRCs were asked to provide information on the social and economic conditions in their countries. In particular information was gathered on educational expenditure for both private and public education, the live birth rate (and estimate of health status), the percentage of women in full- and part-time employment, unemployment rates, gross domestic product, average disposable income, infant mortality, the ratio of hospital beds per 1000, and the percentage of households with telephones. This information was expected to contribute to the construction of an index of development.

National Language and Culture

Differences in linguistic and ethnic diversity were also expected to provide important contextual information for understanding performance. NRCs were asked to provide information on the major mother tongue languages spoken in the country, the nature of the official languages, the proportions of children whose home language differed from the language of the school, the presence or absence of any political debate on language policy, and the extent to which minority cultures were represented in the content of the curriculum.

Information was also gathered under this section on a series of variables which might be described as contributing to a concept of a culture of literacy. This included information on daily newspaper circulation (and language), the numbers of books published, library circulation, and book sales at the national level. The latter all represent a measure of the extent of availability of literacy resources and an estimate of the societal "press" for literacy.

The final section of the questionnaire asked the respondents to identify any special feature of their system which in their estimation would assist the interpretation of the results for their country. NRCs were directed to consider specifically the relative level of reading ability in their country and the spread of differences between pupils.

Administration and Data Management

Data preparation for the NCSQ was managed by Dr Hans Wagemaker in the New Zealand National Center.

Despite considerable efforts from NRCs and a more minimalist approach used in the construction of the final form of the questionnaire, some of the information was difficult to obtain in some countries. Completed questionnaires were eventually received from 31 of the 32 countries which participated in the study. It was evident that in some of the less developed countries, data of the type and in the format requested was difficult to obtain. Nevertheless enough information was received to provide a rich contextual background for interpreting differences between countries in their levels of achievement.

Appendix E

Intercorrelations of the Composite Development Index

Table E.1

Intercorrelations for Six Indicators of the Composite Development Index (CDI), Total Achievement Mean Scores for Population A and B, and the Corresponding Mean Values ($N = 32$)

	1	2	3	4	5	6	7	8	Mean
1. GNP (Per capita in $ US)	–	.94	.69	-.73	.78	.63	.60	.64	10,076
2. Expenditure on education (per student in $ US)		–	.57	-.64	.76	.56	.46	.51	1,824
3. Life expectancy (in years)			–	-.93	.54	.85	.73	.73	72.5
4. % Low birth weight infants				–	-.66	-.78	-.69	-.69	7.6
5. Mean newspaper circulation (per 1000)					–	.57	.47	.61	238
6. % Adult literacy						–	.64	.70	92
7. Total score Pop A							–	.83	500
8. Total score Pop B								–	500

Appendix F

Rationale for Scores Used

In studies of this kind, it is sometimes necessary to exclude one or more items from analysis after testing for reasons not anticipated prior to testing. It may be necessary, for example, to remove an item from analyses in all countries if it did not function in practice as intended. Or, if test completion rates are uniformly low across many countries, a decision may be made to not analyze responses to the last few items on a test.

Occasionally, an item is problematic in a particular country, perhaps because of errors of translation or some unanticipated country-specific consideration. When test results are analyzed using item response theory (IRT), it is possible to exclude items from analysis in particular countries without compromising the comparability of achievement measures across countries.

The purpose of removing items from analysis (either entirely or in particular countries) is to ensure that results reflect as accurately as possible student achievement levels in each country. In particular, the purpose is to ensure that students' results on individual items are providing information about the achievement domain being measured, and are not contaminated by differences in how tests have been translated or administered in different countries.

In this study, the question of excluding items from analysis arose as a result of known differences in testing conditions (e.g., times allowed for test completion) in different countries and because of an unusual level of non-completion of the test in some countries. Given the high non-completion rates, consideration was given to the possibility of basing each student's measure in the three reading domains on only the items obviously attempted by that student, excluding unanswered items at the end of the test. In this way, the influence of different testing conditions in different countries on students' reading scores might be reduced or eliminated.

Although a case for basing achievement measures on only obviously attempted items can be made, and may be appropriate in other IEA studies, this was not done in the current study for the following reasons.

1. The instructions to students were clear, that they should answer every item, that they should work quickly, and that they had 40 min to complete the test. Those students who followed these instructions and completed all items may well have been disadvantaged when their scores were compared with

255

those who devoted all their time to the early part of the test, or were able to confine themselves to items they were sure about.

2.   The time limits were agreed to by all NRCs and the Steering Committee during the test construction phase and were believed to be realistic. Students were allowed more than one minute per item.

3.   In some countries where many items were "not reached" it was observed that students frequently omitted items early in the test. Thus, it is not clear which items were omitted and which were "not reached."

4.   It is reasonable to suppose that many students failed to finish the tests because the longer and more difficult passages tended to be concentrated towards the end of the test sessions.

It is recognized that the style of response to formal tests may differ from one country to another. Thus, it is possible that scores may have been higher in countries which had many students who did not complete the test. Their traditions may have encouraged them not to respond when they were unsure. For these countries, the scores in this book may be an underestimate. Under the circumstances there is no ready way of estimating their scores precisely.

Appendix G

Adjustment for Age Differences

It is clear from Tables 2.2 and 2.3 that the mean ages of the national samples of students varied somewhat from one country to another. Some variation was expected, as the target samples were selected by grade, not age. However, in Population A one country tested a sample whose mean age was 8.89 years, while four others had mean ages well above 10 years. At the Population B level, one sample had a mean age of 13.93 years, while seven others, mostly developing countries, had mean ages over 15.0 years. Indeed, these countries tested older students by agreement.

To what extent would these departures from the defined samples affect the national means? Can these means be adjusted to compensate for these differences? There is no easy answer to these questions, as cross-sectional surveys do not normally provide enough information to make a reliable adjustment. However, the need for some such compensation was keenly felt by many in the project, so an approximation was attempted, using three independent approaches. Fortunately, all three converged on a similar outcome, so there are reasonable grounds for taking their results seriously.

Regression Method

At each population level the correlation between the mean age of each country's sample and its mean overall score was calculated, and a regression equation used to estimate new mean scores with age equated. Those countries with much older students and relatively low scores were deliberately omitted from these calculations. The observed correlation for Population A between age and achievement was .21 (N = 25). The values for the slopes and intercepts were computed, the predicted scores were determined for each country and the residuals worked out. These were added to the country means, and the new values were taken as an approximate estimate of the country achievement means, on the assumption of equal age. This analysis produced scores which were very close to the original means for most countries. The only large changes were in Canada (BC) (+14), the Netherlands (+9), Portugal (-10), Venezuela (-15), and Indonesia (-16) (see Table G.1). Thus a difference of 12 months produced a change of 18–20 points. Overall, the reported means had a correlation of .99 with the means adjusted for age. At the 14-year-old level, the observed correlation between country mean age and mean composite score was again .21, and the resultant adjustments produced the following changes: Canada (BC) (+18), Italy (+16), Hungary (+14), Spain (+12), Belgium (Fr) (+11), Portugal (-20), France (-16), Venezuela (-18), Zimbabwe (-17), and Nigeria (-12). The remaining adjustments were relatively small (see Table G.2).

Table G.1

Mean Scores Reported in Chapter 2 and Scores Adjusted for Age
Differences for Three Domains for Population A

	Narrative		Expository		Documents		
	Mean Scores	Adjusted for Age	Mean Scores	Adjusted for Age	Mean Scores	Adjusted for Age	Score Difference
Belgium/Fr	510	509	505	504	506	505	-1
Canada/BC	502	516	499	513	500	514	+14
Cyprus	492	492	475	475	476	476	0
Denmark	463	463	467	467	496	496	0
Finland	568	569	569	570	569	570	+1
France	532	527	533	528	527	522	-5
Germany/E	482	487	493	498	522	527	+5
Germany/W	491	496	497	502	520	525	+5
Greece	514	521	511	518	488	495	+7
Hong Kong	494	491	503	500	554	551	-3
Hungary	496	503	493	500	509	516	+7
Iceland	518	518	517	517	519	519	0
Indonesia	402	386	411	395	369	353	-16
Ireland	518	525	514	521	495	502	+7
Italy	533	532	538	537	517	516	-1
Netherlands	494	503	480	489	481	490	+9
New Zealand	534	530	531	527	521	517	-4
Norway	525	525	528	528	519	519	0
Portugal	483	473	480	470	471	461	-10
Singapore	521	528	519	526	504	511	+7
Slovenia	502	503	489	490	503	504	+1
Spain	497	493	505	501	509	505	-4
Sweden	536	536	542	542	539	539	0
Switzerland	506	507	507	508	522	523	+1
Trinidad/Tobago	455	458	458	461	440	443	+3
United States	553	549	538	534	550	546	-4
Venezuela	378	363	396	381	374	359	-15

Table G.2

Mean Scores in the Booklet and Scores Adjusted for Age
Differences for Three Domains for Population B

	Narrative		Expository		Documents		
	Mean Scores	Adjusted for Age	Mean Scores	Adjusted for Age	Mean Scores	Adjusted for Age	Score Difference
Belgium/Fr	484	495	477	488	483	494	+11
Botswana	340	341	339	340	312	313	+1
Canada/BC	526	544	516	534	522	540	+18
Cyprus	516	515	492	491	482	481	-1
Denmark	517	517	524	524	532	532	0
Finland	559	559	541	541	580	580	0
France	556	540	546	530	544	528	-16
Germany/E	512	515	523	526	543	546	+3
Germany/W	514	521	521	528	532	539	+7
Greece	526	534	508	516	493	501	+8
Hong Kong	509	498	540	529	557	546	-11
Hungary	530	544	536	550	542	556	+14
Iceland	550	548	548	546	509	507	-2
Ireland	510	516	505	511	518	524	+6
Italy	520	536	524	540	501	517	+16
Netherlands	506	515	503	512	533	542	+9
New Zealand	547	540	535	528	552	545	-7
Nigeria	402	390	406	394	394	382	-12
Norway	515	514	520	519	512	511	-1
Philippines	421	427	439	445	430	436	+6
Portugal	523	503	523	503	523	503	-20
Singapore	530	537	539	546	533	540	+7
Slovenia	534	534	525	526	537	538	+1
Spain	500	512	495	507	475	487	+12
Sweden	556	556	533	533	550	550	0
Switzerland	534	531	525	522	549	546	-3
Thailand	468	457	486	475	478	467	-11
Trinidad/Tobago	482	489	485	492	472	479	+7
United States	539	532	539	652	528	521	-7
Venezuela	407	389	433	415	412	394	-18
Zimbabwe	367	350	374	357	373	356	-17

Growth from 9 to 14 Years

The second approach taken was to estimate the amount of growth in all three domains, from 9 to 14 years, as indicated by gains on the common 14 anchor items, answered by students in both age groups, and then to divide by five to obtain an estimate of the amount of growth per year, on those items. This method produced the enclosed table of p values for each population, with the amount of growth calculated on the right.

Table G.3 shows that an overall gain of 23.7% was demonstrated over five years on these common items. No doubt this figure would have been somewhat higher if there had not been a ceiling effect evident on some of the

Shark items. On the admittedly debatable assumption of equal increments in achievement over each of the intervening five years, from 9 to 14 years, one would arrive at an estimate of growth of 4.74% per year, which is equivalent to 19 score points on the Rasch scale. If the two easiest Shark items were omitted from this calculation, the corresponding gains would be 5.15%, or 21 score points. These figures are very similar to those produced by the regression method (18–20 points per year).

Table G.3

Changes on Anchor Items from 9 to 14 Years

Passage	Item	Population A p value %	Population B p value %	Difference %
Temperature	1	73.1	86.7	13.6
	2	26.3	66.4	40.1
	3	38.8	69.1	30.3
	4	40.8	75.3	34.5
	5	63.6	89.8	26.2
Marmot	1	53.0	75.6	22.6
	2	49.0	81.0	32.0
	3	40.9	68.6	27.7
	4	40.0	71.6	31.6
Shark	1	78.4	89.8	11.4
	2	75.3	90.6	15.3
	3	74.6	86.5	11.9
	4	69.6	86.9	17.3
	5	68.0	85.6	17.6
Mean				23.7

Empirical Comparison of Adjacent Age Groups

The empirical way to check the size of the gain in test scores over 12 months is to administer the tests to adjacent age groups from the same schools. Such a study was undertaken by the chairman of the steering committee in a small sample of five New Zealand schools with the Population A tests, administered under standardized conditions. The samples consisted of 212 students in Standards 3 and 4 (9- and 10-year-olds), in the same multigrade classrooms. As there is no difference in the curriculum or reading materials for these two grades, and as they were taught together in the same composite classes, the normal situation in New Zealand, it was assumed that variations in performance would be attributable to age, not to grade.

The results of this investigation showed that 10-year-olds performed slightly better than 9-year-olds on all items, and that an increase of 12 months of age was equivalent to a 6% gain in Total Score at the median (Table G.4). In schools where the 9-year-olds performed well there was an apparent ceiling effect which reduced these gains; in low scoring schools the gains were larger. While these figures might be found to vary slightly in other schools and other countries, they are reasonably consistent with the findings obtained in the other two methods. A gain of 5–6% per year, or approximately 20 points over 12 months, is a reasonable estimate of growth. Hence the adjusted scores produced in Tables G.1 and G.2.

Table G.4

Percentage Mean Scores on Population A Tests (Overall) for 9- and 10-year-olds by School

School	9-year-old mean	(N)	10-year-old mean	(N)	Growth (%)
A	73.5	35	78.1	31	4.6
B	67.0	31	70.5	32	3.5
C	62.0	9	70.0	12	8.0
D	51.4	11	59.6	15	8.2
E	50.0	21	62.9	15	12.9
Total	63.7	107	69.8	105	6.1

Appendix H

National Panel Ratings of Expected Literacy Levels

Eleven countries took part in an exercise to establish expected literacy levels in their society. The purpose of this study was to provide an additional framework against which to evaluate the reading literacy scores obtained by Population B students. In brief, the Steering Committee proposed the following system for setting proficiency levels in each country. A panel of informed judges was selected and asked to take the Population B test, then to rate each item in relation to two defined standards of literacy appropriate for their country. For example, the percentage of "barely literate" students who were expected to respond to each item correctly was recorded by each judge, and the percentages summed across all items in a domain and averaged to obtain an expected mean proficiency level for the domain, following the method proposed by Angoff (1971). The actual mean scores were then compared with the expected scores to determine what percentage of students fell below the "barely literate" criterion. A similar procedure was used to determine the percentage who were considered "high-level literate."

Summary of Procedure

The following steps were outlined for the NRCs by Dr Nadir Atash of Westat Associates, USA, who advised the Steering Committee.

Select a Panel of Judges

The NRCs were asked to select a panel of 20–40 people representing business, universities, schools, personnel officers, health administrators, and others likely to be sensitive to the literacy demands of public documents and widely used reading materials in their society.

Convene a Meeting of the Panel

The judges were sent background materials and asked to convene for a full working day (or two half days) to take the Population B test and to rate the items.

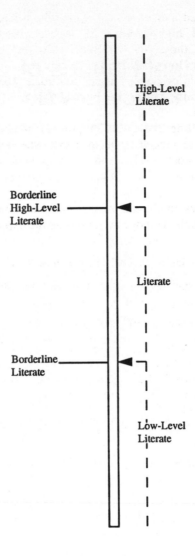

High-Level
Literate

Borderline
High-Level
Literate

Literate

Borderline
Literate

Low-Level
Literate

Figure H.1: Cut-Off Points for Distinguishing Three Levels of Literacy

Define Reading Literacy Proficiency Levels and Reference Groups

The NRCs chaired a discussion in which the definitions and borderlines of "barely literate" and "high-level literate" were clarified with examples:

1.   In general terms, those people falling below the "barely literate" cut-off point were considered "low-level literate." They were judged to be unable to read essential materials commonly used in a society in order to maintain a household, raise a family, perform a manual job, and use basic community services in that society.

2.   Those people falling above the "high-level literate" cut-off point were those readers who were judged to be able to read, understand, analyze, and draw generalizations about abstract concepts, couched in difficult prose or in complex diagrams (e.g., legal documents, government policy reports, professional journals).

Figure H.1 shows in diagrammatic form the two cut-off points on a literacy continuum which the judges used to rate the expected levels of literacy in their country.

Familiarize the Judges with the Reading Literacy Test

Panel members read through the whole of the Population B test, and responded to each question.

Obtain Judgements for the Practice Items

Two passages were used to provide practice and feedback to judges on their ability to rate the difficulty of the items. When making their ratings, judges were asked to consider each item in relation to two questions:

1.   What percentage of barely literate readers in my country would respond to this item correctly? and

2.   What percentage of borderline high-level literate readers would respond to this item correctly?

Obtain First-Stage Ratings

Judges then rated all 89 items of the test, and recorded on a chart their judgements of the percentage of both kinds of readers in their country who would be expected to achieve each of the two levels of literacy on each item. These were referred to as first-stage ratings.

Compute First-Stage Literacy Levels for Each Domain

A computer program was used to add the percentages across all items in each domain.

Obtain Second-Stage Literacy Levels for Each Domain

Each judge was provided with his/her first stage mean literacy levels, as well as those of the other judges. Discrepancies were discussed, and extreme values justified or changed. Revised levels were then recorded for all judges, and the median of the panel was established for both levels of literacy.

Compare with Obtained Scores of 14-Year-Olds

These medians became the recommended literacy levels for the country, to be compared with the actual scores obtained by the 14-year-olds of that country. This was done separately for each domain. The results of these comparisons are presented in Chapter 2 (Tables 2.4 and 2.5).

Further details can be found in the Technical Report (Beaton, 1993).

Appendix I

Reliability Coefficients

Table I.1

Reliability Coefficients (Cronbach Alpha) for Domains and Total
Scores: Population A

Country	Narrative	Expository	Documents	Total Cronbach Alpha	Total Equivalent Forms
Belgium/Fr	.83	.79	.77	.91	.84
Canada/BC	.85	.83	.79	.93	.87
Cyprus	.85	.80	.78	.92	.88
Denmark	.91	.91	.89	.96	.88
Finland	.81	.75	.75	.90	.85
France	.83	.77	.72	.90	.84
Germany/E	.85	.87	.82	.93	.87
Germany/W	.85	.86	.82	.94	.86
Greece	.83	.78	.78	.92	.84
Hong Kong	.84	.73	.77	.91	.85
Hungary	.82	.85	.79	.93	.89
Iceland	.86	.85	.81	.94	.90
Indonesia	.73	.69	.68	.97	.84
Ireland	.86	.81	.79	.93	.90
Italy	.84	.82	.80	.93	.86
Netherlands	.83	.81	.77	.91	.84
New Zealand	.88	.82	.82	.94	.91
Norway	.89	.86	.84	.95	.90
Portugal	.81	.77	.79	.91	.84
Singapore	.84	.73	.76	.92	.90
Slovenia	.84	.83	.80	.93	.89
Spain	.84	.83	.80	.93	.89
Sweden	.87	.88	.85	.95	.91
Switzerland	.85	.85	.80	.93	.88
Trinidad/Tobago	.85	.82	.79	.93	.90
United States	.86	.77	.73	.92	.87
Venezuela	.78	.76	.73	.89	.78
Median	.84	.81	.79	.93	.87

Table I.2

Reliability Coefficients (Cronbach Alpha) for Domains and Total Scores: Population B

Country	Narrative	Expository	Documents	Total Cronbach Alpha	Total Equivalent Forms
Belgium/Fr	.87	.80	.82	.93	.87
Botswana	.48	.46	.73	.77	.80
Canada/BC	.86	.82	.81	.93	.87
Cyprus	.84	.82	.81	.93	.91
Denmark	.87	.82	.81	.93	.94
Finland	.82	.70	.72	.90	.90
France	.82	.74	.74	.89	.88
Germany/E	.88	.81	.79	.92	.86
Germany/W	.86	.79	.77	.93	.90
Greece	.81	.78	.77	.91	.82
Hong Kong	.80	.75	.71	.90	.88
Hungary	.83	.79	.78	.92	.92
Iceland	.86	.82	.81	.93	.92
Ireland	.88	.82	.83	.94	.91
Italy	.85	.78	.81	.92	.89
Netherlands	.86	.79	.83	.93	.84
New Zealand	.89	.85	.84	.95	.95
Nigeria	.77	.73	.84	.91	.76
Norway	.83	.79	.80	.92	.82
Philippines	.79	.77	.82	.92	.90
Portugal	.79	.73	.73	.89	.88
Singapore	.78	.74	.71	.89	.90
Slovenia	.79	.71	.71	.89	.85
Spain	.85	.77	.75	.91	.87
Sweden	.86	.80	.81	.93	.91
Switzerland	.86	.79	.77	.92	.91
Thailand	.86	.78	.84	.93	.72
Trinidad/Tobago	.88	.85	.86	.95	.92
United States	88	.84	.80	.94	.92
Venezuela	..79	.76	.72	.89	.70
Zimbabwe	.70	.69	.83	.89	.85
Median	.85	.79	.80	.92	.89

Appendix J

Variables Included in Chapter 7

Table J.1

List of Variables Included in Chapter 7. Short Label Refers to the
IEA Reading Literacy Study Code Book 05/13/92

1. Student Process Variables

ASBORBO	Freq. borrowing books
ASHWKT	Time spent on homework
ASSSRA	Reading aloud
ASSSRC	Reading in class
ASHWKF	Helped with reading homework

2. School and Teacher Process Variables

ATSSCT	Comprehension Instruction
ATSSPT	Phonics Emphasis
ATSSER	Encouragement to read
ATSSAE	Assessment emphasis
ATSSIA	Taking student interest into account
ATSSAL	Assessment of low order skills
ATSSLE	Literature emphasis
ATSSGM	Graded materials
ATVISIT	Visit school library

3. Student Background Variables

ASSEX	Sex of class, % boys
ATOTLAD	% of other language students

4. Teacher Characteristics

ATSEX	Teacher sex
ATYEARS	Teacher experience
ATEDUC	No of years teacher education
ATSSTE	Teacher readership/expository
ATSSTL	Teacher readership/literature
ATSSTP	Teacher readership/professional
ATSAC	Cognitive aims
ATSAA	Affective aims
ATSSHD	High demand and structure

5. Proximal teaching conditions

ATTECLAR	Time teaching this class
ATINSTD	Instructional time
ATTERED	Time practice reading
ATCLSIZ	Class size
ATNHELPD	Proportion needing help
ATBOOKD	Available books per student
ATCLLIB	Classroom library
ATBODIT	Classroom Library N of books
ACDAYLO	Days of instruction lost
ACTABS	% of students absent

6. School Characteristics

ACENRSD	Total enrolment
ACPNTEAD	Teacher student ratio
ATSCHLI	School library
ACSLIBC	School library, no of books
ACSLIBA	School library, no of books added
ACPWEOD	Hours per year school is open

7. Community variables

ACTYCOMD	Type of Community
ACFSCR	Community Resources

8. Home Background Variables

ASBOOKS	Books at home
ASNEWS	Newspaper at home
ASMEALD	Meals per week
ASSSHL	Home Literacy Interaction
ACPACO	Parental co-operation

Table J.2

Deviation in Rasch Score from the "International Class Mean" Level for Population A. Results for all Domains and for Regression Models on System Variables only, on System Variables Controlling for Community and Home Factors and on System Variables Controlling for the Full Set of 48 Questionnaire Variables

Model	System Variables			System, Community & Home					System and Full Set		
Figues:	7:1	7:2	7:3	7:1-3	7:4	7:5	7:6	7:4-6			
Country	Nar	Exp	Doc	Mean	Nar	Exp	Doc	Mean	Nar	Exp	Doc	Mean
BEF 152	9	5	4	6	2	-2	-4	-2	18	7	6	9
CAC 160	2	2	1	2	-17	13	17	-16	-11	-5	-12	-9
CYP 319	-10	-39	-27	-26	-8	-37	-24	-29	-13	-43	-28	-28
DEN 208	-28	2	14	-4	-44	-11	-2	-19	-43	-7	-3	-18
FIN 71	66	58	69	64	56	48	59	58	50	42	53	48
FRA 136	30	22	26	26	32	24	28	28	38	28	32	33
GER1 149	-1	26	23	16	4	30	27	20	7	33	33	24
GER2 101	-12	21	22	10	-5	25	27	15	-16	14	19	6
GRC 176	9	-6	-15	-4	18	1	-5	4	17	0	-6	4
HKO 167	-13	-22	52	6	11	-1	78	29	-10	-20	60	10
HUN 144	0	11	7	6	-6	7	2	1	2	14	10	9
ICE 283	20	19	23	20	3	6	7	5	5	8	9	8
INS 174	-107	-113	-136	-119	-56	-72	-88	-72	-45	-60	-78	-60
IRE 122	15	4	-7	4	12	1	-10	1	13	4	-6	4
ITA 154	31	28	14	24	44	39	26	36	44	33	22	33
NET 99	3	3	-20	-5	-11	-8	-39	-16	-17	-15	-41	-24
NEZ 176	30	13	18	20	16	2	6	8	14	1	3	6
NOR 191	28	36	23	29	12	23	7	14	15	25	9	16
POR 165	-19	-28	-32	-26	4	-10	-11	-6	5	-11	-11	-6
SIN 206	13	-8	1	2	14	-7	3	3	5	-8	-4	-2
SLO 140	2	-16	3	-4	1	-17	2	-5	0	-14	3	-4
SPA 324	0	14	9	7	-2	13	8	6	-3	14	7	6
SWE 234	39	56	42	45	21	40	23	28	14	35	15	21
SWI 229	11	30	23	22	2	23	14	13	5	25	16	15
TRI 248	-48	-48	-62	-53	-43	-44	-58	-48	-28	-34	-44	-34
USA 298	48	20	48	38	36	10	37	28	30	9	31	23
VEN 162	-118	-89	-123	-110	-95	-69	-101	-88	-92	-73	-100	-88
SUMMA	0	0	0	0	0	0	0	0	0	0	0	0

Index